DANIEL AND ALLA ANDREEV

OTHER BOOKS BY DANIEL H. SHUBIN:

History of Russian Christianity in 4 volumes:
1. From the Earliest Years through Tsar Ivan IV
2. The Patriarchal Era through Tsar Peter the Great: 1586 to 1725
3. The Synodal Era and the Sectarians: 1725 to 1894
4. The Orthodox Church of the 20th Century: 1894 to 1990

Leo Tolstoy and the Kingdom of God within You

Skovoroda
The World Tried to Catch Me but Could Not

Helena Roerich
Living Ethics and the Teaching for a New Epoch

Russia's Wisdom

Tsars and Pseudo-Tsars: Russia's Era of Upheavals

Monastery Prisons

The Gospel of the Prince of Peace

Kingdoms and Covenants

Attributes of Heaven and Earth

Rose of the World (Tr.)

The Grey Man (Tr.)

Daniel and Alla Andreev

Life, Love, Persecution, Survival, Perseverance, and the Production of *Rose of the World*

By

Daniel H. Shubin

Cover Photograph taken by Boris Chukov, February 24, 1959, about a month before the death of Daniel at the age of 52 years.

Daniel Leonidovich Andreev
October 20, 1906 – March 30, 1959

Alla Aleksandrovna Andreeva (Bruzhes)
February 12, 1915 – April 29, 2005

ISBN 978-0-9662757-8-0
Copyright 2015
Daniel H. Shubin
All rights reserved.

Email: peacechurch @ jps.net

TABLE OF CONTENTS

INTRODUCTION	9
PREVIOUS INCARNATIONS OF DANIEL ANDREEV	13
EARLY LIFE	23
THE EARLY YEARS OF SOVIET RUSSIA	39
THE YEARS OF WORLD WAR TWO	133
POST-WAR YEARS	155
DANIEL ANDREEV – ARREST AND INTERROGATION	167
ALLA ANDREEVA – ARREST AND INTERROGATION	213
DANIEL ANDREEV – THE PRISON YEARS	233
ALLA ANDREEVA – THE LABOR CAMPS' YEARS	319
THE FINAL YEARS OF DANIEL ANDREEV	339
THE LATER YEARS OF ALLA ANDREEVA	387
THE FORMATION OF *ROSE OF THE WORLD*	391
APPENDIX 1: INTRODUCTION TO *ROSE OF THE WORLD*	397
APPENDIX 2: INTERVIEW WITH ALLA ANDREEVA	413
BIBLIOGRAPHY	421

An Excerpt from the Poem *Through Nature*, Part of the Ensemble of *Russian Gods*, Chapter 17.

Others confirm the present day.
Let them! Let them!
Whoever is decaying, there in the depths,
In their most clandestine grief.

    Our yesterday of all the nations,
    I spoke of antiquity.
    Now about futurity.
    About these evenings,
    Now about this dawn.

About what is sprouting in the furrows,
The plow breaking in the new epoch,
The seed like a quiet star,
And the sunshine like God.

    I am not a conspirator, not a bandit,
    I am an announcer of that future day.
    But those who burn incense to the present day,
    They do fine without me.

1955

Daniel Andreev in the military during World War 2, about 1942.

Alla Bruzhes, 1931
(Photo taken by Paolo Svischov)

INTRODUCTION

DANIEL LEONIDOVICH ANDREEV

Daniel Andreev was a complex genius encompassing many spheres of comprehension and development. He was simultaneously a mystic entity having a connection to and communication with the realms beyond the terrestrial and mundane material sphere of our own, and he traversed the heavenly regions and the nether regions, and recorded them. Daniel's life beginning at age 14 was infused with a series of encounters with the spirit realm, where he was saturated with the fullness of spirit-deity. This allowed him to transcend the mundane and secular progress of contemporary existence

Over the years after leaving the Literary Institute in 1925, and up to his conscription into the military during World War 2, in 1942, Daniel spent innumerable hours at Moscow libraries delving into world history, religion, philosophy and political science. His personal library at his apartment consisted of over 2,000 books. He had an unfathomable memory in the social sciences and the ability to synthesize information. Daniel's character was also molded over his lifetime in addition to his mystic experiences and education with his arrest, requiring the perseverance and endurance needed to survive his 10 years of extreme prosecution and suffering in Soviet interrogations and high security prisons. Along with this was overcoming his spinal handicap causing spondyloarthrosis, and the accompanying pain, with the necessity of wearing an iron corset.

Daniel was a theologian of the Bible with his own original concepts of deity, the Logos-incarnate Jesus, angels, sin and redemption and judgment. Daniel was fluent in all the major denominations of Christianity, and Islam, Buddhism, and Hinduism, and discusses these religions and their positive and negative contributions to world society. At the same time, Daniel proposes his own meta-religion, one that transcends all religions and yet permits their existence as subservient to his supreme ideal.

If there was a single experience or event in Daniel's life that could be isolated as being the most definitive in molding his ideology, it would be the year or so that he was assigned to the funeral corps while in the military during World War 2. Because of his spinal handicap, Daniel was unfit for active duty and so was first assigned to the supply train behind the troops heading toward Leningrad to break the blockade. After the Germans withdrew from the city, Daniel was assigned to the funeral corp. His duty was to record the remains, if identifiable, of the dead and then bury them in the field, in unmarked graves. The work and difficult and horrifying. Many of the dead had been lying in the snow frozen for several months and now with the spring they were thawing, and with the weather warmer the bodies were putrifying. They were gathered and piled on carts, covered with canvas and hauled to some open pit just dug.

Daniel stared at the horror of war before his very eyes and all of this left its indelible impression on his psyche. The scene of massive death and the job of disposing bodies as objects, objects that were once living humans just like himself, molded his attitude toward war and military service, making it repulsive and objectionable.

When Daniel died at the age of 52, he no doubt thought his memory would terminate likewise, as well as all his writings. But 30 years after his death, Daniel resurrected to life through the publication of his poetry and *Rose of the World*, including a present movement in Russia to implement its concepts into a functioning organization in order to better Russia.

ALLA ALEKSANDROVNA ANDREEVA

Alla Andreeva (Bruzhes, Ivashev-Musatov) loved Daniel because he was a genius in the field of literature and was a person not of the ordinary category. At the age of 20, she married someone 15 years her senior and the marriage failed. Alla then meets Daniel, and at the moment they meet an indivisible and lifelong connection was created. They met in February 1937, but due to the difficulty of Soviet life and then World War 2, it was not until June 21, 1944, that Alla moved to live with Daniel and soon after filed for divorce from her present husband. After Daniel's discharge from the military, they registered as a legal couple on November 4, 1945. Due to health and finances, plus their 10-year incarceration, they did not have a formal church wedding until June 4, 1958. They were inseparably together – except for the 10 prison years – until Daniel's death March 30, 1959.

Alla remarried in 1963 to an old friend of the family, and he died in 1977. They had a fun-filled marriage. Alla died April 29, 2005.

As far as the mystical or spiritual facet of Daniel was concerned, it is apparent that Alla knew little about it, or could not identify with it, or decided early that this was an inherent part of Daniel and so leave it alone. Alla did read Daniel's poetry and later in her life would recite his poetry to audiences in Europe and Russia.

Notes on Translation

Much of this volume is an original translation or paraphrase into English directly from original Russian sources. The author has done his best in this area, and especially the translation of selections of Daniel's *Rose of the World* (Роза Мира) and Alla's *Sailing to the Heavenly Russia* (Плаванье к Небесной России), and the other quotes from people's memoirs and letters and diaries, and especially Boris Romanov's Russian biography.

No text has been inserted into the translated passages, except if located in [brackets].

Russian names differ for male and female. With the first name or last name, the male usually ends in a consonant or the letter –o. With the female, the ending is always with an –a, or a –ya. The only exception are foreign names, such as Kemnitz. With the male patronymic, the ending is with –vich. With the female, the ending is with –ovna or –evna.

In Soviet Russia, it was not unusual for the wife to continue using her maiden name throughout her marriage. Not all women changed their last name to be the same as their husband. This will be noticeable in the text where the wife's family name is different from the husband's.

Structure of this Volume

The book is organized chronologically, first into major sections of their history, and then on a year to year basis.

Rose of the World (in italics) is the book composed by Daniel Andreev.
ROSE OF THE WORLD (small capitals) is his concept of a meta-religion to be instituted in the future as the deliverance of humanity.

Previous Incarnations of Daniel Andreev

The earliest previous lives or incarnations of Daniel are difficult to ascertain because they are just fragments entered in his diary or notebooks: a mention of a place, maybe the era, or description of his vocation, or something characteristic of the era, but without specifics.

The following is a list of Daniel's previous lives as much as can be ascertained from his available compositions and primarily *Rose of the World*:

1. Atlantis: either the mythological island or elsewhere.
2. Gondwana: not the legendary landmass, but a certain meta-culture that included the islands of Java, Sumatra and southern India.
3. Urartu, as a member of the Nairi. This would have been in the 13th – 11th centuries BC.
4. India – in the northern region during the era of the imperial dynasty of Gupta. There Daniel was a snake charmer. This would have been in the 4th – 5th centuries AD.

5. The land of *Daimons* or England of the 13th century. This is mentioned in 2 different places and probably refers to the same incarnation, as he mentions England as a place of rebellion against authority with bloodshed, which is also a trait of the world of *daimons*.

Daniel's next incarnations are in the south of India, in Travancore, during the 17th century or thereabout. He mentions his satisfaction with having led 2 lives in India, and the 2nd incarnation being subsequent to the first, but Daniel had to deal with redeeming the karma of the first Indian incarnation in the 2nd.

He reflects on his previous life in Travancore, where he was a Brahmin, a poet living along the banks of some lake and in the mountains, at the blue summits of the Anai Mudi in southwest India. It was particularly there in the south of India that karma or fate defined his path as a poet and poetic genius in his subsequent life. So did Daniel become after he died in Travancore and reincarnated.

This is recorded in the following vision in *Rose of the World*, and which also includes journeys through other worlds in the interval.

> I do not know where and when I will die this time, but I know where and when I died the previous occasion before I was born in 1906 for a life in Russia. Of course, this knowledge does not have common significance and can only interest those who are capable of bearing it with trust in my witness and who in the process feel a karmic connection with my destiny. But my knowledge of certain stages of the route between my previous existence and the progressing, based on my objective interest, is wider. I can and must explain of their existence from what I was able to gradually remember.

My previous death occurred about 300 years ago in a country that had another type of meta-culture at its head, one very ancient and mighty. My entire present life, from earliest childhood, wearies me with homesickness, a lonesomeness for this ancient homeland. Maybe it is so consuming and deep because I lived not just one life in this country, but 2, and therein very satisfied ones.

But departing from *Enrof*,[1] 300 years ago, during my entire route through *Shadanakar*,[2] initially I felt liberated from a destiny of any redeeming post-mortem descents into the depths of these strata where places of torture unfold, lasting sometimes entire centuries or even millennia, having to deal with the karmic knots with which they tied themselves during life. Initially I was able to untie these knots while still in *Enrof*, with prolonged torments and bitter deprivations atoning for those crimes and errors I committed while a young man. And so the first time I died with an unburdened soul, although from a religious point of view this country was truly fated to await a post-mortem horror. But I already knew that due to my exclusion from the caste system and my 40-year life among the outcasts, I was able to redeem all. Death was easy and full of hope.

This was my declared hope and such did not deceive me. Regarding the first hours, even regarding the first few days of my new existence, I was not allowed to remember, even to this time I cannot. But however, I remember a few localities of that new stratum where subsequently I resided for a long while.

There is one meta-culture for everyone. This stratum, however, is very diversified. In the ancient tropical, immense meta-culture, which twice enveloped my life, it was similar to its nature in *Enrof*, but softer, without the

---

[1] The name of our corporeal stratum, understood as equivalent to the contemporary astronomical universe.
[2] The planet Earth, having the name *Shadanakar*, is one of the heavenly bodies of *Enrof*

extremes of its cruelty and majesty, and without raging tropical rains and devastating arid deserts. I remember how the white towering clouds, in extraordinarily powerful and triumphant forms, hung almost motionless over the horizon, billowing up to the apex of the sky. Nights and days rotated, and all these gigantic radiant towers stood high over the land, hardly changing their features. But the sky itself was not blue or light-blue, but a green-blue. And the sun there was more beautiful than the one we have. It as if played with various fluctuating colors, slowly changing them, but I still cannot explain why the light from this origin of coloration did not cause the same color on the objects upon which it shined. The landscape remained almost the same, but the prominent colors were green, white and gold.

There were rivers and lakes. There was an ocean, although I did not have the chance to see it. Once or twice I did stand on the shore of a sea. There were mountains, forests, and open ranges that reminded me of our steppes. But the growth of these zones was almost transparent and so light, just like the forests in the northern regions of *Enrof* during late spring, when leaves just begin to cover them. The crests of the mountains ranges, and even their slopes, seemed to be just as tranquil and semi-transparent, as if all of this was the ethereal flesh of those elements that compose the physical body of *Enrof.*

But birds and fishes and animals were not aware of this stratum. People remained as its sole inhabitants. When I say people, I refer not to that type who are is just like ourselves residing in *Enrof,* but the type that we will become after death in the first of the worlds of Enlightenment. Finally, I was then assured that the comfort which we absorb into our thoughts from old religions regarding meeting our close ones is not legend and not a deception, as long as what we do in life does not draw us into the bitter regions of redemption. Some close friends met me, and the joy of association with them again became the content of entire periods of my life in that stratum.

It is very ancient, even when angels resided there long ago, before the creation of humanity, and it is called *Olirna*.[3] This musical word seems to me an appropriate appellation, and with credit to those who named it. Association with close friends did not consist of any kind of discredit, bitterness, trivial worries or misunderstandings, as we would defile this here. This was an ideal relationship, in part due to our conversation, but for the most part in silence, which is characteristic here with association with the few with whom we were united, and especially if it was a profound love, and especially in profound minutes.

In *Enrof* we were completely free of any worries regarding sustaining our existence, this had such a negligible effect. Because the weather was not always the best, we still needed shelter but only the minimum. It seemed to be this way in *Olirna*, but not necessarily in other meta-cultures, but I do not remember in detail. The most beautiful of plants was our food, and we drank directly from springs and streams, and they each had a unique flavor, if I remember correctly. Clothes in *Enrof* were beautiful, vivid, a light gray but still radiant, sewn out of wool, silk or linen, and it seems that our body actually created its own clothes, but it is an ethereal body that we here will not even recognize. But in the worlds of Enlightenment and in *Enrof*, life cannot exist without such a body.

And for me, all of the initial time spent in *Olirna* was saturated with worry over those still remaining in *Enrof*. I left behind children and grandchildren, and the old lady – my wife there, and all of my valuable possessions, for which I violated the laws of the caste system and

---

[3] The first of the worlds of the ascending series.

became an untouchable. This severance from them contributed to my constant alarm of their fate. Soon I learned to see them as cloudy figures wandering through thorny trails of *Enrof.* And then after some time passed, I finally met my wife again, and she was just as young as she was early on, but more beautiful. Her journey in *Enrof* was consummated several years after mine, and now the joy of our meeting was not clouded in any manner.

New methods of revelation and senses for perception opened one after another within me. Not those senses of sight and audio, which in the ethereal body completely coincide with their relative organs of the physical body. No! These senses of sight and audio acted from the first minutes of my residency in *Olirna*, and it was particularly due to them that I was able to perceive *Olirna*. But that which we call spiritual vision, spiritual audio and profound memory; that which majestic sages strive to unveil in *Enrof;* that which is revealed there but just by a few among the many millions – is that which in *Olirna* is revealed gradually to each person. Spiritual vision and audio destroy the barricades between many strata. The lives of those whom I left behind on earth, I perceived particularly through these new senses, but not distinctly, but I still perceived them.

I was much consoled by the flourishing nature; I had not seen in *Enrof* such beauty before my eyes ever. But it is strange that I did not lack anything in such a nature, and soon I realized why: it was the diversity of life. Sorrowfully I remembered the singing and chirping of birds, the buzz of insects, the oscillation of fish, the beautiful forms and unconscious instinct of the higher animals. How much our association with nature, the animal world, means for us was only here explained to me. However, those who knew more than I, impressed on me hope, that the ancient, nebulous fantasy of humanity about the existence of strata where animals become educated and highly intelligent – is not a fantasy, but a premonition of truth. Such strata exist, and in time I will enter them.

Other than association with people and enjoyment of nature, time passed at work on my own body: the necessity is its preparation for transformation, because the route from *Olirna* into the next, the higher world, lies not through death, but through transfiguration. And I understood that the verses of the Gospel that narrate about the ascension of Jesus Christ somewhat allude to this event. The resurrection from death changed the nature of His physical body, and with the ascension from *Olirna* it will transfigure a second time together with the ethereal body.

Daniel also described a meeting with a girl from another Indian caste, one that he depicted in a poem at some early time, and the appearance of a long-time foe whose name was Yuri. Daniel writes about this in *Rose of the World* in the 3rd person:

For the sake of her love you abandoned questionable blessings. You were then excluded from the caste and banished. You met again in other strata, but in one of them Yuri imposed on you a horrible mistake. To summon Yuri took immense strength. He then fell lower than *Arga*.

Arga, according to *Rose of the World*, is the 4th of the strata of purgatories, the stratum of black smoke, where sinners redeem their bad karma.

So did all of Daniel's trans-physical journeys indicate a tie with his personal life, and which were journeys through worlds of the past, with each one becoming more and more acute and defined each time it surfaced from the depths of his subconscious. Daniel also wrote in *Rose of the World* of his divine assignment, a missions that he obligated himself to accomplish, while in one of these other worlds:

> Revealed in front of me was the opportunity to withdraw backwards, to the region of another meta-culture that was to this point unknown and alien to me, but still completely young, but with an immense future. Something rather agitating, turbulent, gloomy, emanated from this immense, multi-layered mass, nebulously accepting or pulling me from a distance. The assignment that I accepted was supposed to have a relationship to the great task evolving far beyond the boundaries of this meta-culture and with the responsibility in the distant future to encompass the world. Already, thousands of souls were in preparations for participation in this task.
> So I selected this opportunity in particular. I now understood that I placed upon my shoulders this burden, and which would be prohibitive for me to discard. So from the *Gotimna*[4] of India I was transferred to the *Gotimna* of Russia. There I was supposed to finish preparing for the execution of my mission, which my *I* accepted from above.

In front of me is a junction of paths: it appears to every person who enters this stratum. Once the selection is made it is impossible to change the long centuries that will be spent in one of the many worlds that are here chosen. I could freely select one of the 2: either an ascent into the heavenly India, the end forever of the route of reincarnations, and its exchange for the route of an ascending transfiguration traversing strata of a different form of matter; or else the other one, which also consists of several that exist in *Enrof*, but not as the result of bundled karma, since it was unbundled, but as a means of materializing the tasks to which only I was assigned, and with which I was entrusted, and which I freely accepted.

---

[4] The garden of supreme destinies, because here the destinies of souls are foreordained.

Later Daniel composed some poetry regarding this other life of the past that occurred in India.

> The blinding wind of May,
> Excited, the camp cried out,
> We have arrived from the Himalayas,
> To the turbulent Hindustan.
> From these days a new has started,
> Life, did I recognize you then?
> Like a child the first word,
> You sealed on my lips.
> All flowered, jungles were thin
> And over the blue sea the hills
> Messengers of enemy tribes shouted,
> In the red midnight darkness of cities.
> But I died. I changed my face,
> The days that were, but not history past,
> And like the quiet snow of the north,
> My face turned pale.

Daniel also mentions Italy in passing in a prison notebook, calling it a place of overwhelming promiscuity. But nothing more.

One interesting statement was recorded by Victor Vasilenko in his memoirs, in regard to a conversation he had with Daniel:

> He related to me especially a lot about *Monsalvat*, about the cup of the Holy Grail. He spoke of the troubadour who dedicated his entire life for the search of *Monsalvat* and at the very end died somewhere in the east, beyond Iraq, and so never finding it.
>
> Daniel, writing about *Monsalvat*, said that in a previous life he approached the Grail. He saw the church from a nearby cliff, but he was not allowed any closer.

In his notes on his journeys to the spirit realm, there existed a region he called – personal. This experience he was able to express in poetry and scattered in various other compositions. One of these was his previous lives, as he wrote in his poem *Ancient Memory*:

> I changed cycles
> The days of existence
> But they were no longer.

A few months before his death, Daniel wrote his final poem, and part of the poem deals with his expectation of a future incarnation in a world of perfection for both himself and his wife Alla:

> The third request: so it is destined
> For me to again be incarnated,
> Allow me to be born in such a country,
> At such a time, when the waves
> Of divine creativity and veracity of souls prevail
> And the Dark one cannot state: Silence!
> Give to both of us, wife and myself,
> Earth to touch in such a country,
> Where temples are built, and the entire nation
> Ascends to you generation after generation.

Early Life of Daniel Andreev

1896

Not everything was so clear to Daniel Andreev regarding his origin. He wrote in his diary, "I knew little of my biological parents."

According to general opinion, the marriage of Leonid Nikolaievich Andreev and Aleksandra Mikhailovna Veligorski was seldom happy. He was from Oryol, in central Russia, and was attending law school in Moscow, and writing poetry and drama in his spare time. They met in 1896 at a summer estate in Tsaritzino, just south of Moscow. Leonid wrote to friends:

> During the summer I took some classes at Tsaritzino and lived with some marvelous people, with whom I felt at home, just as I do with you. I spend entire days just residing at their home.

This was the home of Pavel Mikhailovich Veligorski, and he introduced Leonid to his brother-in-law, Philipp Aleksandrovich Dobrov, married to his older sister, Elizaveta Mikhailovna. The other sister of the Veligorski home was Aleksandra and another brother was Petro who lived in Nizhni-Novgorod. One special person who would be critical in the family later was Aleksandra's mother, Efrosina Varfolomaievna, who had the nickname of Businka.

Even before his marriage, Leonid acknowledged in one of his letters:

> The Dobrov family has awesomely become for me a strong support in all of my sorrows and has provided me moral strength. If it were not for these Dobrovs, I would have assimilated into the world.

1898-1901

In 1898, Leonid is again in Tsaritzino with the Dobrov family. The happy summer ends quickly. He spends his time writing dissertations and stories, squandering time in taverns, and subsequently jails, and in the meanwhile quarrelling with his future bride while at their home. At the beginning of 1899, Leonid admitted himself into a hospital to recover from neurasthenia. Aleksandra visited him regularly at the request of her mother. Leonid was disorganized and imbalanced, suffered depression and melancholy, and had drinking bouts, but success was still granted him. In 1901, he published his first volume of short stories. Critics wrote and spoke highly of them.

1902-1904

On the night of January 31, 1902, the police entered the home of Leonid and searched it, looking for letters to Maxim Gorki. Leonid had written to him:

> It is not a good time for me to marry. Yesterday my brother just disappeared without a trace. Apparently he is sitting in Butirskaya Prison. My mother just wails over the event. The center of the city is occupied with soldiers and Cossacks, the streets are blockaded. I bumped into some long and black carriages under a strong convoy of Cossacks and I wept. This place is

suffocating me, but I cannot postpone my wedding. Relatives have arrived here from all ends of Russia, many old people included.

Leonid and Aleksandra married February 10, 1902, at the Church of St Nikolai the Wonder Worker, along the Arbat in Moscow, which was thick with snow that day. His best man was his bride's cousin, a corporal of the Voronezh infantry, Mikhail Aleksandrovich Dobrov[5]. Aleksandra was 21 years of age, 10 years her husband's junior, when they married. Every person who knew her spoke and wrote of her if not joyously, then with clear kindness, calling her young and nice, happy and considerate. Everybody testified that she would bring much happiness to Leonid Andreev. The Russian poet Valari Veresayev, a person not inclined to complements, nevertheless noted, "I have not met a better wife and friend that a writer could have."

Maxim Gorki remembered her as a thin, fragile young lady with nice clear eyes, contrite and silent. He spoke of her as a rare woman with an intelligent heart and loved to refer to her as Dame Shura[6], and this was flattering to Aleksandra, as she later recorded in her diary, coming from such a famous writer.

During their honeymoon, fleeing the Moscow turbulence, the Andreevs traveled to Odessa and then the Crimea, where the weather was warmer. Gorki had a winter home in Oleyiz, where they stayed for about a month, and then returning to Moscow. For Leonid, the years he spent with Aleksandra, were happy ones; they seemed to pass unnoticeable and quickly. During these initial years of their marriage, his fame as a writer increased in Russia. Often Leonid would read his short stories and poetry to his brother-in-law Dr Philipp Dobrov, and they were also the best of friends. On a few occasions, the Andreevs and Dobrovs vacationed together in Finland.

---

[5] Later in 1906 he was arrested and sent to Siberia for revolutionary activities.
[6] Shura is a diminutive of Aleksandra in Russian.

On Christmas Day of 1902, their first child was born in Moscow, Vadim Leonidovich. But then it became impossible for Leonid to continue to live in Moscow and he relocated to St Petersburg in October, 1905, as he could no longer tolerate the scene of tortured bodies and brutality. As much as he wanted to believe that this revolutionary year was a gracious rain upon Russia, the reality was intolerable for him. Subsequently Leonid was arrested and spent almost 3 weeks in Taganskaya Prison in Moscow and, after his release, the family moved from one apartment to another. Due to Leonid's anti-militarist views, as described in his short story *Red Laugh*, published in 1904, and other anti-war articles, he was threatened, "We need to butcher this swine."

1906

From Petersburg, Leonid departed for Berlin, but only for a short while. In May 1906, he migrates to Helsinki, Finland, and settles there. The Russian police discovered his location and trailed him. Fearing arrest he again departed for Berlin, arriving there August 14, 1906, and the heat was intensive that year. The travels took their toll on the expectant mother, Aleksandra, with their second child. Leonid did all he could for the care of his wife, moving to a city outside of Berlin, Grünewald, close to Brandenburg, with doctors available. There in their apartment, he continued to write his short stories and poetry. Aleksandra's mother was living near them at the time and so was Leonid's mother.

Daniel Leonidovich Andreev was born October 20, 1906, in Grunewald, at their apartment. Aleksandra however began to fever after childbirth, and her temperature rose to 106. Her condition worsened and the doctors could not help, except to give her morphine for the pain. Aleksandra Mikhailovna died 7 days after childbirth, October 27, 1906. The grandmother took the newborn and left for Moscow to the family of her other sister, Elizabeth Dobrov. Traveling was difficult, as Daniel himself was ill. Eventually, the body of Aleksandra was moved to Moscow and she was buried at the Novo-Devichi Monastery on December 5, at a cemetery plot that Leonid had purchased earlier for his family.

Leonid in complete despair took his older son and mother and departed from Germany to Cyprus, where Maxim Gorki was residing at the time. He began to drink again, unable to recover from the shock of losing his wife and the departure of his son to Russia. Leonid blamed the Berlin doctors in the death of Aleksandra, unable to help to decrease her fever, but it was useless.

Maxim Gorki agreed to be the child's godfather and Daniel was christened on March 11, 1907, at the Church of the Savior Transfiguration, on the Arbat in Moscow. Leonid remained in Cyprus, unable to travel to Russia due to fear of arrest at this time, so Daniel's uncle, Pavel Mikhailovich Veligorski, stood in his place. A letter written by Gorki was read at the conclusion of the ceremony stating his desire to be Daniel's godfather.

In later years, some critics of Leonid Andreev surmised that he blamed the death of his wife on the new-born son, and as a result the grandmother had to remove him from the father's presence. Leonid was likewise in turmoil that an Orthodox priest was not available at the time to perform last rites and communion for his wife on her deathbed.

1907-1910

The following year, in August 1907, Leonid managed to travel to Russia and visit his son and also his wife's grave. One of Leonid's early plays was also being performed in Moscow in October, but he had an altercation with the director, Konstantine Stanislavski. The play was still performed, although not to the satisfaction of the playwright.

Dr Philipp Aleksandrovich Dobrov was not only a relative, but a longtime and close friend of Leonid. After finishing medical school at the Moscow University, Dobrov spent the balance of his life – almost 50 years – working at the First City Hospital, and it seems that every person in Moscow knew him. When Daniel arrived in December 1906, to live with his new family, Dr Dobrov moved to a larger apartment at the Spasso-Peskovski intersection. Later they would move to an even larger apartment at Mali Levshinski, which residence Daniel would remember the most.

Dobrov was already 40 years of age when Daniel arrived, and the family was a happy one. The Dobrov home was always surrounded by writers, artists, musicians, singers, and so many that it often seemed that his vocation was not medicine, and he also played piano. It was very much a comfort to Leonid that Philipp and Elizabeth agreed to adopt Daniel as their son and raise him. For all practical purposes, Daniel grew and respected them as his parents and the house on Mali Levshinski was his home and the one he remembered all his life. While incarcerated at Vladimir Prison, Daniel wrote a poem titled *Old Home*, dedicated to the memory of his uncle:

> Two giant dogs,
> Guarded the quiet court,
> Where flowers and grass reached to the knees,
> In the rooms there lived
> Life, thoughts, books
> Beyond the walls.
> Children's game with fans
> Blowing this way and that way
> And the agitation of sleep's riddles,
> While the adults argued
> And hearing names of leading figures
> Of all the ages.
> And on the outside of the door,
> Pleasant and trustworthy,
> The plaque read: Dr Dobrov,
> And calm and moderately
> Life continued here joyously,

Widely.
O, my father, not with blood,
Do you install a will!
My dear uncle: mentor and friend!
Among the blessed
The best days
Sustained my infantile spirit.

The house was unsightly from the outside, having two-stories, with a wooden second floor and it was definitely old, with a history of having been a residence for Napoleon's soldiers during their short occupation, and then rebuilt in 1832. The entire first floor of 7 rooms was occupied by the Dobrovs, and a kitchen that was located in the cellar. The house had a yard with a few large trees.

It was the grandmother Veligorski who provided a happy childhood for Daniel, doing for him what she could not do any more for her daughter, and so her life and love was concentrated on raising Daniel. He and the rest of the household referred to her as Businka. She was a dedicated Russian Orthodox and would raise Daniel to be equally religious and a devout adherent of Orthodoxy. She also impressed on Daniel that this was his home and his uncle and aunt were to be respected as his parents.

The following year Leonid remarried. His new bride was Anna Ilyinichka, and they subsequently had 3 children: 2 sons Savva and Valentin, and a daughter Vera. In 1907, he acquired a private house for his new family in Vammelsuu, Finland, (today known as Serovo), along the Chornoi River, not too far from the Gulf of Finland, about 40 miles north-west of St Petersburg. Leonid's fame likewise increased as he continued to write his short stories and poetry, and he was soon able to return to Russia, working regularly in St Petersburg. The drawback was that whenever Leonid was in Moscow he would visit his Aleksandra's grave and descend into depression and drink again.

Leonid still firmly wanted son Daniel to be close to him, so at least during the winter of 1909-1910, Daniel lived with him and

Vadim at the house on Chornoi River. All that remained in Daniel's memory is that the house had many windows, along with the winter snowfall and the ice-cold Finnish wind. His brother Vadim was convinced that Daniel could not adapt to the father's house because he was still worried about and had a warm feeling toward the Dobrov home, where he had been living. After the winter was over, grandmother Businka came to the house and took Daniel back to Moscow, it was obvious to her that Daniel had a resentment toward his step-mother Anna. The next opportunity that Leonid saw his son was 2 years later in 1912, and he was again back at the house on Chornoi River, but this was during the summer that year. In later years Daniel would write about the enjoyable occasion he experienced that summer. Daniel returned to Moscow to the Dobrovs in autumn.

Daniel would also visit Petersburg with father Leonid. He later told the story of how the 2 of them were walking, and Daniel tightly holding his father's hand, when suddenly Leonid stopped and began talking to someone. The person was tall. Daniel began to tug on his father's hand, but he stood firm while talking. Finally the 2 adults bid farewell to each other, and then Leonid told Daniel, "This was the poet Aleksandr Blok." Of course this surprised Daniel that his father knew such a famous person. In April 1910, Leonid visited Leo Tolstoy at his estate near Tule, Russia.

1911-1914

Leonid traveled to Italy for the winter of 1913-1914, returning to Petersburg that spring.

Grandmother Businka passed away in spring of 1913. Daniel had contracted diphtheria and while caring for him, she contracted it herself and then died; her resistance and immune system was weak already as opposed to the strong boy. Daniel was quarantined and isolated from the death of his grandmother until his recovery. The following summer of 1914, Daniel was again with his father at the house on Chornoi River, and he contemplated suicide, even at the age of 8 he missed his grandmother that much. In later years he would remember the event and wrote a poem titled *Nemerecha* regarding it.

> Yes, from my childhood years;
> From my childhood sorrow,
> At the shores of the Baltic's pale waters
> I understood death as a distant summons
> From beyond the sea,
> As a white, white distance steamship.
> There, beyond the seas is the sun and Cherubim,
> And I, in despair, will meet my mother in paradise,
> And my beloved grandmother,
> And the Good Sorceress hovering over them.

This occurred the final year they spent at the Gulf of Finland, it was the year before the war. That summer, its seaside strolls and sparkling stars of the night, left a permanent impression on Daniel. In July 1914, they visited Naantali, Finland, near Turku, traveling there aboard Leonid's schooner, the trip taking 2 weeks. Philipp Dobrov and family and also Vadim were there vacationing. While there they heard about the beginning of World War 1. The Dobrovs returned to Moscow with both Vadim and Daniel, the father feeling they would be more safe there.

The 2 boys slept in the room that formerly belonged to grandmother Businka. The Dobrovs likewise surrounded young Vadim with their love. Since he was now 12 and without a mother of his own, the family did their best to compensate, even though step-mother Anna had been doing her best.

When summer ended, Vadim began to attend Polivanov School and which was next door, at the corner of Mali Levshinski and Prechistenka. Vadim wrote about his brother Daniel, that he was tall and slender, with a high forehead, shy, not physically strong, and was afraid of heights. Vadim soon began to feel homesick and lonesome for his father, and would not stop talking about him. In November the Dobrovs decided to return Vadim to his father for a week. During the journey to Petersburg, they already had a premonition that once Vadim left, he would not return.

The Dobrov home was anything but quiet. It was always filled with Dr Dobrov's patients, associates, friends, and friends of friends. The large dining room table was always filled and crowded. Daniel was the youngest in the household and he was spoiled and mischievous. Cousin Shura (Aleksandra) was 14 years his senior, and Aleksandr was 6 years his senior. Daniel preferred to play with girls, often wearing their dresses when playing children's games at home. Daniel did not miss his brother or father, his new mother conducted schooling for him in the home and she provided him with lessons to keep him busy during the day while she was at work. They nicknamed him Danya.

1915-1916

About this time, Easter of 1915, Daniel began his sketches in notebooks of imaginary fictional characters with dinosaur attributes, and attributing to them names, such as Ipsilofodon, Stenakodon, and several more dozen fossil animals figured as humans, whatever his imagination could create. They would later surface in *Rose of the World* as demonic powers. That same year Daniel began to wrote poetry and prose, just at the age of 9 years, and he had less of a desire to complete regular studies and music lessons. Daniel likewise hung on the walls of his room the drawings he created of his imaginary dynastic rulers, those that he preserved in his notebooks.

Leonid did not appear again in Moscow until summer 1915, since his previous visit in 1910. However, his visit with son Daniel was short. In memory of his visit, Daniel composed a short poem:

> A sad hymn of farewell,
> A quiet hymn of the fields,
> A ringing hymn of greeting,

A long hymn of avenues.
All the hymns merge
Into one strange sound:
It will at one time shake,
And at another time still the air.

Leonid also succeeded in a 2nd visit to Moscow that year, arriving October. But every time he was in the region, his business with literary and theatrical affairs took the primary purpose. Since Leonid's life was convulsive and spasmodic, he spent little time visiting his son at Dobrovs. He wrote much, he nervously lived through the war, all of his compositions directed toward the destined and inevitable revolution he felt Russia was drawing toward, and this stifled within himself the constant alarming melancholy. From another facet, if he did not write, he was not living. During these years Leonid Andreev was one of the most famous of all Russian authors – prose and poetry, but he felt himself misunderstood and oppressed. He admitted in a written statement in October 1915:

> Almost all of my best things I wrote during the interval of my greatest individual disorder, during the periods of my most difficult psychological experiences. That persecution to which I was subjected over the past 7-8 years in Russia overwhelmingly reduced the quality of my work. Do any of the critics still recognize me? No one anymore, it seems. But some readers still love my work, even if they do not know who I am. But who are they? Either the ill, or else the suicidal, those close to death, or just the lower classes. People have confused ingenuity with worthlessness, life with death, health with illness. They are garbage, just as I am.

This diagnosis did not only pertain to himself or to his reader, but also to his contemporary Russia: WW1 was in progress, the country was in political and economic upheavals, and a revolution was on the horizon. To escape the psychological turmoil, Leonid spent his time with his new wife Anna and son Vadim and the 3 newest children: Savva, Vera and Valentin, at their house on Chornoi River, and he would often go on cruises in his yacht.

The final time Daniel saw his father and brother was in July 1916, at the Dobrov summer estate at Butovo, south of Moscow. They were there 3 weeks and then Leonid and Vadim returned to Petersburg. Leonid visited Moscow for the final time October 14, 1916, for the premier of his play *Requiem*. He was only there for a week. With the victory of the Bolsheviks in November 1917, Leonid considered this the victory of the power of evil and destruction, and he foresaw the advent of impunity for mass murder now that a drunk satan had ascended to the throne of authority over Russia. From his home in Finland, Leonid wrote fervently against the new Soviet government. Of course, the events of 1918-1919 caused Leonid to devolve further into depression.

The greatest of Russian writers of the era, Leonid Nikolaievich Andreev, died unexpectedly and suddenly of heart failure, September 12, 1919, in the village Neuvola, Finland.[7] He died at the home of his friend F.N. Falkovski and was buried in Marioki, Finland, near his home, 48 years of age. The news of his death reached Moscow in a laconic telegram with a small obituary in newspapers, and most would not believe it. So was the era, the newspapers were saturated with news anyway of the civil war and the new government. The Dobrovs likewise would not accept the news until they received a letter from Paris, from his widow Anna Ilyinichka. Paris now became the new home for Anna and the 3 other children. (Vadim eventually moved to Paris after his term in the White Army in Russia's Civil War.)

Daniel Andreev, continuing to grow and mature, and not seeing his father after 1916, from the age of 10, could no longer imagine him as a genuine human, especially with all the fame that surrounded the man, but as a mythological figure. So was Daniel referred to: son of the famous writer Leonid Andreev.

---

[7] now in Russia and known as Gorkovskoi, located just above St Petersburg

Vadim remembered his uncle Dr Dobrov in the following manner:

> Uncle Philipp in his complex character was a typical Russian intellectual. He would sit with guests until midnight discussing the revolution, God and humanity. The heart-to-heart talks and psychological goodness and kindness were here united with almost Puritan severity and self-control. The immense cabinet was with filled bookshelves and soft sofas, with a large Bechstein piano – Philipp Aleksandrovich was an excellent pianist. Least of all the cabinet would remind people that he was a doctor. The visiting room, which was located alongside the cabinet, was where he treated patients, and when not in use, it was where I did my school lessons. In the dining room, separated from the cabinet by a thick curtain, on the wall hung a portrait of father, one that he painted himself, and at the time with a bald chin, the Leonid Andreev of that era. The house was filled with much furniture, large cupboards, gigantic drawers, and racks.

All who visited the Dobrov home remembered the host with ecstasy. He was hospitable with all, not only because of his character of a self-denying and self-sacrificing doctor, but as a person with a famous and profound personality. It was this principled atmosphere that Dr Dobrov created that nourished Daniel.

All the Dobrovs were musically inclined. Dr Dobrov's sister, Sophia Aleksandrovna, was an organist. Visitors at the Dobrov home included the composer and pianist Aleksandr Skryabin and the opera singer Feodor Shalyapin. Daniel was also exposed to the music of Richard Wagner at the home. Cousin Shura Dobrova taught drama at a local school, but she was never able to become an actress herself because of stage fright.

Daniel was the youngest, and they all loved him and spoiled him, and at least until the post-revolutionary reality made life for the family difficult, his childhood was happy. As his future wife Alla recollected from her conversations with him in later years:

> He thanked God for this to his final days and remembered many happy and amusing episodes from his childhood. For example, a private tutor would visit Danya and he provided him 2 rewards at the end of one week for his success in his studies and conduct. One was a tablet with the Sanskrit alphabet and the other was a ticket for a ride around Moscow, first by horse carriage and late by streetcar. The Sanskrit letters mesmerized the boy with a love of India, and riding around Moscow strengthened Daniel's congenital love for his native city.

Based on Daniel's notebooks, we can recognize some of the children's games that he would play: cup-and-ball, hoop rolling[8], croquet, and the card game solitaire.

Often Daniel would spend summer months together with the Muraviovs, a family that was close friends with the Dobrov, at the estate of their grandmother in the village Scherbinino, about 10 miles outside of Tver. Daniel was sent there together with Olga Yakovlevna, another cousin now living in the same house as the Dobrovs. The childhood friendship of Daniel with the Muraviov sisters remained through the end of his life. As a teenager, Daniel had incidences of infatuation, the first being the 16 year old Irina Muraviov, whom Daniel fantasized of marrying one day, although the girl never suspected such a thing, and so he wrote in later years. Daniel wrote a poem about another passing infatuation:

> She reads in her hammock,
> She laughs, there in the patio.
> While I, squatting on the sand,
> Watching the trees, weaving the branches.

---

[8] Or hoop trundling

She descends to play croquet,
Together we knock with our sticks.
No hope, no hope.
I am only 8, she is 13.
She is taking a stroll in the meadow,
She calls to the adults,
And I drag myself home alone,
Skipping across the gate.
Onto the terrace where she sits
Watching the day end.

Daniel Andreev after his release from prison, at Gorachi Kluich, 1958

Alla Andreeva at the Mordovia Labor Camp

THE EARLY YEARS OF SOVIET RUSSIA

1917-1918

In 1917, Daniel turned 11 years of age. The revolutionary events he comprehended not only from the conversations of adults, but that life changed rapidly, the events of today quickly superceded the events of yesterday. October 1917, bonfires were burning at all the major intersections of Moscow, armed people crowded around them. When the Junker infantry began their revolt against the Bolsheviks, Dobrov's quiet intersection was filled with Moscow militia and bonfires at night. The Junkers and Bolshevik soldiers would battle each other in public. Gunshots were heard all over Moscow, increasing toward the evening, and canons echoed. During November, fighting was prevalent in all the streets: broken walls, beaten windows. Soldiers lined all the streets. The talk at Dobrov's table was about Kerenski being ousted, the new leaders were Lenin and Trotsky, how was Russia to survive, how was Moscow to progress. Ration cards were issued: in December it was a quarter-pound of bread per person per day. In January 1918, the Patriarchal treasury was pillaged by the Soviets. The new style calendar was installed February 1, and the next way was February 14.

That year, 1918, was the first year in Moscow history that the Kremlin was closed for Easter services.

At the end of May that year, members of the Cheka entered Apartment 9 of the house next door to the Dobrovs and arrested all the members of a counter-revolutionary group that called itself *Union to Defend the Homeland and Freedom*. At 2 o'clock in the afternoon, a truck drove up to the house and some members of the Cheka jumped out, broke into the apartment, and took the alleged conspirators, they were hardly unaware of what was occurring to them.

Daniel recorded these revolutionary events in his notebook.

After the revolution, the Dobrovs lost several rooms of their home to the state as residences for others: from 9 rooms they were down to 3, even with same number living there, and the kitchen and bath became communal. But all of Moscow was this way, living in small quarters. Dr Dobrov's cabinet became living and dining room, even with the piano in the center, while Daniel's bedroom was divided in half with a curtain: he on one side and the girls on the other. The 3rd room was occupied by Dr Dobrov and his wife.

1919-1920

In 1919, Arseni Mitrofanich, a cousin whose father died of typhoid fever, moved in with them. In 1923, a nun of the Novo Devichi Convent, Feoklusha, who had no family and was displaced when the convent was closed by the Soviets, moved in with them.

This year of 1919 was especially difficult for the Dobrovs. That spring Dr Dobrov was infected with typhus, and it was not until sometime that summer that he recovered. The coming winter was expected to be famine-stricken and freezing with heavy snowfall. That winter, everything superfluous or unnecessary was burned in the furnaces for warmth, whatever would ignite and fit.

Daniel's education began in September 1917 at a private school for both genders supervised by Evgenia Albertovna Repman, whose grandfather arrived in Petersburg in 1816 from the Netherlands and started schools. The Moscow branch was founded in 1907 and was advertised as, "one of the foremost and democratic, practical institutions for the best education." Daniel was 10 years of age. During the years 1918-1919, students and teachers changed quickly at the Repman school, and it was only the persistent and firm who survived. However, once the Soviet school system was implemented in the new Soviet Union, Repman became likewise a Soviet institution and new procedures and subjects were introduced. The teachers, who were dedicated Orthodox Christians, were no longer able to impress the students with the necessity of attending communion or studying Orthodox catechism. But Daniel excelled in all the subjects taught, except he was a failure in mathematics.

Daniel would walk to school. He was dark complexioned, a long nose, and it seems that when he met a gang of other boys on the Arbat, they would corner him and call him a Jew, and demand to see his cross.[9] He would not show it to them and just fight his way out.

In Daniel's school notebooks we can find prototypes of all his subsequent books. Meditating, he would compose poems already in his early teens, and with new words created that would apply to his future cosmology:

A child playing near a poplar – this is Titan.
The planet seemed to me as children.
And I gave it a nickname, and proud one: *Orliontana*.
I heard in its sounds the power of mountains,
The distant rivers, the worlds.
From where? Whose will creates the resonance?
The child no longer knows what the edge is called,
The giant cliffs, the substance of another system,

---

[9] Russian Orthodox always wore a cross around their neck.

Whose flesh are the enormous Andes,
Urals and Himalayas.

So did Daniel record his childhood compositions, seeing in them unrecognized revelations of other worlds.

His first composition that is still preserved in his school notebook is the history of the country *Mishinii*. Here the author creates something rather like a chronological narrative of 2 ruling dynasties: the Yurasovski and the Klimski. Divided into paragraphs and narrating their wars, internecine strife and revolts, the characteristics of the changes evolving into one replacing another on the throne and the alternating possession of authority. The composition also testifies to Daniel's familiarity with the popular *Lectures on Russian History* of professor Sergei Feodorovich Platonov due to many parallels between them. It is fully possible that he started his chronicle after his first history lessons at school. In his infantile naivety, but acuteness, he lists about 40 fictitious reigns, and this in itself makes the historical epic of *Mishinii* impressive. His dedication to his Orthodox religion is also apparent in the narratives as well as the role that religion plays in the progress of history. Some of the wars also appear to incorporate events of the Russian revolution and subsequent civil war. The glorified and credited rulers are those who loved and worried over their homeland and observed God's commands.

On the wall in Daniel's room hung a map of a hemisphere of a planet that he had invented. It was called *Yunona*. Alongside it hung hand-drawn portraits of his imagined rulers of *Yunona*. A complete series of such portraits and similar maps accompanied Daniel's notebook with the title, *Short Description of the Country of the Planet Yunona*. If his chronicle of *Mishinii* was a historical composition, then the description of *Yunona* was a geographic. This newer text always reflected more experience and adult exposure than the former. All of such qualities are also noted in *Rose of the World*. With the same mythological thoroughness he attempts with *Yunona*, Daniel does the same with the structure of *Shadanakar*, his *zatomisies*,[10] *sakualas*,[11] *shrastras*,[12] and etc. Here is also the *Orliontana*,[13] that he mentions in his poetry, with a description of its geography and history. Daniel also indirectly reflects on Russian history in *Orliontana*, which, as he states:

> It abounds with all possible sectarian groups, political parties, and there often occurs revolutions and revolts, which are suppressed nevertheless and usually with the help of other countries. In the recent past, there occurred a colossal revolution. This revolution is popularly known as the Great *Orliontanski* Revolution.

So already during his adolescent creation of mythology, the opaque and naïve beginning of his mystic epos – *Russian Gods* – can be viewed. For future wife Alla, this was a testimony of Daniel's inherent or innate tie with another reality. She wrote later in her memoirs:

> The stream of letter-sounds and word-formations which later materialized in a ripe poetic creation was already being instilled into the child. When a person becomes familiar with Daniel's childhood notebooks, it becomes only so apparent the other powers were preparing the child, that his early and prenatal literal encounter with death was an early closeness to another world and one that would occupy him forever. And it seems that his entertaining games with words were also complex exercises in the audio communication with these other worlds. This direction to other worlds appeared in him unusually early.

---

[10] The *zatomises* are the higher strata of all the meta-cultures of humanity
[11] The system of 2 or several diverse-materiality strata, tightly connected together structurally and meta-historically.
[12] The other-spacial material strata, connected with certain zones in the corporeal body of the planet Earth.
[13] The world of spirits of mountain summits; queen of the snow-capped heights.

Then he was attracted from that time on to astronomy. Nights he would climb upon the roof and for hours stare and gaze at the star-filled sky. Father Leonid heard of his son's enthusiasm in a letter from him, and he responded to the Dobrovs, "Surrounding all of you are wars and revolutions, but he writes me an entire letter about nothing but stars."

The books Daniel read during his adolescence, and lived-out in his imagination, as revelations, even after decades, remained deep in his conscience. Daniel read Yogi Ramacharaka's book, *The Inner Teachings of the Philosophies and Religions of India*, at the age of 13, and Daniel later admitted that this book, "Played a very great role in the history of my development."

Daniel devoured Ramacharaka's writings during the year of 1920, but there is no evidence whether Daniel knew this was William Walker Atkinson, an American attorney from Pennsylvania, writing under this pseudonym. The writings caused Daniel to believe that he had a previous birth and life in India, and impressed on him that all forms of religion are equally good, and that the present humanity is distant from its original spirituality. Atkinson's books circulated in Russian translation before WW1 and became popular due to the people's desire of a spirituality they could not acquire in Orthodoxy, the sectarians, or the atheists. Daniel's reading included Hatha Yoga, and he would practice the breathing exercise as discussed in the book. But it was *Inner Teachings* that defined several of Daniel's views to at least some measure and he introduced them into *Rose of the World*. Concepts of cosmic breakthrough, spiritual cognizance, theory of reincarnation, the thought that humanity in its development must attain a genuine and original religious spirituality, the reality of the existence of higher powers, the growth of the cognizance of humanity as a brotherhood, and more ideas that Daniel obtained from Ramacharaka now became his personal own, and he would live them in his inner person during the years of his incarceration.

Ramacharaka's books became the accidental kernel that sprouted the concept of divine announcement. Daniel wrote in a notebook:

Only in accidental valuable moments do we recognize within ourselves the existence of spirit and at such moments do we sense that we stand before the awesome figure of the Unknown. Such moments can occur when the person is immersed in profound religious contemplation or when he delves into a poet's compositions, what is proclaimed from soul to soul.

From this moment forward, Daniel would intently await and listen to the message disclosed to his inner soul, the news he must proclaim. But Daniel would never become a theosophist, but he united all of his concluded concepts with the fundamentals of Russian Orthodoxy in a poetic picture of a universal ideology.

Dobrov family life during the initial years after the revolution was especially difficult, alarming and dearth. But it was this way for everybody. Dr Dobrov worked hard, attempting to feed a large family that could not adapt to this new form of existence. He started to also moonlight with the preparation of medicines. People found out about this and ordered his home-made medicines; Daniel would deliver them throughout Moscow.

1921-1922

The year 1921 was also difficult. The civil war continued, while peaceful people struggled for survival; just to reach the next day was an effort and each day was different. That August, intense summer heat overwhelmed central Russia and parched the fields. In the provinces of the southern Volga, famine began. People heard horrible news from Petrograd. Aleksandr Blok died of illness, the Soviet government refused him an exit visa to seek medical care in Europe. A conspiracy was uncovered against Soviet authority and the conspirators were arrested and shot, a total of 96. The famous Russian poet Nikolai Gumilev was shot, along with professor Vladimir Tagantzev and his wife Nadezhda Felixovna. This shocked the Dobrov family, due to their close association with this circle of Petrograd poets and scholars.

In August 1921, Daniel experienced an ecstatic state that seemed to be what he read from Ramacharaka – a state of enlightenment, a breakthrough of spiritual cognizance or illumination, even though at first it was not fully comprehendible. Daniel counted this as his first entrance into the mystic reality of another realm. He writes about this in *Rose of the World*.

> The first event of this type that played an immense role in the development of my inner world, in many ways a very defined role, occurred in August 1921, when I was not yet 15 years old. This happened in Moscow, toward the end of the day, at the time when I much loved to aimlessly wander the streets and pointlessly fantasize. I stopped at a parapet in one of the city squares that surrounded the Cathedral of Christ the Savior, one that overlooked the shore [of the Moscow River]. It was a marvelous view that opened over the [Moscow] River, Kremlin and the region beyond the river, with its dozens of church bells and cupolas of many colors. It was about 7 o'clock and the church bells were summoning parishioners for matins. The incident of which I speak opened in front of me, or more correctly said, over me unveiled some turbulent, blinding, unattainable world that enveloped the entirety of the historical reality of Russia in an awesome unity with something of disproportionate size hovering over it.
>
> Many years I was nourished by icons and ecclesiastical ideas, and now gradually I was floating away from them into a circle of special cognizance. Intellect for a long while could not compare with all this, trying to create new and newer designs which somehow had to harmonize the contradictions of these ideas and

interpret these images. The process quickly entered a stage of meditation, bypassing that opportunity for my contemplation of the event. This construction seemed to be erroneous, my intellect could not access the same level of the ideas impressed from the event, and so it required another 3 decades saturated with supplemented and profound experiences for the abysmal depth that was unveiled in my early youth to be properly understood and explained.

Daniel also wrote of this event in a poem:

> Early youth. Fifteen years.
> Moscow summer, quiet and not hot.
> In my soul an ancient light flickers
> From the first-throne light.
> Squares surrounding the Church of the Savior,
> Distant and from the distance a silver speech
> Calmly carrying a native sorrow
> A forged evangel from across the Moscow River.
> I wander about the narrow side streets.
> The five domes glisten reflecting various colors,
> There at the high ambo, I seek
> The burning fire of Orthodoxy.
> In obscure dreams of good and evil,
> The scattered heart long meditates,
> The ancient, partially understood praise
> To the great martyrs and patient in persecutions.
> I see: over the medallion of the green sunset,
> Quietly flying from the roof
> Of the Kremlin, storks of a pink color
> Like silk, soft is the sound of the street.
> In the old vestibule – incense, chants.
> This quenches the strengthening mind,
> Eternal truth regarding the Sun over the world.
> This soul at the exit of its years,
> Still whole like nature,

It whispers an irreconcilable, No.
To the apostate nation.
I amble about the city aimlessly,
I see the Kremlin under the streetcar noise,
The peaceful city stared directly into my eyes,
Perhaps for the worldwide destiny
Destined, Moscow, Moscow!
No, not Moscow, but the Kremlin.
Crosses, towers, domes,
Over each church
The reflection of the sunset.

There was one square alongside the Church of Christ the Savoir, where the empty pedestal of Tsar Alexandr III stood. Daniel strolled through the area many times and even with his nursemaid. But now the area took a different form, and so did the Kremlin in the distance with its crosses, towers and domes. All of a sudden he noticed architectural ensembles that earlier he did not, but now symbolizing the heavenly Kremlin of which he wrote in *Rose of the World*, these great centers of the future religious culture.

> I was hardly 15 years of age when these forms first began to appear in front of me, and it was a year later that I attempted to codify them permanently with the assistance of a pencil. I was not an artist or an architect, but the forms of these ensembles, their exterior and interior, such magnificence, that they wanted to be compared to a chain of mountains of white and pink marble, with the summits crowned with gold medallions while their slopes were covered in flowering gardens and forests. All of this was redefined in my mind from the previous decade of my life and changed my view to another.

Being raised in a house where many artists lived, Daniel loved to draw, but he had a skeptical approach to his artistic abilities.

His cousin, Aleksandr Dobrov, recently completed architectural school, and so did a close friend, Aleksei Shelyakin. Daniel was likewise attracted to architecture, and he collected postcards with views of different cities. But in order to become an architect, it was necessary for him to learn mathematics, a subject totally alien and incompatible to him. As a result, his love for architecture remained in him as unfulfilled mental images of temples of the Sun of the World and mysterious garden-lined cities of the era of ROSE OF THE WORLD.

During the final years of classes, Daniel and a few friends in a humorous fashion created among themselves what they called KIS – Circle of Exceptional Sympathetics, an informal private fraternity. In one respect it was a parody of the Soviet secret regiments with their letter-designations, such as the Cheka and KGB. The KIS-circle of friends – or Kisovski as they called themselves – kept in contact with each other for many years into the future, supporting each other in their individual relative difficulties, and even to the final months of Daniel's life.

On January 3, 1959, Tatyana Olovyanishkova wrote to Daniel:

> "Today I was looking at some old photographs and noticed our Kisovski group. You look well. I am sure you remember all the strolls and trips we took during our Kisovski era."

1923

The last day of school for Daniel was June 19, 1923. The name had changed to Moscow Public School #26, but the students continued to call it Repman. Daniel wrote a poem dedicated to the memory of the end of his education, titled *Waltz*.

> The old school, native and stuffy
> She began to sing, and behold,

> A waltz rocking airy echoes,
> The hall of blinding brightness.
> The grandfathers of reverent calm,
> The eldest of the teachers,
> All the boys and girls dressed in white,
> Welcome, future. To joy, to maturity,
> Do we hear your moving summons,
> The slow whirlwind of pedals.

After the last day of school, the Kisovski friends decided to take a short vacation to Senezhskoi Lake, a reservoir about 40 miles northwest of Moscow. One of the classmates, Nelli Leonova, had a family summer house there, about 4 miles from the lake. The friends ran along the lake, helped the local farmers gather hay, played croquet. In September, Daniel and another classmate, Ada Magidson, together composed a poem to memorialize their summer vacation, titled *Osiniada*.

Daniel's childhood and adolescence and his generation coincided with the revolutionary demolition of the entire traditional Russian life. This demolition was signified by war, a fracture visible to all that evolved into a complete rupture of the country beginning in 1917. At times it would seem that the hurricane would ameliorate, and life flowing again in a proper order would unite the ruptures and make it again as solid as granite. But the sensation of what was occurring was a mysterious reflection of some untraceable cruel struggle, where the participants were raising this bizarre figure of the power of darkness. All of this appeared to him in his school years and became all the perceptible. This sensation was intuitive, poetic and mystic. The terrible and ruthless surfaced from behind the masks of regular people, and who acted as though this was very ordinary.

His wit, his imaginary living pictures, humorous compositions, happy strolls into nature, passing the time in his Kisovski circle, was not only the abundance of adolescent strength, but the attempt to shelter his private world from the attacks of the ruthless reality of the era.

Explaining trans-physical journeys, Daniel speaks somewhat about mystical lasciviousness, where it originates and how it displays its influence.

> If similar journeys occur along demonic strata and so without a guide, but under the influence of sinister aspirations of your individual soul or the treacherous summons of demonic principles, a person, awakening, does not remember precisely anything, but carries from his journey a luring, deceptive, sweetly-horrifying sensation. Out of this sensation, as though from a poisoned seed, only the same type of activities can sprout, which for a while bind the soul during its existence after death to these worlds. Such wanderings occurred with me in my youth, they drew such activities after themselves, and it was not due to any merit of mine that the further radiant path of my life on earth led me further and even further away from these failures into the abyss.

Daniel possessed theories of 2 abysses – the abyss of the celestial world and the abyss of the demonic stratum. In our impulsive drive to the celestial it is difficult to avoid the dangers to end up in the sinister abyss. But this is better than a sinking existence in some inescapable quicksand. A person can still tear out of and dart from the sinister abyss. The sinister abyss that unveiled itself in his presence as a youth acquired the features that he unveils in his compositions, the details that were impressed upon him.

Among these contemplators of the celestial, he names Ivan the Terrible as one that was able to draw himself into the demonic abyss,. In a poem about him, named *The Ruin of the Terrible*, he speaks also of a personal experience. His Ivan experienced the adolescent visions of the Heavenly Kremlin and Sun of the World, playing as a child in the Kremlin garden, where he traversed the tribulations of both abysses. The poet does not want to reject the horrible test, on his path it is unavoidable.

> I will not reject this evil burden,
> These descents into the bosom of fiery powers.
> Only one is worthy of the morning,
> Who passes through the night and is victorious.
> Who at his turbulent edge of existence
> Unraveling the knot, traversing the desert,
> Drinking the jet of a flaming spray,
> A river of Gehenna, and heavenly rivers.

His address not only pertains to a inner experience, but also of the turbulent historical experience of Russia. This sinister period covered the years of his life at ages from 18 to about 22, a personal growth of despair, a growth surrounded by insanity, upheavals, crimes and suicide. But Russia was able to survive the calamitous era. War communism, bloody, cold and famine-stricken, final ended. In 1921, the Soviet government announced the NEP – New Economic Period. Moscow with its pot-holes and worn out building facades, eaten alive by the civil war, slowly resurrected, but the city lived in anxiety. The noise of civil war artillery ended, but now the ideological war arose and was ruthless. The Cheka acted cautiously, no one saw their arrests. The struggle against religion expanded, including any religious philosophy. Unwanted writers and philosophers were exiled from the country. Included in the lists of the Soviet's antirevolutionary literature were the massive libraries of religious philosophers: Plato, Kant, Schopenhauer, Nietzsche, Vl. Solovyov. In the library shelves that were previously reserved for religion, now appeared only anti-religious books.

1924-1925

But Daniel and his Kisovski friends continued to have a sense of optimism, that although all seemed bad, it would soon end. They aspired to hear the summons of the future and continued to believe in love, happiness, laughter and humor. In January 1924, Daniel with some classmates traveled to the village Dunini, near Zvenigorod,[14] west of Moscow, to ski. It was a joyful vacation.

On January 22, 1924, Vladimir Lenin died. Red flags were hung from buildings, cold frost enveloped the city and affected its entire population and that of the entire country.

Rose of the World speaks of the spiritual dissonance that began in Russia in the 18th century, that the compositions of Lermontov, Dostoyevski, Vrubel and Blok were its various historical stages. Daniel finds this dissonance among many authors, whom he also identified as messengers or announcers. Speaking of them, he turns first of all to his personal experience.

> There is a genius that creates its human image, and there is a genius that destroys its human image. The first of them, traversing every type of fall and failure during adolescent years, increases the wealth of its soul and eventually attains a maturity and gradually is liberated from this downward and backward draw and the tendency of self-destruction is annulled, so that in old age it will reveal its image of individuality, all the more and even more harmonic, transforming the memory of its fall into a wisdom of knowledge of good and evil.

Daniel saw the images of mystical lasciviousness in the Luciferian canvases of artist Mikhail Vrubel and in the verses of Aleksandr Blok. These 2 artistic geniuses stood side by side for

---

[14] A small city just west of Moscow, and the Moscow River flows through it.

Daniel, and they particularly represented the demonism of the era, deceit through their debased art and poetry. They made Daniel nauseous.

Daniel nonetheless grew up with Blok's poetry, it was regularly read aloud in the Dobrov home. Father Leonid also felt he possessed an inner family relationship with Blok and highly respected him. Blok's words that, "the revolution occurred not only here, but also in other worlds," was not a metaphor for Daniel, but a precise description of the event. One chapter in *Rose of the World* is dedicated to Blok, titled *Fall of the Messenger*. Daniel presents Blok's fate as a complex tragedy, a spiritual descent down a staircase of mystic levels. In Blok's poetry, Daniel recognizes the urban landscape of the *Duegguer*;[15] he hears the summons of lunar demons of the female gender. The atmosphere of Blok's poetry was mystical, and Daniel vicariously lived the experiences mentioned, as though they were real and not just literature; it was a part of his hidden private life. So it was obvious to Daniel that Blok did not just visit the *Duegguer*, but even sang about it. In Blok's verses Daniel clearly saw the materialization of the *Duegguer* illusions, and in Blok's literary compositions, Daniel everywhere found reflection and images of the demonic worlds.

In order to understand what occurred with Daniel during this sinister period, it is necessary to grasp what he writes about the fall of Aleksandr Blok. Daniel dedicates both love and sorrow to him in *Rose of the World*. Daniel relives Blok's fall as though his own.

> Blok his entire life remained a noble, deeply orderly, sympathetic and good person. He never did anything incorrigible, unforgivable or criminal. The fall was expressed in the external stratum of his life, in the plan of actions that were only a series of drunken evenings, lascivious nights with intoxicated gypsies. People that slither along the superficiality of life do not understand

---

[15] One of the strata of the demonic *stikhials*, having a special significance for humanity.

in essence why such a horrible fall could occur, of what ruin we can speak? But to understand someone else's failure as a fall can only apply to those who themselves have a place from which to fall. Those who sit in life's gutter and mire imagine that this is the normal order of things and is fatal for all.

Subsequently, Blok's fall is forgiven. Daniel mentions in *Rose of the World*, that after a short term of residency in purgatory, together with his father Leonid Andreev and Afanasi Fet, and other excellent but fallible people, he is included in the *sinklit*[16] of heavenly Russia.

Other than Blok and Vrubel, Dostoyevski also accompanied Daniel in his sinister journeys, whom Daniel considered the first of the greatest Russian artistic geniuses. Daniel likewise read as many biographies of Dostoyevski that he could get.

In *Rose of the World*, Dostoyevski is named among those who transformed the memory of his failings into the wisdom of knowledge of good and evil, and likewise placed him with the great contemplators of both abysses. In the souls of Nikolai Stavrogin of *The Devils*, and Arkady Svidrigailov of *Crime and Punishment*, Daniel saw the gloomy glare of the *Deuggeur*. Daniel stated that Dostoyevski guides us as Virgil led Dante through the very darkest, hidden, sinful, and pitch-black descents, not leaving even one corner – undisclosed, and not one demon – hidden and secretive.

Among the great contemplators of both abysses – the celestial and the demonic – other than Ivan the Terrible, Dostoyevski and Vrubel, *Rose of the World* names Lermontov as the 4th. At one time Daniel felt he should have designated Blok as the 4th instead, but his personality was of a smaller scale than the others and his impact was less.

---

[16] Masses of enlightened human souls that are residents of the higher strata of the meta-cultures.

Daniel's mental exhaustion forced him to wander Moscow's midnight streets. Often his intimate friend and classmate Yuri Popov would accompany him. Their sleepless strolls often occurred in the lunar darkness. Daniel would refer to Yuri as the sinister friend of his hated adolescence. Yuri was the sole companion and trusted friend of those nighttime strolls. In his own unfortunate adolescence, Yuri began to drink and over drink to indulgence. He later became an artist, but at the beginning of WW2, Yuri climbed to the top of a roof in an intoxicated state to extinguish a lamb, and then slipped and fell and died as he struck the pavement. The event had a psychologically devastating effect on Daniel, accepting some of the responsibility due to his earlier association, and never forgetting about it. He wrote to wife Alla from prison:

> For example, I still carry in my memory one great, very serious guilt pertaining to the late Yu. Popov. At the time I could not release it, and now after many years he is no longer alive, so it will remain. How to remit it, I do not know where, when and how. But as long as it is not remitted, a sharp, burning feeling of this guilt will reside in me alive, although it seems entire days will pass and I will not recollect this. But that I do not recollect it is due to my absentmindedness, a lack of depth of what occurred.

Daniel did not cease to ask himself similar torturous questions all his life, feeling he was somewhat culpable in his friend's death due to his drinking.

So during this sinister period, Daniel descended into deep depression and the thought of complete self-destruction entered his mind: a series of actions leading him downward and subsequently suicide. He was unable to complete his task, but only wounded himself with a knife and not very seriously. Daniel described such actions as the ministry of evil, and suicide was the complete demonic summons. Daniel sensed himself under the control of darkness and temptation, wandering in a twilight zone. At the same time he felt a Someone sheltering him the entire time from this extreme self-annihilation.

In one of these actions that led downward toward his self-destruction was a bizarre attempted to kill a dog, or perhaps he did succeed. He describes the action in *Rose of the World*.

> There was one incident in my life which I would like to share with you here. This is difficult. The matter is that a few decades ago, I executed this knowingly, even deliberately, an ugly, vile action pertaining to one animal who is in the category of man's best friend. This occurred because at the time I was passing through a certain stage, or better said, a zigzag of an inner path, toward a higher level of darkness. I decided to practice, as I at the time expressed this – a ministry of evil – an idea not fully developed in its stupidity, but which enveloped my imagination and inclined me toward a chain of actions, one more torturous than the other. I wanted to know, finally, if there was in the world some type of action, no matter how base, vile and inhuman, that I would not perform it particularly as the result of my weak character and no resistance toward cruelty. I have no mitigating circumstance as an excuse, that I was a thoughtless child or maybe I fell into bad company. I do not remember having any bad company or surroundings. I was a fully mature adult and a student. I performed the act and on the certain animal that I mentioned, and it is no longer around. But living through the incident seemed so devastating that it changed my attitude toward animals with an unusual force and forever. In general this also contributed to my inner upheaval. And if this shameful blemish did not remain on my conscious, I, perhaps, would not now be suffering such a loathing toward every torture or killing of an animal, often even to losing total control of myself.

This sinister zigzag of his inner path had an effect on his student studies. After completing Repman school, Daniel prepared to enter Moscow University, but they would not allow the son of the counter-revolutionary writer to take the entrance examination. So in 1924, Daniel entered the Valeri Brusov Higher Literary Institute in Moscow, founded just a couple years earlier in 1921, but closing in 1925.

Literary life here boiled over. Students and associates came and read the poetry of Sergei Esenin and Vladimir Mayakovski. Valeri Brusov taught at the institute himself, teaching classes in ancient literature and the science of poetry. Daniel was hardly able to attend his lectures as Brusov died October 9, 1924. The following year the institute was closed and replaced by the Soviet Higher State Literary Courses, or VGLK.

A portion of the students continued their studies in literature courses. Most of them were in the evening but any and all were able to attend, and so many of the students were those who were not able to enter a state university due to genealogy or political affiliation of the parents, as occurred to Daniel initially. As a result the students were a mixed bunch who all were drawn to literature. During the day students would congregate at the Rumyantzevski library, studying, as Daniel did, devouring books on world literature, history, philosophy and religion. One person during Daniel's attendance who later became a close friend was Vadim Safonov, from Kerch, Crimea, and he would also spend time at the Dobrov home.

Soon after, Daniel was accepted into the All-Russia Union of Poets, which was headed by VGLK professor and poet Georgi Arkadyevich Shengeli. The Union integrated poets and novices of diverse interpretation and calibers, and existed until 1929. But in reality, it was of little help to the young poets, except for them to congregate and continue friendships developed in earlier years.

The summer of 1925, Daniel spent in Sudak, on the Crimean Peninsula, at the residence of Evgenia Albertovna Repman. Former students of her school would gather there, and also assist here, since by now she was paralyzed in both legs, and they would likewise provide some financial security for her, now having lost her school to the Soviet school system. Along with him was a classmate Zoya Kisilova and professor A.A. Fomin, and also Gleb Smirnov who became later good friends with Daniel.

1926

In Spring 1926, Daniel unexpectedly received a letter from brother Vadim, the first correspondence in about 10 years, since their father passed away. Vadim finished school in Helsingborg, Sweden, and then in October 1920, traveled to France and then to the south of Russia where he joined the Volunteer White Army in the Russian civil war against the Bolsheviks. At the end of the Civil War, Vadim traveled to Batumi and thence to Constantinople, where he began teaching. From there he traveled to Sofia, Bulgaria, and reached Berlin, Germany, in April 1922. His paternal grandmother was still living in the region and he moved in with her. Vadim attended Berlin University and taught Russian art history, and he published his first book of poetry in 1924. He returned to France and entered the Sorbonne, again teaching Russian art history. In 1926, while in Paris, Vadim married Olga Victorovna Chernova, from a family of Russian art and literary renown.

Father Leonid's wife Anna Ilyinichka with their subsequent 3 children were also living in Paris at the time, but news about them was difficult to acquire, and especially with the Iron Curtain now formed around the USSR. As a result, Daniel felt himself a spiritual orphan, isolated, yet enveloped by unexplainable dreams he could not interpret, his ascension to mystical moods and experiences. This letter overjoyed Daniel with news of his family, including his half-brothers and half-sister. As a result, Daniel quickly responded in a letter, now having an address to which to write:

During this same interval so much has also occurred in my life – mainly the inner. I so much want to see you, speak with you! I have accustomed myself to isolation, and it oppresses me all the harder, but I so much want a brother. I recently lived through one very unpleasant event, when I placed in a stupid position by some vile person, and whom I fully trusted. But this was a punishment for me, because the same type of vile act I imposed earlier on some other person, learning to lie. I wonderfully survived, played my role successfully, and even very much because the result exceeded all my expectations. But this is base and below me from my side, but I still was punished for the matter. I will explain the entirety of this entangled and repulsive event when I see you.

But right now I am occupied with much, and I have bills to pay (those cursed creditors!). In the meantime I was working much on my novel. Know that I have come to the conviction that I will write 2 or 3 novels over the course of my entire life. And not long ones either, since I have been writing this one now 2-1/2 years, and it will only have about 150 pages, and I am now 1/3 of the way through it. I sit entire weeks at my manuscript and I now have 16 thick pencil-written notebooks. I think I will continue to revise and revise, and a hundred times, until in my old age I finally produce something. But it will be 5 or 6 years before it goes to print.

I also wrote verses and as a result I ended up in the Union of Poets. Right now it has been over a month since I wrote any verses, I am too occupied with my prose and my studies.

At home it is all the same as it was in the past: interesting, peaceful and content. Good and interesting people surround me. All of this is quite pleasant. But nonetheless, I am infinitely desperate for changes, but changes of a plain variety, mainly to leave and reside on my own, completely alone, so I can be my own boss. This will occur and I hope, sufficiently soon, and when I say – soon, this means within a year.

Tell me more of your affairs when you have a change to visit. I hope you will respond to this letter. Brother, you are so dear to me! How so much I want to see you! We have so much to talk about. I kiss you! Why did you not write sooner?

The reference in this letter is to Daniel's novel *Sinners*, on which he started before he began attending the Literary Institute. The nights working on his novel were dispersed occasionally with some composition of poetry.

Having completed school, life for the adult Daniel in the large Dobrov family, even though they loved him much, was nonetheless uncomfortable. The apartment was overfilled with residents, it was difficult to find any space to be alone in order to write. For most of residents it was just a place to sleep. When cousin Aleksandra (Shura) Dobrova married Aleksandr Victorovich Kovalenski in 1922, 5 years her junior and still a student, he moved in. Then for a while Daniel shared a room with cousin Aleksandr (Sasha) Dobrov. Then Sasha married Irina and she moved in, and Daniel ended up sleeping in the kitchen. He got accustomed to it and rather enjoyed it, and had some nights to write. Dr Dobrov still had patients he cared for once a week.

In 1915, Kovalenski started medical school at the Moscow University, and at the same time was taking classes in physics and aerodynamics, all at the same time. In 1918, Kovalenski was diagnosed with spondylitis,[17] and spent an entire year in bed and then 7 additional month wearing a plaster corset, and at the same time suffered with epilepsy. After marrying in 1922, he returned to his studies, but due to his illness he transferred to the St. Petersburg Bekhterev Psychoneurological Research Institute, taking classes in physics and mathematics, from which he graduated in 1925. He then began studies in literature. It was

---

[17] Or, Pott's Disease

nothing less than the higher literature courses and Kovalenski's ideology drew him into a close friendship with Daniel. Kovalenski also had musical talent and played piano in order to help him develop his right hand, having lost some of his dexterity in his spinal illness.

From 1926 to 1930, Kovalenski published about 30 children's books, for the most part being verses and rhymes. But as with many authors of the era, Kovalenski was torn between making a living with his books conforming to expected Soviet standards, or not compromising and risking estrangement. Kovalenski was nicknamed Bisha in the Dobrov household. He and his wife Shura had a loving relationship and she considered her husband a genius.

Even in such cramped quarters the family resided friendly, able to laugh and joke. The older Dobrovs fully understood Daniel, always the youngest in the family, and were willing to forgive him much, and he, spoiled by his beloved aunts, was obligated to help the family during these difficult years, so every month Daniel contributed some hard-earned funds.

Some person brought to the Dobrov home a pair of statues that were figures of the gargoyle on top of the Cathedral of Notre Dame. They were placed in the bedroom of Sasha Dobrov, and where Daniel likewise slept for a while. Sasha's mother, Elizaveta Mikhailovna, objected to the statues because of her superstitions that they were creating a bad environment for the household and she attempted to discard them, but only one went into the trash. Daniel objected, saying that they were just art and that her fears were nonsense and superstitious. Daniel hid the remaining gargoyle in his corner of the house.

After a while, Daniel realized that some sinister power resided in the statue, and he told this to Galina Rusakova, who only laughed at him, and in the same manner that he had laughed at his aunt Elizaveta. Daniel took the remaining gargoyle and broke it apart and discarded it.

The gargoyle, as Gothic representations of diabolic hordes, forever remained for Daniel a symbol of sinister worlds, an infernal defilement. Then Daniel began to notice such statues all over Moscow, in the parks, railway stations, on the top of buildings. All of a sudden Daniel felt the presence of some unclean defiling power in the Moscow of the time. He was now 20 years of age, and he sensed a demonic force that birthed a smoky-dark twilight that was so easily attempting to lead him astray.

At one time Daniel loved Moscow, but the city was now not the same. Wandering along the streets only lighted by a gloomy moon and a few streetlights, he now saw a demonic city: Moscow whether day or night with no decoration during the decade of the 1920's. It was a moon-like female demon that illuminated it. She inhabited the empty squares and hidden apartments and railway stations. So did he gaze at the capital at night, penetrated by rays of the *Duegguer*. During these sinister years the element of *Duegguer*, as Daniel described it, saturated the night streets ruined by civil war. Atheist morality with insolent authority suppressed religious morality. Free love was propagated during the early 1920's, with legislation directed toward the annihilation of the family as a legal entity, legalizing abortion without restrictions, and allowing divorce at the request of either party and with impunity. In 1924, Mikhail Bulgakov led a column of nude people across Red Square, carrying banners containing revolutionary slogans. The newspapers carried the stories. The Soviet young people's newspaper, *Komsomolskaya Pravda*, published an article on the topic, The Sexual Question and the Young Communist.

Daniel recorded in his diary on September 12, 1926, how totally nude people with only a scarf around their shoulders would ride on streetcars, absent of any sense of shame. The *Duegguer* celebrated, and it was not just painful for Daniel. When the results of the new legislation and attitude of unrestrained sexual activity were submitted, state authorities put the brakes on it. The statistics of divorce and remarriage were beyond anybody's expectations, with many marrying one day and divorcing the next, and repeating this regularly, innumerable heartbroken women, increase in suicides, tens of thousands of unwanted pregnancies culminating in abortion or in abandoned children or children left to die from exposure. As a result laws to attempt to institute morality were legislated by the Soviet state at the end of the 1920's.

Moscow, having living through war communism, civil war, NEP, people changing apartments, where survivors huddled side by side with both the genuine and imaginary victors, resided just as did the balance of the country, not only impoverished and hungry, but with a feeling that the definition of good and bad had changed on them. During its nights and in dark corners a demonic city mistress definitely reigned. It was along this moonlit Moscow that 20 year old Daniel rambled. He subsequently composed a poem about it.

> At twenty years of age I wandered, as one dead,
> I gazed as a raven,
> The agitated caw sounds loud in the dusk,
> Due to the anger that prevails.

It was especially during these gloomy years that Daniel frequently and regularly entered Russian Orthodox Churches, attending matins and vespers. Those classmates of his who remembered his wit and sharp humor, happy and superior character, were now surprised at rumors of Daniel's religiosity. It seems to have been an unexpected beckoning. Orthodox clergy were being deported to concentration camps, churches were being closed, former seminarians were now writing anti-religion brochures. But the majority in a customary manner were silent.

One of the evils that affected Daniel was his marriage to someone he did not love, Aleksandra (Shura) Gublyor, and this occurred almost unexpectedly for him and which was a surprise for his family. She was also a student at the literary institute and they were taking the same courses. Daniel and Shura married at the end of August 1926, at the Church of the Resurrection at Yuspenski Vrazhke. She was from Kiev and a year his junior: he was 20 and she was 19. She was apparently infatuated with him, or it seems, and pursued him everywhere.

Shura would accompany Daniel in all his wanderings about Moscow, attend all the Orthodox churches with him, wherever time would draw him. But he did not love her. He was stupefied, going around in circles with her on a spiral descent.

Aunt Elizaveta Dobrova described the event in the following manner:

> At the institute he became acquainted with one girl, and saw here at courses and would visit her home. But she never spent time with us. On occasion she would walk in, stay for a minute and they would quickly leave together. During his 2nd year of studies, her visits increased and she had no consideration for the time of day. She would come by at 2 or 3 o'clock in the morning, wake him in bed and take him somewhere, saying that it was some important business matter. She constantly called on the telephone, and based on the conversations that I overheard I concluded that she did not interest him at all. It also seemed to me that this was unpleasant for Daniel.
>
> We were sitting one evening and he was reading to me something he composed, and then be abruptly stood and went out of the room and came back in and went straight to me and said, "Mamachka, I am guilty of doing something to you. So will you ever forgive me?"
>
> I answered, "Danya, my child, what is the matter?"
>
> "Mamachka, I married."
>
> "My dear child, why did you do this?"
>
> "Mamachka, it had to be this way; we love one another."
>
> "But why did you do this clandestinely, so we did not know?"
>
> "While in church during the wedding ceremony I felt that I did not do what was proper. It was so difficult for

me, that you were not in church, and all the time it seemed to me that you would enter."

Seeing him in such a difficult condition, of course, there was nothing I could say. My biggest mistake was in genuinely believing that they loved one another. Of course, he did not love here, but whether she loved him, I can not say. In short, after all the hustle and bustle, by the end of the 2nd month of their marriage, they separated. Now they have acquired a civil divorce, and then they need to deal with the church. I must say that all of this caused Danya stress and exhaustion.

Shura however was unable to decipher the mystical Daniel, and all she saw was the literature student, the unusual and extraordinary poet. She was young and pretty and believed in her happiness. But Daniel was something else that she was not, and she did not see it.

Their marriage was never consummated. After the wedding they went to her residence and Daniel unexpectedly fell ill – scarlet fever. He laid in a high fever that night. Shura let the Dobrov's know about it and cousin Shura immediately came over and took Daniel home. Once he recovered from the illness, he never returned to her.

The early winter gloomy but invigorating weather brought some restoration to Daniel after his illness. He again wrote at nights. After the rupture with Shura, Daniel could not return to his literary classes. Aunt Elizaveta wrote to his brother Vadim:

I need to tell you that it is not easy to get along with Danya anymore. He has become introverted, his character is now stubborn, if not actually obstinate. If something gets into his head, it is next to impossible to rationalize with him. He decided that his studies at the institute, where he has attended the past 2 years and was highly complemented by the professors, that he has nothing more to be gained by attending and so decided to withdraw. How hard we have tried with all of our family strength to convince him not to do this, but it was all futile.

The matter was not his obstinacy, and the household, recognizing this, did not further insist that he stay there. It was obvious that he did not want to bump into Shura. He did not blame her for the incident, but blamed himself, feeling he deceived her and then failed her. It seem to be unbearable for him to see her again, to explain something that she would not remember or not understand anyway, and which he did not himself completely understand.

It was toward the end of 1926 that Daniel's life turned around for the better. He saw the opera, *Tale of the Invisible City Kitezh and the Girl Fevronia*. The city Kitezh was popular in Russian mythology and folklore, having sunk into Svetloyar Lake near Nizhni-Novgorod when attacked by Mongols in the 14th century. Again Daniel saw a mystery surrounding the tale, a city that could not be approached, submerged in the depths of Russia, and protected by the hierarchies of light. Daniel associated the city with his concept of eternal womanhood, the global soul. In *Rose of the World* this figure received the appellation of *Zventa-Sventana*.[18] This female figure Daniel also identified with the Virgin-Mother Mary, as opposed to the prostitute figure of Moscow. Now he repulsed the influence of the demon *Duegguer*, the mistress of the city leading all astray along a dangerous path. So it was here in Moscow, the red city, where he saw an apostate people, having accepted this exchange of good for evil together with blaring slogans and promises of a earthly paradise of socialism, and which caused this change in him.

The Virgin-Mother answered Daniel's prayers, to save him who had gone astray. Later, Alla Andreeva wrote of this event:

---

[18] The great monad born of God expressing eternal Womanhood, the Bride of the planetary Logos, Jesus Christ.

Daniel told me how amazingly his liberation from this sinister hand occurred. This literally occurred in one moment. He beautifully remembered how he entered the front portion of the former hall at the Dobrov home and then as though suddenly something sinister just plainly fell off of him. All then seemed completely lax and defined. Daniel said that Dr Dobrov was in the room at the time, and he saw and understood what was occurring. They did not say anything to each other, but both understood. This seems to me so unusually important.

For a long while, Daniel was not able to explain what occurred to him, or to write about it in an intellectual manner.

Subsequent to this Daniel composed *Twelve Gospels*, a poem pertaining to the Easter season events. Alla recollected how Daniel read the Gospel account to her:

Especially about the resurrection of Christ and the appearance of the Lord to Mary Magdalene. He read it in such a manner that to this time I still hear his voice, and that which occurred two thousand years ago, I felt that I was actually present there invisibly in the garden of Gethsemane.

1927

In Spring 1927, Daniel went to Leningrad. He regularly visited his father's old apartment, now most of it communal, and he became familiar with his 2 cousins on his father's side, who were living there.

While there Daniel visited an exhibit and museum dedicated to his father that was organized by the Pushkin House. Daniel was very impressed with all his father's artifacts, photographs, illustrations in his plays, books and manuscripts that were on display.

The following is a vision in Daniel's life that is not dated but seems to apply to this era, and he records it in the *Rose of the World*:

> Many years ago, long before the Second World War, when I was still very young, I had a vision of an unexplainable, beautiful image that persistently remained with me: it was as though visible from an infinite distance, a bluish pyramid constructed of crystal, through which the sun was shining. I felt its immense significance, waves of grace, strength and beauty emanated from this shining concentration, but I could not understand the meaning of this image. Later, even with my limited human comprehension, I thought this was a refractive reflection of the Global *Salvaterra*.[19] What a childish thought! The person whose soul touches the reflection of the Global *Salvaterra* will have integrity and be prophetic. And then it ended, and such a reflection did not have any tangible aspect at all.

1928

In Spring 1928, as Easter drew near, anti-religious propaganda was more blatant and extreme. Easter Sunday that year was on April 15. The evening of April 14, Daniel went to attend Easter services at the church next door, Intercession of the Virgin Mary at Levshin. Patr Tikhon occasionally performed liturgy at this church, and after his death, Daniel wrote that the patriarch was one of those who entered the *sinklit* of the heavenly Russia.

Daniel's 2nd revelation occurred during that Easter Sunday and which he describes in *Rose of the World*:

---

[19] The name of the summit and heart of *Shadanakar*, the highest of its *sakualas*.

The second incident of this series that I encountered was in Spring 1928, in the Church of the Intercession at Levshin corner. I remained in the church after Easter matins. This liturgy which begins about 2 o'clock in the morning, was special, as popularly known, due to the recitation once a year of the First Chapter of the Gospel of John – In the beginning was the word. The gospel passage is repeated by all priests and deacons participating in the service, from the different ends of the church, in order, verse by verse, in various languages, those utilized and those obsolete. This early liturgy is one of the pinnacles of the Orthodox – and in general Christian – calendar of worldwide services. If matins can be compared with the sunrise that occurs at the ends of the liturgy, then it is a genuinely spiritual noon, full of light and worldwide joy.

The inner event of which I speak occurred was completely different from the first in its content and in its tenor. It was much wider and as though connected with the panorama of all humanity and with the encounter of worldwide history as a single mystical current. Through the celebratory movements and sounds that were being performed in the liturgy in my presence, it gave me a sensation of that higher realm, that heavenly world, where our entire planet is presented as the great temple and where eternal liturgies of enlightened humanity are performed without interruption in an unimaginable majesty.

But these individual bursts of divine revelation did not provide Daniel the arrangement for a complete picture. They only remained as testimonies of a mystical reality, not providing him that fullness of attaining what he was aspiring. But the light-filled visions came to him as a rule for the most part during liturgies at or near a Russian Orthodox Church.

Soviet persecution of the Orthodox Church became all the more ruthless. Campaigns began in 1927 for the removal of ecclesiastical bells from their towers. Daniel described it as a storm from the Soviet authorities causing a repression leading to national apostasy. Young people were especially and easily susceptible to the anti-religious propaganda. They participated in the destruction of churches, in humiliating and ridiculing priests. A quiet monk walking the street would have rocks thrown at him. After Easter that year 1928, the Soviets executed arrests at the Troitzi-Sergeev Monastery, they arrested Fr Pavel Florenski. Any public display of religious association or belief in God was easily considered a criminal offense. Daniel composed a poem about it.

> Days after days, affairs, worries, loneliness,
> Beaten apart seeking wisdom in books.
> Days fall aside, like a shot, their dead end,
> Will not silence the chorus of boredom.
> All of life is icy frost.
> Trying to keep Hosanna on my lips.
> I will not withdraw, yet cannot skip forward.
> I seem to be those distained in John,
> Not cold and not hot.[20]

This poem was composed in 1928, when Daniel again began to seek his purpose in life; but it seems that once he found what he sought in himself, later he lost it. The mundane existence affected him daily. Leaving the classes in literature, he considered himself obligated to something else other than writing, to involve himself in some occupation so he could have a regular income and provide for the household. Little was provided him from his father's publications, which was his sole support, and yet he was having a difficult time to access all of what he felt was his as inheritance. Daniel's fate especially depressed his kind and loving aunts – Ekaterina and Elizaveta, who could not stop worrying over him, and still having the

---

[20] Rev 3:15-16

responsibility over the Dobrov household. Aunt Elizaveta wrote to his brother Vadim:

> Nonetheless I consider it in general a necessity for Daniel to study, and likewise indispensable for him to adjust to some regular and correct vocation. I cannot agree that a proper vocation is his writing, and rightfully so, since he can sit for entire days, and at other times will do nothing at all for long periods until he decides to write. You are a writer and I hope you can understand, to do this for a living is impossible for him.
>
> In regard to our life in general, I can say that I work less than before, just unable to do much anymore. Our family has become large: the 2 of us, plus Shura and her husband, Sasha and his wife; Katsya now in her 5th year living with us, but she works and helps us financially. We also have an orphaned girl whose father died about 4 years ago. Also Feoklusha the nun who has nowhere else to go. What a large family all in just a few rooms. Katsya is the cook, and I am the laundress. But it seems all the responsibility falls on my shoulders.

On March 29, 1928, a nation-wide celebration was held in honor of the 60th birthday of Maxim Gorki, and now that he returned to the Soviet Union to reside here permanently. It was organized by the highest of Soviet government directors.

Daniel then turned to his god-father for help, and needing someone desperately close to Soviet authorities to testify that he was the genuine son of Leonid Andreev. Daniel's birthright was contested because it occurred in a village near Berlin, Germany, and Leonid was not in good standing at the time with Russian authorities. What certificates were available, if any at all, were questioned. Daniel hoped a document signed by Gorki would prove his birthright and allow him access to all of his father's royalties, and of which Daniel was in desperate need. Gorki only mentioned to Daniel that he would do what he could and perhaps find him a job in some company needing a writer. However the association between the 2 ends here.

The summer 1928, Daniel spent in Tarusa, a small city on the Oka River about 100 miles south of Moscow, in Kaluga Province. It is an ancient city once famous during the era of the Great Chernigovski Principality of the 13th to the 14th centuries, with many ruins, and then part of Moscow Principality of the 15th to the 16th centuries. There during the late 19th and turn of the 20th century many of Russia's intellectuals and off-beats would gather and rest and exchange ideas. As a result, it was likewise used by the Soviet government as a place of exile for unwanted dissidents, with the nearest railway station over 15 miles away. Electricity and telephone were still not connected to Tarusa in the 1920s.

Daniel's reason was to cleanse his faculties using Russia's nature and to listen to the silence. His friend Kovalenski accompanied him. The green quiet city with its hills overlooking the Oka River, the bright cupolas on its churches, impressed Daniel. He would wander and roam in the meadows outside the city. This was his first occasion to be isolated in forests and meadows, after all his years in Moscow and Petersburg, with time for personal meditation apart from city regimen and the effects of Soviet influence.

A few years later, Tarusa would fall victim to Soviet anti-religious activists, and the churches would close and be defiled with slogans. In September, Daniel wrote to Vadim:

> I spent summer in the Kaluga province along the Oka, in a extraordinarily beautiful plant. It was so awesome. For several years now I have not left Moscow, and now I have landed in this fairy-tale world of beauty. The nature here is intoxicating, and in its intoxication there is not one drop of bitterness.

With the attraction of Daniel to the nature of the region, within a year he would continue further south to Trubetz and then

Trubchevsk, to their virgin green expanses, also part of another ancient principality, to sense his native and mystic connection with ancient Russia.

Returning from Tarusa, Daniel went to Leningrad. After his visit Daniel returned to Moscow and wrote a letter to brother Vadim:

> Recently I arrived from Leningrad, where I went to register for military service. For the meanwhile I do not know if they will allow me a postponement for a year or not. I will have to return there at the end of October a second time. I lived there with Levi and Lyusi, in my father's old apartment along the Moika. I was able to develop a close relationship with Levi, he is one of so few people who can speak the same language as I do. We converse for hours without end long into several nights. He is a very interesting person. We also spoke about you, and he mentioned his fervent love for you. I told him I plan to write to you upon my return to Moscow and he asked that I give his regards to you.
>
> But Levi's affairs are rather vile. What is occurring with him is the same as what is with many: he drinks a lot, is mentally detached and morally dissipated. It is horribly pathetic. Essentially he is a good and fine person. Now I need to add that his health deteriorated, and for some undetermined period he is confined to a hospital. Other than him, I saw Larisa and her husband, also Anna Ivanovna, Rimma, and others.

Several of Daniel's relatives on his father's side lived there, cousins Larisa Pavlovna and Anna Ivanovna Andreeva; his aunt Rimma Nikolaievna Andreeva, his cousin Leonid Arkadyevich, named after Daniel's father, and who also bore a striking resemblance to him, and of course all of their children. With cousin Leonid, who also studied mysticism, Daniel also was able to develop a friendship.

Returning to Moscow from Leningrad, Daniel again dove into literary pursuits, although he continued to feel he was not just a writer, as he records in a letter to brother Vadim:

> Now begins the winter routine: city, work, notebooks, books. I really wanted to at the end of October, when they will probably conscript me into military service, to finish my notorious novel, but it seems, I will not. It seems to be a bad family trait, to start something that will be almost impossible to finish. Other than this, every year the demands on my life tend to increase along with my demands on myself and to my child.[21] There is still a lot more I need to rework, recast some characters, and polish.
>
> The relationship with mama,[22] aunt Shura and her husband are now excellent. My house has become my conscious. Do you understand? And even more, it seems, I cannot exist long without it. Even after 2 weeks of being in Piter,[23] I got anxieties.

Good relationships at home and an inner balance helped Daniel write, and his compositions highlighted meaning in life. Most of all his efforts were extended to the novel, *Sinners*. He also wrote some poetry, including the long *Red Moscow*. He began *Catacombs* poetic cycle, which was not completed until 1941. Even though none of *Catacombs* has survived, the subject was the departure of the Russian Orthodox Church underground during the 1920s, during the era of heavy religious persecution.

In between Daniel continued to study the mysticism of the orient and middle-east. The books that were located in his personal library included *History of the Ancient East* by Vladimir Turayev, the popular *History of Chaldea* by Zinaida Ragozina, all of which volumes were much studied by orientalists. Included in his study was the *History of Religion*

---

[21] referring to his book in process of writing.
[22] His aunt Elizaveta
[23] Diminutive for Petersburg, referring to Leningrad.

and Secret Religious Societies of the Ancient and New World by Pierre Daniel Chantepie de la Saussaye. Daniel studied the secret religious world, the hidden knowledge of the priests of Babylon and Egypt, Buddhism, mystic Hinduism, while developing his personal convictions and concepts in the process.

1929

In 1929, church bells ceased to ring in Moscow. During the summer Daniel traveled especially to Radonezh to listen to bells at the Troitzi-Sergeev Monastery, which was the last monastery in Russia where the bells still rang.

The battle against ringing church bells was, of course, in the interest of the working class and began with a secret edit of the People's Commisariat of Internal Affairs, *Regarding the Regulation of Bell Rings*. The prohibition was church bell ringing in all the cities, and subsequently Soviet authorities began to remove the bells from their towers and sent to factories to be melted. The bells were removed at Troitzi-Sergeev Monastery in November 1929. In addition to this, they started demolition of old Moscow Orthodox churches, including the Church of the Intercession at Levshin, next door to the Dobrovs, an edifice so respected by the Dobrov family and with which Daniel was familiar since childhood. The Soviets also attempted to change the calendar into first, a 5-day week and later into a 6 day week, but this failed. However, they did remove Christian holy days from the calendar, denouncing them as religious propaganda, and installed new days that commemorated events associated with the advance of Socialism.

The follow summer of 1929, Daniel did not spend at Tarusa as he originally thought to, but in Ukraine. He mentions Tripolye as the place, which is in Kiev province, 40 miles south of the capital city along the Dnepr River, but he does not say with whom, but more than likely it was with some of the older Dobrovs to visit some family. However, in *Rose of the World*,

Daniel relates to us about the *stikhials*, the living spirits of nature, and recollects his travel.

> Personally with me all began during a 1929 sweltering summer day near the small city Tripolye in Ukraine. I was happily exhausted after a several-mile roam over open fields and along streams and windmills, and which allowed me a wide open view at the bright-blue branches of the Dnepr, and at the sand covered islands between them. I climbed to the top of a neighboring hill and suddenly was literally blinded. In front of me, not stirring under the descending waterfall of sunlight, a sea of sunflowers spread out further than my eye could see. At his very second I sensed that over this majestic scene, an invisible ocean of some kind of rejoicing living happiness was oscillating.
>
> I walked to the very edge of the field and with a pounding heart, I pressed 2 leafy sunflowers to both cheeks. I watched in front of me, at these thousands of agrarian suns, almost exhaling love toward them and toward those whose joy I was feeling at his field. I felt something strange. I felt that these invisible entities with joy and with pride are leading me as a distinguished guest, as if to their marvelous celebration, something like a mystery play[24] and feast. I carefully took a couple of steps into the thickness of the sunflower growth and, closing my eyes, heard their contact and their summoning rustle was barely heard and flaming divine heat surrounded me.
>
> So it began at this point. True, I recollect the encounters of this type that pertain to the earlier years, as a child and adolescent, but they were not so enveloping. But those earlier and later, not occuring every year, but sometimes it was several times just in one summer, they occurred in the midst of nature and

---

[24] Also Miracle Play, a theatrical exhibition with a Biblical event as the topic.

absolutely when I was alone. These were strange minutes when I was intoxicated with joy. They appeared for the most part where behind me was 50 miles that I had walked on foot, and when I unexpectedly entered some spot that was unknown to me, and which impressed me with the abundance of foliage freely growing. Entirely, from head to toe I was embraced with ecstasy and agitation. I climbed through wild growths, through marshes warmed by the sun, through thorny bushes and finally threw myself onto the grass to caress it with all my body. What was most important was that during these minutes I unambiguously realized how these invisible entities loved me and penetrated through me, whose existence was mysteriously connected with the foliage, water, and meadows.

So did Daniel describe this penetrating sensation of what lives in all nature, not only a special mysterious life, but what displays a completely other type of spirit-inspiration that is distinct from the observer. He saw invisible entities – the *stikhials* – in this poetic penetration of nature, and which altered his attitude and it became more profound a spirit-experience. In this manner Daniel was molded, seeing everything everywhere as possessing a mysterious metaphorical existence. After a few years the Tripolye vision would be transformed into further descriptions of mystical worlds of bright and demonic *stikhials* revealed to him.

Daniel's general approach in nature is recorded in *Rose of the World*:

> I stayed away from all types of machines or operating equipment, and especially transit, lest I take advantage of it instead of walking. After my roams I would return to my room in the local village for a few days and listen to the roosters and the children and the people in the streets, and read literature with some depth in it, and then again departed into the wilderness.

Of course, some of the local populace considered me a vagrant, lazy, because they would be working in the fields, while I would be hiking or camping. But this did not affect me because they did not know my situation. Since I felt I was right, I ignored their opinions.

Returning to Moscow at the end of August, Daniel immediately and sharply sensed the approaching autumn with its cold fogs, with its morning routines and icy dews, yellow frost-covered grass. But life was still at its fullness for Daniel with its flowering meadows, marvelous summers, and memories.

That autumn, while the church bells were silent and the newspapers were loud, the iron fist grabbed the peasantry, defining the common enemy as the kulak, the peasants who still privately owned farms. The terrifying era of collectivization began, the dispossession of their property, which only prepared the region for a merciless famine, an extermination by hunger. The rights of the peasants were removed and the Soviets announced a compulsory work of socialism. The kulaks were forced off their farms and into massive reinforced-concrete housing units.

1930

One of father Leonid's closest friends and fellow poet, Ivan Alekseevich Beloyusov, died January 7, 1930, and subsequently, another close friend poet, Aleksei Evgenyevich Gruzinski. They were all of the same circle of literary associates and close fiends with the Dobrovs. Beloyusov also helped Daniel in regards to acquiring literary rights to his father's books, and he became close friends with his son Evgeni over the years, since 1924.

Kovalenski, Daniel's friend, by now was a respected writer of children's books and a member of the Commission for the creation of a new line of children's books for the Soviet school system. He was able to get Daniel some work in this area and in April 1930, he was likewise writing children's books. It was not inspiring, required much assiduous concentration, and interfered with his own work, but he needed the money.

In spring 1930, Daniel also started on a poem titled *Solstice*, which become one of his primary plans to complete by the end of the year. Daniel never completed *Red Moscow,* but attempted to salvage as much as he could by incorporating it into *Solstice*. By September, he had 600 lines composed, as the first part of the book, but as with many of his other poetic endeavors, it was never completed. Based on information available, *Solstice* was a poem about the Russian revolution and Civil War, which Daniel compares to the Time of Troubles and the imposters of the era.

All the while changes were occurring in the Dobrov household. Superficially nothing seemed to be any different, but they occurred. Sasha Dobrov divorced Irina. Another woman Margarita appeared, joyful and kind. It seemed the household had a different set of interests than Daniel, but it was still large. Feoklusha deified Dr Philipp Dobrov, attentively striving to cater to him and assist him. Dr Dobrov would walk every day to his hospital on Pirogovskaya, while in the evenings he would stop at patient's homes on his way home, and almost always it was a charity work.

Regarding his military obligation, Daniel fell into the category of non-infantry preparation. This was military instruction in Moscow for 1 month a year for 2 years, and he was content with this assignment. Daniel did not sense any inclination to war or military service, but he felt that since the obligation existed, and while there was no war, the matter was not so important and he was willing to comply with the requirement.

During the decade of the 1930s, Daniel devoured the poetic literature of Vladimir Mayakovski, Sergei Esenin, Victor Khebnikov, Maximilian Voloshin, Ilya Selvinski, and Aleksandr Tikhonov, and he especially considered himself a student of Boris Pasternak. Regardless of their views being completely contradictory to his, this was immaterial. What was important is their experience reflected in poetic composition. Along with the poets, Daniel read Russian histories, his favorite authors being Aleksei Chapigin, Yuri Tinyanov, Wilhelm Küchelbecker and Aleksandr Griboyedov. Daniel also read Mikhail Sholokhov's *Quiet Don*, which impressed him. Osip Mandelstam he did not like. All of this helped Daniel in this development of the meta-history of Russia as he records in *Rose of the World*. One author whose works that Daniel searched for 1-1/2 years but could not find was Innokenti Annenski. Soviet censorship stopped production of any literature not promoting the socialist agenda, and suppressed the distribution of existing copies and their removal from libraries.

At the beginning of August 1930, Daniel along with friends and classmates, Aleksandr Kovalenski, Varvara Malakhieva-Mirovich, and Yuri Beklemishev, departed for Trubchevsk, in southwest Russia near the Ukraine border, along the Desna River. Trubchevsk is one of the oldest of Russian cities dating back to the 11th century and contains a wealth of historical antiquities. The beauty of the surrounding virgin forests overwhelmed Daniel's imagination, cranes would fly into the local lakes where Daniel would roam for the entire day, the summer heat was intensive.

This first summer he spent near the Nerussa River, a small tributary that emptied into the Desna River on the east side of the city Trubchevsk. His first visit to the region was short and they returned to Moscow. Alla recollects Daniel's description of his Trubchevsk vacations in her memoirs:

> Every year Daniel went to Trubchevsk and there wandered about his beloved forests. As he explained to me, he had special places in the forests, and each one dedicated to one of his friends. But the attitude of Daniel to nature, his acceptance of nature, was extraordinarily serious and profound. Almost all the poetry on this topic were born tied to his hikes in the forests near Trubchevsk, a small ancient Russian city about 2 hours drive by bus from Bryansk.

In Trubchevsk, Daniel became very close to one family. The head of this family was a school teacher, artist and music-lover, Protasi Panteleevich Levenok. This entire family became almost Daniel's own family. The first memorial plate to be installed in Russia after Daniel's death to commemorate him was on the front of their house. One of Protasi's daughters, Evgenia, even thought she would one day be Daniel's bride. These were people who, with their warmth, humility and sincerity, deeply personified their native province, and about which the balance of Russia only dreams.

Daniel did notice the initial negative effects of collectivization during his stay in Trubchevsk. The peasants did not want to be relocated off their individual farms to the collective farm – kolkhoz. This attack against the peasantry went hand in hand with the anti-religious propaganda. The churches were plundered, the icons were desecrated and then broken and burned, priests were oppressed; the silos and grain storages were confiscated. Freight trains full of peasants were moved by the Soviet government to the east and north, boxcars filled with unfortunate people being relocated, with barbed wire over the windows.

Subsequently every corner of the Soviet Union had some enemy of the people hiding, some wrecker, some contra-revolutionary, somebody against the class struggle. The philosopher and theologian Alexsei Feodorovich Losev and his wife were arrested for being participants in a non-existent underground Russian Orthodox Church, for his vocal opposition to socialism, and his book, *Dialectical Myth*, an expose of the flaws and faults of Marxism. They were sentenced to 10 years incarceration and he was sent to work on the White Sea–Baltic Sea canal. Later his sentence was reduced to 5 years. The evidence that Daniel read *Dialectical Myth* is based on content in some places in *Rose of the World* that reflect Losev's convictions of a Holy Russia.

Alla Bruzhes, the future Alla Andreeva, was a 15-year old school girl at this time and just finishing middle school. She recollects the fear of this period.

> They arrested my uncle, and for 1-1/2 years I stood at the window every night and waited for them to come for my father. Eventually the tragic-comedy ended. An automobile drove into the yard. I was completely convinced that they came for my father, and this was after 1-1/2 years standing at the window every night. Then the vehicle turned around and left, it was just making a delivery. I went into hysteria.

1931

Daniel returned to Trubchevsk in the summer 1931, but instead of following the Nerussa River, he roamed along the Navlya River, another tributary a few miles north of the city. In *Rose of the World*, Daniel described his wanderings in the Trubchevsk region.

> These were strolls that encompassed the entire day, from dawn to dust, or 3 to 4 days together with a sleeping bag and overnight stays in the forest, wandering the roads between the villages and the footpaths in the fields; through meadows, forest preserves, villages, watermills; taking slow river ferries, with accidental encounters with local residents and willing conversations; spending nights either with a campfire along the river, or in some field or haystack, or anywhere in a village hayloft.

Sunburned and wind burned, eaten by mosquitoes, exhausted, Daniel returned into the city after his few days of rest and listening to the morning call of roosters, and children's voices, and having read calming, profound and virtuous books. Then he would go back to wandering.

In Trubchevsk he made an acquaintance with one woman, Marfa Feodorovna Shavshina, age about 80, who lived alone. Before the revolution, she would wash clothes for the local and traveling salesmen, and now she sold herbs and did some bootlegging. She was not able to read or write.

It was particularly during this intensely hot summer that something occurred that would also tie Daniel's soul to the Trubchevsk wilderness, what he considered the best moment of his life. This is related in detail in *Rose of the World*.

> The content of this consisted in that the universe – not the world only, but particularly the universe – unfurls as though in its own higher plane, in this divine spirituality, which penetrates and envelopes it, removing all tormenting questions regarding suffering, struggle and evil.
>
> In my life this occurred on the night of a full moon, July 29, 1931, in these Bryansk forests, along the shore of the medium size river Nerussa. Normally I aspire to be alone when I am with nature, but on this occasion what happened was that I was a participant in a small common excursion. There were just a few of us, young adults and adolescents, and one of us was a novice artist. Each of us had a knapsack on our shoulders filled with provisions, while the artist also had a traveling album for sketches. All we wore were pants and shirts, while some even removed their shirt. We walked in tandem as the Negroes walk along the animal trails of Africa, without speaking and quickly. We were not hunters, not scouts, not explorers searching for something to dig from the ground, but plainly friends who wanted to spend the night along a campfire at some popular reaches of the Nerussa.
>
> Like the sea, as far as we could see, the pine forest turned into a broad-leaved forest, as this always occurs

in the Bryansk forests along low flowing rivers. Centuries' old oaks, maples, and ash towered, and aspens surviving with their sturdiness and height, appearing like palms with their crowns at a head-spinning height. Willows had their branches reaching over the streams. The forest stepped up to the river precisely with loving cautiousness. The wilderness silence was broken only by our barely noticeable footsteps, a few footprints we left. We followed paths left behind by lumberjacks or woodcutters, who would cut wood for the winters and haul them into Chukhra or Neporen on sleds.

We reached a local swimming area before the evening hours of a hot, cloudless day. We swam long, then gathered brush and started a campfire about 6 feet from the quietly trickling river, under the shade of 3 old willows, and we cooked ourselves an ordinary meal. Darkness set. From behind the oaks the low July moon shined, completely full. Little by little the conversations and the stories ceased, the comrades one by one fell asleep about the crackling campfire, while I remained vigilant at the fire, quietly waving a tree branch like a large fan to defend myself from mosquitoes.

And when the moon entered into my direct vision, and the overhanging branches of the willow tree lighted a pattern on the ground from the light, the hours that will remain in my life as the most beautiful of them all began. Breathing quietly, throwing myself on my back on a pile of straw, I heard how the Nerussa was trickling, not behind me, but just a few steps from me, but it was as though directly through my personal soul. This was the first extraordinary incident.

Solemnly and silently all that existed in the world, all that could exist in heaven, trickled right through me, poured into me. It was a bliss that was barely endurable for a human's heart, and I felt as though uniformly-constructed balls were slowly rotating, while floating in a world-wide round dance, but through me. And all that I could imagine or contemplate, was embraced by a joyful single unity of myself. These ancient forests and transparent rivers, people sleeping at the campfire, and other persons, and nations of close and distant countries, city mornings and noisy streets, churches with sacred images, seas incessantly agitating, and the steppes with its waving grasses, all was really and actually in me the entire night, and I was in them all. I laid there with my eyes closed. And beautiful, white stars, and not at all like what we always see, but larger and brighter, also floated from within the entire global river, as white watery lines. Although I could not see the sun, it was just the same and it also flowed somewhere close to my periphery. But it was not its radiance, but some other light that I have never seen before, that penetrated all of what there was, all that floated through me and at this time soothing me like a child in a cradle, with an all-satisfying love.

Attempting to express in words all that I encountered cannot be done because language is too lacking and insufficient a manner. How many times I have attempted by means of poetry and artistic prose to transmit to others what occurred with me that night. And I know that any attempt of mine to do so, and this is also one more, will never provide another person to understand the true significance of this event of my life, not its scale, not its depth.

Daniel's mystic experience on this July evening was again described in a personal letter about 2 years later to a long time female friend, Evgenia Fedulova, and which included his task for *Rose of the World*.

An inexpressible veneration then enveloped me, and not a bloody crush, but a magnificent one like the star-filled sky, the universe became harmonious. I turned to the moon, perhaps with that feeling that raised the hearts of distant ancient nations to it. Dew settled on everything, all sparkled, the meadows seemed to be covered with waving sheets, and when I again turned and laid at the campfire, the branches of the willows shined, as though covered with varnish. And further, beyond them, secret expanses saturated with a blue color departed into the divine silence, the sparkling meadow, the black unknown regions of the forest's edges, the sandy shallow river banks, during the day they are yellow, but right now they were blue. I was lying focused on one branch, weakly shaking over my head due to the heat rising from the campfire. The stars flowed along and it seems that my entire soul was like a river being poured into the ocean of this divine, this perfected night! Birds, silenced in the thickness of the trees, people, fallen asleep at the protecting fire, and other persons, the people of distant countries, the sun-filled cities, rivers with slow-moving barges, gardens with flowering roses, seas with ships, innumerable churches dedicated to various names of the Sole, all of this was united into one. Nonetheless there were minutes when the boundary between myself and not-myself were erased.

On its own, I suppose, I am not pretentious – God save me! – toward cosmic cognizance, but what I lived through that night was just a crumb that approached me, but nevertheless he confirmed my approach to it. I want to hope that this will not be final time for something like this to be near to me, but it seems its repetition will not be soon. During this summer the entire composition of my inner world and even the course of external circumstances amazingly made this self-revelation capable and possible.

Evgenia Fedulova later reflected on Daniel's description of the event;

Daniel had a difficult time to express in words this state that he lived through, when the cosmos unveiled itself within him, since it always seemed larger and more significant than he was successful in explaining.

As with rivers in India that are considered sacred, Daniel in a literal sense deified the rivers of the Trubchevsk region that he visited: Desna, Navlya, Nerussa, and he personally sensed this. What he wrote in *Rose of the World* about these rivers' souls was the poet's encounter while roaming along their banks that led into the translucent waters. Not only verses, but a definitive teaching about the *stikhials*, the souls of rivers, evolved from these encounters. As Daniel wrote in *Rose of the World*:

The world that is truly inexpressibly enticing is translucent through the speeding waters of the peaceful rivers. There exists a special hierarchy. From a distant past I am accustomed to label it the souls of rivers, although I now understand that this expression is not exact. Every river possesses a certain soul, unique and unrepeatable. We see the external surface of its eternally flowing tangible body like the gush of a river, but its genuine soul is in the heavenly Russia or in another heavenly country, if it flows along the lands of another culture of *Enrof*. But the inner layer of its body, the ethereal, which penetrates beneath it, is incomparably more lively. And where it appears almost with complete consciousness, it is located in a world contiguous with ours and named *Liyurna*. The bliss of its life is confined in that it uninterruptedly provides both streams its gushing body of a large river, and this is the sea, but the body is not depleted, but all gushing and gushing from source to mouth. It is impossible to find the words to express the fascination of these entities, such joys, laughter, nice, immaculate and peaceful. And no type of human kindness can be compared with their kindness, except for the kindness of the brightest and most loving of all the daughters of humanity. And if we should be so fortunate and blessed to accept the *Liyurna* with soul and body, submersing the body in the gushing of the river, the ethereal body in the gushing of the *Liyurna*, and our soul into its soul, shining in the *zatomis*, you will exit on to the shore with such an immaculate, illuminated and joyful heart, as extensive as possibly a person could have possessed prior to the fall due to sin.

His immersion into the depths of eastern religion and mythology at the time is repeated in all of his encounters, and the sunset seen somewhere along the Desna River with its majestic shorelines reminded him of visions of heavenly Russia.

While Daniel roamed the overgrown shores of the Nerussa, workers in Moscow were preparing to demolish the Church of Christ the Savior. They plundered the gold cupola and all that remained was a metal carcass. On December 5, 1931, at high noon, the first explosion occurred, and then half-an-hour later the next, and the explosions continued until all that remained was a pile of bricks. The intent of the Soviet government was to build a gigantic Palace of the Soviets in its place. It was never built.

1932

At the beginning of 1932, Daniel initially decided to go into public service, as he laconically describes:

I entered the work force at the Moscow factory Dynamo, as editor of the factory newspaper *Motor*, where I first worked as the newspaper proofreader, and then later as the factory representative on a newspaper regarding socialist life. I was only in public service for 6 months and left on my own decision, not finding within myself even the smallest inclination of either newspaper work, or any type of public service. I never returned to any type of public service.

The reason for his resignation, as Alla Andreeva would later relate, is that letters and notes having an anti-religious topic would arrive for publication in the newspaper. Next door to the factory the Rogozhko-Semeonovski Monastery was located, and the monastery was demolished to make room for factory expansion, and the Church of the Birth of the Virgin Mother, also next door, was closed even against the protests of parishioners. Daniel could not get himself to include the Soviet propaganda that justified the demolition of the monastery and closure of the church in the factory newspapers, and the notices he received he would place in a box under his desk. The Union of Militant Atheists continued to submit articles for publication, but when the box was completely filled and Daniel could no longer hide his clandestine refusal of publication of articles that were against his conscience, he gave notice of his resignation.

At the same time, Daniel becoming familiar with such a large factory, with its mechanical rhythm of general labor, with the working class, with the craftsman, and many who were working here well before the revolution, opened to him a side of life about which he earlier knew little. Daniel learned of the laws directing factory production and increase of Soviet propaganda directed at the workers now part of the initial 5-year plans of the New Economic Period. As a result, Daniel had a vision of a gnashing monster with strange appellations personifying the ruthless will of the Soviet state, as he describes in *Rose of the World*.

> In February 1932, during the period of my short-term service at one of Moscow's factories, I became sick at night, running a high fever, and I had a certain experience where, of course, the majority did not notice anything except my delirium, but for me it was awesome in its content and unconditional in its conviction. The essence of this experience I designated in my books and will designate here under the expression of the Third

Yuitzraor.[25] This is a strange and entirely not a Russian word, but I was not the one to invent *Yuitzraor*, but it was thrust into my cognizance at some time. The meaning of this gigantic essence is very simply, it can be rather compared with the monsters of the ocean depths, but incomparably more massive in size. I would define it as a demon of a great dominating government. This night remained with me for a long while as one of the most torturous encounters that I have known in my personal experience. I think that if I was to accept into utilization the phrase – infra-physical outburst of psyche, then this encounter would fully apply.

Life became all the more difficult. At home the entire household was ill that winter of 1932. Dr Dobrov was now 70, overworked and he self-diagnosed his condition of angina pectoris. Aunt Ekaterina's son Arseni died alone in Nizhni-Novgorod of an unknown cause. The books of Leonid Andreev were no longer published and any income that Daniel was receiving ended, although a few of his father's plays were still performed in some of the provincial capitals, but the royalty from them was meager. After his resignation from Dynamo, Daniel more often worried about an income, now having to face a reality he did not earlier when matters were better in the Dobrov household.

About this time Daniel became friends with an ecstatic, unstable, unlanded person, a poet – as he considered himself – named Victor Mikhailovich Vasilenko, whom Daniel brought into the Dobrov household. Vasilenko was an enthusiast of western art, a means of distancing himself from his Russian village roots, and he composed simple sonnets. Daniel found in his new friend an empathetic soul, a person Daniel felt could identify with him. Vasilenko lived nearby with his parents, and he would wander regularly into the Dobrov residence and sit for hours with them late into the night. They would discuss poets and authors, such

---

[25] The potent, intellectual and extreme ruthless entities residing in strata intermixed with *shrastries*. From the point of view of a person, this is the demon of massive and despotic government.

as Blok, Voloshin, Gumilev, Fet, Dostoyevski, and the topics of God and religion. Ten years later, Vasilenko would write of his conversations with Daniel:

> He loved to read books on theology, and those at the time which seemed unusual, and he told me of the time once as a child he had the opportunity to visit Optinski Monastery. One special distinction about Danya was that he did not like large crowds. Seldom were there more than a handful of people in any gathering of ours, and often it was just the 2 of us.
>
> Daniel read to me all that he wrote. I remember how he described his previous life in other worlds. He related it, as he would raise his head and half-close his eyes, with his beautiful character, with his the pale face and soft voice. He always spoke slowly, without any type of expression, not jumping from place to place, not making any sharp motions. He was always deeply concentrating, attentive, calm. But I would seem to annoy him. This was the early 30's. I told him how I would often fall in love with some girl, and then the relationship would fall apart. I would cry to him and he would comfort me.
>
> Daniel was very handsome, tall, well-built, flexible, with these intimidating eyes. But what was primary is that I sensed in him some great inner strength. And at this time he was easy to get along with, and there was no reason to ever say anything stupid. Women also loved his company. But his attitude to them was rather aloof and respectable. He was easy to like.
>
> Several times and for long whiles he would explain to me of his life in some kind of other world. There were 3 suns there: one was blue, the other was emerald, the 3rd was something like ours, and they would rise at different times. What would occur is when one is setting the other is rising, and the sky would flare in amazing, fantastic colors that would reflect on everything, on houses, forests, and meadows. The people there lived very happy:

there were no wars, no crime. He spoke of beautiful edifices, a happy sea, that all the residents of this world love poetry and art. I asked him, "Just like in a paradise?" After silent for a moment he replied, "Yes. Just like in a paradise." He spoke of some type of love he felt for a girl on one of the planets. She was young and pretty, and he met with her often at some type of marble pavilion. Happy animals would wander alongside them. They were similar to tigers, with arched, velvet backs, but they were led by they hand and harmed no one. Birds also flew about and which would land on your shoulders, and would wipe their beaks on your cheeks. While others would let you hold them in your hands, and people fed them with some kind of seeds, which he could not see. These marvelous fruits grew there, and women brought them and they would depart. People laid on stone beds in light clothing and read books.

He would recite verses majestically, not just reciting them, and had a impressive memory. He possessed some type of special penetrating, singing method of reading.

In his narratives, Daniel was always falling in love with blindingly-beautiful girls, this seemed to be his fantasy. In one description he wrote of the morning dawns and the evening sunsets, when the 2 suns would coincide opposite to each other. Brilliantly did he describe this. He said, "The blue sun unwillingly yielded its place to the gold. And we just melted, watching how the blue and gold streams of lights would merge. The blue would fade, vanish, and the gold would fill it entirely with its soft radiance. Weeping willows – these were the trees, Victor, that also grow on other planets, and they are blue, and then they change into gold and seem to be cast from gold. There was no breezes in the mornings, the lakes were motionless, and from the hill we saw how they were filled to the bottom with this golden stream. While my beloved, meeting the next dawn, would read to me verses."

"Tell me, Daniel, do you remember these verses?" I naively asked.

"No, of course," he replied. "But I do remember they were elegant and cultural."

Vasilenko also related that Daniel highly valued Indian culture and to the extent that he felt Hinduism was the highest form of religious display and closest to a spiritual entrance into the cosmos. Daniel also related to Vasilenko that he believed in reincarnation, evidenced by an irrefutable vision of his first life in India.

And yet Daniel sought the India Spirit, not the Himalayan, but his personal, one that would present to him the entirety of its reality, it was the India that he saw in books that enveloped him since childhood. Everything in India interested him, but first of all he saw there a religious country, a poetic illumination, sacred mountains and rivers, multitudes of deities and innumerable temples. A country where almost every encounter is with some other world, Daniel sensed a spiritual life of nature that was his personal, so now he would go roaming barefoot. But he also noticed a discrepancy that annoyed him and he mentioned in a letter.

> Lately I dropped by a theater to watch a film having a large poster with the title, *Journey through India*. But my disappointment was terrifying. The movie was vulgar and talentless. Imagine this. Half the time was spent on showing some kinds of factories, workshops, production processes, and etc. While the balance of the time my eyes were consumed with looking at English aristocracy riding on elephants and visiting ruins. Only for a few moments did I see some half-naked people wearing white turbans descending some stone steps to a river, and saw temples piled one on top of each other dedicated to the holy Vanarasi.
>
> Vanarasi is my dream, one of the most beloved and most painful.

In one of his poems, Daniel calls India – the rainbow of the wandering heart, while Vanarasi is called – the inextinguishable rainbow.

On his 3rd visit to Trubchevsk, in 1932, Daniel came for the entire summer, with the hope to again relive that same extraordinary state that now became for him revelations of cosmic other-worlds. But all of June and the beginning of July were rainy and he was hardly able to do much hiking. Once the weather cleared, Daniel stepped on a rusty nail and an infection began in his heel. A local doctor cut open his heel to relieve the infection and it was 3 more weeks before he recovered and could hike again, but Daniel still limped for some time. He traveled 4 days into the Bryansk forests along the Nerussa River, alone and spending nights under the moon along a campfire, and when he returned he figured he covered a distance of about 50 miles. But the infection again started in his heel, and he had to cut it open to allow the abscess out and for it to heal again.

But Daniel was desperate to relive the previous experience, and he set out again in August, as he confessed in *Rose of the World*:

> I aspired with all my strength to summon this encounter again. In subsequent years I created all those external conditions as they existed back in 1931 when this happened. I even spent the night at exactly the same spots and on the same dates. But all was in vain.

This year Daniel sought the India spirit along the overgrown banks of the Nerussa River and in the Trubchevsk wilderness, that maybe this river would lead to his marveled India, where everything was sacred, everything was inspiration, all had its religious connotation, as he understood the place.

Returning to Moscow from Trubchevsk with a painful and infected foot, Daniel forced himself to lie in bed. He passed the time with his foot soaking in some hot medicinal bath and wrote more poems.

During the autumn of 1932, Daniel became friends with an artist who recently completed art school at the Moscow University, Andrei Dmitiyevich Galinadkin, and they were the same age. Along with him another new friend was Aleksandr Mikhailovich Ivanovski, a son of a priest and also an artist. Galinadkin in the next few years was one of those who would circulate through the Dobrov house in the evenings and listen to Daniel's compositions, and discuss history and politics and literature with him.

December 27, 1932, the Soviet state issued new passports – identification cards, but not to peasants. They were issued solely to Moscow residents, but not all of them, only those whom the Soviet state wanted to remain. Whoever did not receive a new passport had to leave Moscow. Some neighbors of the Dobrovs, the Shakhmanovs did not receive passports and they had to leave Moscow somewhere. Some felt it was because there was a Shakhmanov who was incarcerated at the Petro-Pavlovsk Prison, earlier a member of some Tsarist government bureau.

1933

The following year of 1933 brought discomforting news from Trubchevsk. A famine causing deaths due to malnourishment plagued the region, occurring subsequent to collectivization. It seems that a family of 5 received 100 rubles pension from the Soviet government, while bread was selling for 50 rubles a pound, while some people did not see any bread the entirety of the 1932 winter, or even one potato. The diet of most people was one beet a day and nothing more. Daniel wanted to organize the delivery of some welfare packages, and he helped another family, the Kisilovs, who were already making arrangements, but they could not make any deliveries until April 1933. Even then, nothing was mentioned in any of the newspapers about any famine or malnourishment in Ukraine. Instead, the newspapers were filled with the news of the airplanes in the Arctic delivering men from the icebreaker SS Chelyuskin that was trapped in the ice.

Daniel could not travel only to Trubchevsk, as he figured, but also not to Leningrad. He wrote to his friend Evgenia Reinsfeldt:

> In general, never yet in my life have my intentions and plans been so sharply and steeply upset. I spoke to you earlier about them. And my great undertaking, which I so much enjoyed and believed, turned into fog during the winter. There is only one reason left for me to be happy, and that is that this occurred now and not later. But you know yourself how bitter this is.
>
> Spring is soon to arrive and again the spirit of discomfort forces me at nights to journey, across my atlas, because there is no other way for me. For hours I sit and stare at maps of India, Indochina, the Malaysian archipelago.
>
> Endless days are ahead of me. I am writing a book for publication with the energy industry. It is a series of biographies for young people, a list of scholars and discoverers who excelled, beginning with Archimedes. This would be interesting if I had the time and place to seriously write, to concentrate on the epochs and personalities of these individuals. But they only provide me time up to July 1, while so far I have only done 6 pages. And I have little material with which to work and to get information is difficult. What also ruins my work is that with all of these scholars, their entire life was spent at a desk, the canvas of their life is amazingly dearth as far as external events are concerned, and to create these biographies I need some stuff that is impressive and fascinating, but it doesn't exist.
>
> I am tight with money, so I have taken jobs in just drawing charts. This takes all my evenings and I hardly have time left over to do some reading. But recently I read a very interesting book by one of the finest

contemporary astronomers, Sir James Hopwood Jeans, *The Universe Around Us*. This description of the universe is from the point of view of the most recent theories. It is awesomely interesting!

I hope to travel south of Moscow this summer, to Kalistova, and spend July there.

Daniel's association with Reinsfeldt was limited to letters, but she seemed to Daniel to be interesting, not only because they had common childhood recollections, but common interests. She, as we divine from his other letters, was studying the Arabic language, which made him happy. It was this draw to the secrets of the Orient that united the 2 of them in correspondence, if for no other reason. She lived in Leningrad and he hoped to visit her the next occasion he had to travel there.

Other than Reinsfeldt, another friend from childhood days was also living in Leningrad at the time, Tatyana Olovyanishkova, who was now married to a Morozov. Daniel also corresponded with her.

In December 1933, Daniel again writes a letter to Reinsfeldt, summarizing the events of the year:

Summer I did not travel anywhere, unless you were to consider a few days that I spent with some friends at their summer home. It was this way because my publisher withheld the funds for my book until September. I was supposed to travel to Trubchevsk, but my trip this time would not at all match the pleasures of previous summers, but seemed to offer me only prospects of a very difficult situation. But I cannot escape them anyway, they will screw me in Leningrad where I will go as soon as I am in material need. From February to July, I wrote a book, a series of biographies of scholars and discoverers for young people, which included Archimedes, Leonardo da Vinci, Pascal, Leonhard Euler, Daniel Bernouli, James Francis who invented the turbine, and our academic Nikolai Zhukovski. This was a sufficiently pleasurable work, but toward the end it began to affect my health. I have already collected over 50 illustrations and it is in print. With the money that I am still owed for the book I hope to use to travel to Leningrad. I think this will be in January or February.

Now I work in a different vein – graphics. I create diagrams, tables and other nonsense. If such work was constant, I would do it instead of anything else. I have a friend who works with me regularly, he is an artist. And grateful that the work is mechanical, it is possible for the most part to spend the time in conversation or just in silent meditation, each in his own thoughts.

Summer for me was a break in many respects. The primary is that I am escaping the drive to create a metaphysical and other systems. But it is obvious, these outlooks have a completely useless value. It is possible to create some quantity of them, all of them logical, but at the same time improvable and equally unable to express the true attitude of concepts, ideas and existence in the world. Personally for me more or less those propositions that appear to me most reliable right now are those that are confirmed equally by all the great religious systems. And such propositions are very few. The remaining are matters of the heart, intuition, but not of the intellect. It is a pity that this year I did not succeed in engaging with nature. Such engagements are extremely important for me.

Materially, matters are worse than the previous year, but at least I have a warm corner in my room.

Apparently one of the reasons for discarding his summer plans was because he was overloaded with work until the beginning of winter. The book for Energo-Izdat (Energy Publications), started in February, took serious effort. But his book was never published. Every manuscript was meticulously scrutinized and likewise had to pass an ideological verification. It was not surprising that Daniel's book was not approved by the Soviet censurers, especially with the number of Europeans and Americans included. As a result, it was never released for publication.

Daniel describes another meta-physical experience encountered in 1933 in *Rose of the World*.

> In November 1933, I accidentally, and I mean particularly completely accidentally, entered one church at Vlasyevski Lane. There the akafist of the venerated Seraphim of Sarov was being performed. No sooner did I open the entrance door that immediately a warm wave of descending choral singing rushed into my soul. A state that is extremely difficult for me to explain, much less in writing, enveloped me, An overwhelming power forced me to my knees, although I earlier disliked having to worship on my knees – a psychological immaturity motivated me to earlier suspect that something servile was contained in this maneuver. But now standing on my knees seemed insufficient. And when my hands laid on the worn rug that had been trampled by thousands of feet, some type of secret door of the soul swung open, and tears of a blessed ecstasy burst unrestrainedly from me, incomparable to anything at all.
>
> And I need to truly say that anything following this encounter no longer was very important to me, whatever they might call – ecstasy or rapture. The content of these minutes was my ascent to the heavenly Russia, enveloped by the *Sinklit* of the illuminated spirit streams of an other-worldly warmth, pouring from that concentrated source which justly and precisely possesses the appellation of the heavenly Kremlin. The great spirit that at some time traversed our world in the figure of Seraphim of Sarov, and now one of the most brilliant lamps of the Russian *Sinklit*, approached me and knelt to me, covering me, just like with an epitrachelion, a

priest's stole over me emanating rays of light and a joyful warmth.

During the course of almost an entire year, until this church was closed, I attended the akafist of Seraphim of Sarov every Monday and – amazingly! – I relieved this state each time, again and again, with unweakening potency.

This medium size Church of St Blaise, was built at the beginning of the 17th century and still stands at the corner of Bolshoi Vlasyevski and Gagarinski Lane. It was closed shortly after Daniel's visits ended and turned into a produce packing plant.

His next composition was *Contours of Preliminary Doctrine*, where Daniel attempted to ascertain all that was unveiled to him on the banks of the Nerussa River, in the Church of St Blaise, and what he researched in Hinduism and Buddhism, and produce a organized and defined system from it all. Daniel attempted to organize his ideology in *Contours* more than once: working in it, then shelving it, and again returning to it. Not finishing this volume, he then utilized as much of it that he could in the first 2 parts of his novel, *Night Wanderers*.

Contours never survived, but as with his primary novel, the theme dealt with the theory of the changes of epochs. This is deduced from some correspondence from Daniel's friend Irina Yusova:

> Danya had interesting and original concepts of historical religious cycles that grasped the majority of masses of peoples and even entire nations. It was something kind of like a curved flight pattern: fire the engines, take-off, a spiritual flight, and then a landing. Every cycle could grasp more or less time, more or less quantity of countries and nations, attain more or less of an altitude, or on the contrary, the amount of descent. It is a pity that I do not remember how Danya arranged these cycles in time and space, that is, what years and what nations. I do remember that the colors of the cycles were relative

to their substance: from gold it was blue; from light it was a radiance upward that was crimson, or downward that was scarlet.

His inclination toward astronomy is very obvious in Irina's narrative and perhaps some of it was derived from his study of James Jean's book. Alla Andreeva described Daniel's use of colors in her recollections of the contents of *Night Wanderers*:

A series in orderly fashion of red and blue epochs in the history of Russia. The colors red and blue were conditionally selected, but understandably, for what they reflected: the red epoch is the supremacy of material treasures; the blue is the spiritual. Every historical epoch has 2 levels: what has the supremacy is the shade of the aspiration of the dominating portion of society, and an underground is always present in that epoch as the opposing color. Later, maturing and accumulating power, this underground becomes the supremacy bound with authority, the shade of the subsequent epoch, while the powers and currents that were formally on the surface now go underground.

With the course of historical time, the change of epochs increases speed, while their color becomes brighter. In the depths of history, any material drive did not lose spiritual reflection, but any spirituality did not cut ties with the ground. There remains in view the state structure, and not the aesthetic accomplishment, but this is a manifestation of another order. Although very often this aesthetic accomplishment is promoted not for personal salvation, but for the salvation of the world.

The ancient epochs can be called – lilac, and sometimes bluer, sometimes redder. The closer to our era, the more defined the color.

Using the lights of this theory, we can investigate for example the accumulation of the red strengths of the Decembrists at the end of Tsar Alexandr's reign with his blue shade. And likewise the mystical fantasies of the beginning of the 20th century with the red powers of the authorities arriving on the scene, materializing in the victory of Bolshevism.

As part of the novel *Night Wanderers*, Daniel assembled a special chart with the alternating series of blue and red epochs in history and he would read it to friends.

That same year of 1933, Daniel wrote a medium length poem – *The Silver Night of the Prophet*, pertaining to the well-known journey of the prophet Mohammed to Jerusalem.

1934

The XVII Congress of the Supreme Soviet in early 1934 triumphed the autocratic authority of Stalin. As far as Daniel was concerned, as applying to the nation in general, these were just echoes of redundant rhetoric, slogans and banners, but no information was available for practical issues, such as production and food supplies. The first trollycars appeared in Moscow, and subways started construction. The Church of the Resurrection and the Church of the Assumption were demolished, because they interfered with construction. By this time, Moscovites were accustomed to the demolition of churches for the sake of construction expediency, others had a melancholy attitude and just kept silent.

On August 17, 1934, the first All-Union Congress of Writers opened. All the newspapers wrote about it: ovations to Stalin and Gorki, and Bukharin's report to the new generation of Soviet writers.

Daniel spend the greater part of this summer in Moscow, but occasionally leaving the city. He spent some time at the summer home of his associate Nikolai Konstantinovich Muraviov at Nikolina Gora, a village along the Moscow River about 30 miles east of Moscow. Daniel was able to have many discussions with Nikolai, regarding the poetry of Max Voloshin, whom they both admired, and this year they discussed a recently published book, an autobiography of Mahatma Gandhi. Nikolai's sister Tatyana was also there with Gabriel Volkov.

Back in 1929, Daniel became especially good friends with Gabriel Andreevich Volkov, beginning with their first meeting. He later married Tatyana Muraviova. Volkov studied the compositions of Leo Tolstoy and participated in editing his *Collection of Complete Works*. Tatyana was also involved with Tolstoy, working together with her husband at the Tolstoy Museum on Prechestinka. Her love for Tolstoy was inherited, since her father associated with Tolstoy for a long while and also took part in composing his will and legacy. Daniel would take long strolls near the house in the pine forest together with Volkov.

Daniel likewise lived this year in search of a personal India, departing into unusual states of some inspirational fantasy land, often meeting that sole image that, it seems, would soon appear in a Moscow crowd. He viewed it as the expression of an ideal that was so assuring, one that he believed he would meet in another life where the lock of comprehension would be opened to him, and the possibility of meeting it in this life.

In one of Daniel's compositions he created a semi-autobiographical, semi-fictional, narrative in the 3rd person of an incident that is somewhat ironic and romantic.

> Once he was traveling on a streetcar and at one of the stops he saw a girl standing, leaning against a post, holding in her hands something prosaic, seeming like a can for milk and a bag of groceries, and apparently waiting for her train. Something about her looks struck him and he thought, "Is it her?" So he jumps out of his streetcar onto the street. But being very shy, he decided not to approach her, but looked at her from a distance. He then jumped on another streetcar, the same one she did, to get closer to her, keeping her in view, up to the train station, where she exited, and he following her. She

enters the train station, and he follows her. She is already mixing with the immense crowd and passes through the control point onto the platform. But because he does not have a ticket to pass to the platform he stays behind. But because the gate through which she passed led to the trains going out of Moscow, he then divines that apparently she must return to Moscow. So he goes to this train station regularly and waits at this platform. I do not remember how many days or weeks he went to the train station and how many hours he waited at this platform, just for the opportunity to see her again. But he knew that it would be impossible for him to explain to her in precise terms why he was waiting for her, so he took a copy of this Indian poem, where he speaks about love, about the predestination of a couple, one for another, and other poetic explanations.

When he finally saw her he gave her his notebook and said, "Read this," and asked when she would be back in Moscow. After so many days he again appeared at the train station. And look, there she was. What will she say to him? She returned the notebook to him with the words, "I am married."

This romantic, mystic world of the poet was his 2nd reality. But no matter how much a fantasy it might seem to him, how could he not believe that in a previous life he was a Indian and belonged to the caste of Brahmans, but was exiled from it due to his marriage with an untouchable. On the table in his room stood a photograph of Galina Rusakova, while all his visions seemed to be tied with this comrade on the Moscow streets and Soviet wildernesses. The poetic route through great religious myths became part of his individual myth fabrication and led him to mysteries of the contemporary era, to what was occurring before his eyes in Soviet Russia. In order to interpret this mystery, it was necessary for him to traverse the routes of the human spirit, and not only the Orient, but also the Occident.

Daniel loved the poetry of Maximillian Voloshin, valued it highly, and Voloshin is mentioned in *Rose of the World* as one among others who entered *Sinklit* immediately after death. Daniel called the religious-ethic command of Voloshin a supreme attempt. According to Alla, they only met once, as she records:

> During the summer of 1931, he met him on a Moscow street, Maximillian Aleksandrovich Voloshin, and overcoming his personal and painful shyness for this opportunity, he walked up to him and introduced himself. It was completely understandable that his encounter with Maximillian Aleksandrovich was especially friendly and joyful, and he here invited him to come to Koktebel. But Daniel had no money at all that summer, and by the following year Voloshin was no more alive.

December 1, 1934, Soviet Russia was shattered by the news of Kirov's murder. The murder was discussed among the Dobrovs, but rumors circulated, especially in Leningrad, that the culpable parties were the NKVD, People's Commissariat of Internal Affairs, and Stalin.

1935

On January 16, 1935, in Leningrad, Zinoviev, Kamenev, and 17 of their confederates were accused by the Military College of the Supreme Court in the murder of Kirov. In August, Kamenev and Zinoviev were first sentenced and executed. In May 1935, the Society of Old Bolsheviks was dissolved, and the following month the Society of Political Prisoners (Polit-Kartozhan) and Exiles. The abolition served its purpose and all the unnecessary, useless, interfering, clumsy people – as they were identified – were liquidated. Their possessions were confiscated.

That summer the Dobrov's neighbors were arrested: the Lomakin brothers. The wife of Vasili Lomakin recollected:

When I remained alone, I sat at the sill of the opened window of our room the entire night and with agitation listened to every sound. Will Vasili Vasilyevich return home? So I waited until daybreak. Our sufferings began that day, our difficult tribulations. Transfer to prison, visiting him only through the grating on the door, awaiting his exile, this is what filled my life.

After the arrest of Vasili Vasilyevich and Nikolai Vasilyevich, people would avoid me. All lived in fear of their own fate, while associating with people that had family members in prison was dangerous. Seeing me on the street, my associates would walk on the other side. Very rarely did anyone come to visit me.

The Dobrovs empathized with me in my sorrow. I would return home from work, remain alone in the room, start a fire in my isolated cold room, which was formerly the residence of the Shakhmatovs until their exile. Once the fire was burning, I would watch the flames, my heart would moan in the same mundane torment, tears flowed from my eyes. I knew nothing at all: where Vasili Vasilyevich was or who was with him. During such minutes, Elizaveta Mikhailovna would visit, embrace me and persistently convince me to go visit them. I would go to their apartment, sit at their large family table, become warm from their comfortable and loving attitude toward me. Once her sister Ekaterina Mikhailovna invited me to attend matins with her. We stood in church next to each other and I remember her old, withered face, she also had her share of sufferings and sorrows in her life.

Regardless of the formidable era, visitors still sat at the long table at Dobrov's apartment just as in the past every evening. Up to the time of their own arrest, the apartment was filled with their own and wanderers. Daniel would read his most recent poetry to the group, but otherwise kept silent and did not involve himself in any of the discussions or debates on political or state issues.

Even though Daniel did not consider himself an artist, that year he succeeded in becoming a member of the Gorkom[26] Artists and Decorators. As mundane as the work was, it still gave Daniel some official status, allowing him some privilege of freedom of expression. They tested his experience and assigned him a place to work. The Gorkom consisted of a regiment of artists of the most diverse qualifications, retired people, unsuccessful individuals who could not join an official Soviet union, or those self-taught. For the most part he worked in the Moscow Polytechnic Museum, in the Moscow Communal Museum, the Art Theater, and various pavilions of business and agricultural exhibitions, and public cultural fairs.

In 1935, he spent more time at the home of Evgeni Beloyusov.[27] Evgeni would read his short stories, while Daniel would recite his poetry. He also became acquainted with Evgeni's friends, including Elena Feodorovna Lisitzina, a student at the Literary Institute who would become Evgeni's first wife, and with the Kemnitz couple: Victor Andreevich and his wife Anna Vladimirovna Skorodumova, a ballerina at the Kamerski Theater. The woman was well-read, loved and knew poetry, and had a good conversational ability to discuss poetry, and so Daniel enjoyed her company. Aleksandr Dobrovolski would also appear at the Beloyusov home, with whom Daniel became even closer friends.

Alla Andreeva recollected the movies that she and Daniel enjoyed watching:

> Many of the movie theaters were playing the German 2-part film *Die Nibelungen*.[28] I went to the Arse where an orchestra was accompanying the film with music from Wagner. The film truly was excellent. The first series was called *Siegfried*, and the 2nd was *Kriemhild's*

---

[26] City Committee of the Communist Party of the Soviet Union
[27] He would later marry Alla in 1963, after Daniel's death in 1959.
[28] In 1924, directed by Fritz Lang.

Revenge. I, of course, loved Siegfried, he was perfect in himself. Kriemhild was also beautiful, especially her long curly blond hair, which is something I dreamed myself all my life to have.

Daniel also saw this film as a teenager. Naturally, his perspective was considerable deeper and more complex. He loved Kriemhild, and even to the point that he went to the theater several times to watch the movie. He saw the movie 70 times wherever it was playing in Moscow. The concept of his *Song of Monsalvat* dates to about this time, one of his early unfinished poems.

Daniel began to write this poem in 1935, and in *Rose of the World* he explains his concept and sources for *Song of Monsalvat*:

The heavenly country of the European culture is presented to us in the form of *Monsalvat*, the eternally celestial summit where knights-virtuous persons from century to century are preserved in the cup of blood of the incarnated Logos, which was gathered by Joseph of Arimathea at the crucifixion and transmitted to the wanderer Titurel, the founder of *Monsalvat*.

At a somewhat distance from *Monsalvat*, a transparent castle rises high, created by the sorcerer *Klingsor*: it is the concentration of apostate powers and with its unsurpassable obstinacy it strives to destroy the potency of the brotherhood, who are the protectors of the supreme sanctuary and secret. Such are the 2 poles of the general myth of the European supra-nation from the unknown creators of the ancient Celtic legends, through Wolfram von Eschenbach to Richard Wagner. The supposition that as though the disclosure of this figure was consummated by Wagner's *Parsifal*, is not completely undebateable, and it is still too early to tell. The trans-myth of *Monsalvat* grows, and is becoming more gradiose all the time. Let us hope that more thinkers and poets will arise from the sturdy European nations, whom the meta-historical enlightenment will permit to attain, and it will represent the heavenly country of *Monsalvat* in the manner it is at present.

The poem was never completed, although as much as Daniel was able to compose in the period 1935-1938, the poem consisted of about 2,000 lines. Most of it was composed during the winter and spring of 1936. He was infatuated with his poem, which seemed to him better than other poems he composed. The inspiration over the evenings took the place of any depression, doubts and melancholy due to the events occurring in Soviet Russia at the time. The concept of *Song of Monsalvat*, the mystic myth of the Holy Grail also mesmerized Daniel's circle. His friend Vasilenko recollected:

> He related to me especially a lot about *Monsalvat*, about the cup of the Holy Grail. He spoke of the troubadour who dedicated his entire life for the search of *Monsalvat* and at the very end died somewhere in the east, beyond Iraq, and so never finding it.
>
> Daniel, writing about *Monsalvat*, said that in a previous life he approached the Grail. He saw the church from a nearby cliff, but he was not allowed any closer.
>
> But what evolved here from concrete knowledge, and how much from poetic fantasy, I do not know. But when I heard about the topic of the Holy Grail, I found Daniel to be most interesting. He was not just a master author, he was a poet of the most profound inner content, a content that I have not yet found anywhere else.

The composition of *Monsalvat* with its heroes and friends and the topic of the Holy Grail were all part of Daniel's route of development that would bring him to composing *Rose of the World*.

Elizaveta Dobrova was ill during the spring of 1935, bedridden an entire month. She had pernicious phlegmon with severe bouts of malaria. The household was an uncomfortable place during her illness, since it depended so much on her.

In Moscow, nature was not to be found. In place of demolished churches were trenches for foundations or just empty lots, and the largest of them was the place of the former Church of Christ the Savior. But the more that the old Moscow was demolished, the more the propaganda proclaimed Stalin's plan for reconstruction, and it seems that the demolition was occurring at a faster pace than any reconstruction. Heavy snows covered Moscow that winter and early spring of 1935. At the end of April, Daniel left Moscow for the forests. Sometimes it was easier for him to share his secrets with those at a distance than those who closely surrounded him.

In the middle of May, Daniel responded to his friend Evgenia Reinsfeldt, who shared her recent misfortunes with him. He writes back attempting to empathize with a woman's soul.

> Often I sense that you are very close, disregarding that essentially I know you very little. It seems to me that I, if I do not understand, feel something in you anyway and perhaps this is what is important. And I am convinced that you also have a inner understanding of the vein of my life. Was I tongue-tied in this expression? But this is not important, right?
>
> My life at present passes uniformly and almost completely without inner light, as it is every spring. This is the exact expression of the yearly cycle from July to January: a route of ascent and then decline, and each cycle ends in a state of burdensome depression. I have this year attempted to struggle with especial persistence against this, but I notice little benefit from my effort.
>
> The reasons for this prostration are 4; among them the first is my external character. Two are exclusively internal, while one is, so to speak, spontaneous. This final reason consists in what was already in part expressed in my one poem about India, which I once read

to you. Up to the age of 30 years, I wandered in search of a sole captivating figure, severing within myself all shoots of any conscious pull toward others. This is not only tormenting, but perhaps very much a mistake, one that is irreparable and crippling the soul and life.

What pertains to one of the internal reasons, here the matter consists in that I, due to my intellectualism, willingness and arbitrary traits, am just a poet. And along with this from childhood my voice has not changed pitch, and maybe I need an operation.

Autumn I started a large poem about the epochs of the Crusades, a liberal variation on the topic of the central myth of the later middle ages.[29] It was very liberal and instilled with a meaning that would only apply to a person of our epoch and country. Otherwise, the effectiveness of the poem traverses the 12th and 13th centuries. Along with fictional characters that I introduce into the text, I have also included traditional persons, such as Lohengrin. It will be very voluminous, and I have finished 1/3 of it so far. From a literary standpoint – and of course from others – its composition is far from what I have composed earlier, and fortunately. This is the only poem I am working on and which compels me with a reason to continue my life. I live for the purpose of finishing it. I have little backround information with which to work. I hope to travel this summer but apparently will not be able to go anywhere.

My health very much and more requires some repair, I seem to have completely lost my voice. What little strength nature has provided me, I seem to have lost a good proportion of it. Even at my age, I realize I need to economize and count every penny, having the goal of surviving at least another 10 years. And if conditions should change as far as work is concerned, I may last longer. What is primary is primary: to successfully

---

[29] He is referring to *Song of Monsalvat*.

materialize at least one of the basic items on my agenda, what is directly and persistently in front of my mental vision.

Spring is difficult, torturously difficult in the city! An endless spirit of travel causes my head to rise, and what mortal melancholy affects me due to this cursed focus on one point!

I was able to leave the city 3 times: I listened to the larks, played some solitary games in the open forest, roamed like a barefoot gypsy along the thawed marshes, and did much more, whatever I could in nature. But these one-day excursions in general only provoke a hunger for more.

Please forgive me for such a short and shallow letter. I am assured that my melancholy will end within a month or 2.

But in this letter, Daniel did not explain everything to the end, withholding many confessions. After a few days he wrote to brother Vadim, continuing to reflect on crossing the age boundary of 30, meanwhile providing a short autobiographical portrait. Daniel had also received a photograph of Vadim recently.

Your photograph testifies that we have something in common, and not only much that is external. But life has impressed on you a seal of such sufferings of which I am not aware and cannot be aware, as those upon me, living and having lived always in my native land and in my beloved family. Do not think that my life was without poverty and sorrow. But it has been difficult here in another respect than yours. Outwardly I do not appear younger than you. I think that even with a great inner similarity, we are distinct one from another in many more peripheral traits: in characteristic, in temperament, in tastes and inclinations, and etc.

You asked me if I smoke. Yes, and very heavily. Am I involved in sports? Regretfully I have to answer in the negative. My veins are completely void of any sports participation, and this is very vexing for me also and because my health is completely impaired and sports just might be of help to me, especially if I was active since childhood. My impaired health consists in constant weakness, headaches and other body pains, and the inability to do manual labor, and more. I seem to just ruin myself with my mode of life: a double set of vocational responsibilities (graphic arts and literature), evening outings, irregular sleep. When winter comes along I hope to maybe go skiing.

But what I do is my association with nature, accepting it with all strings attached, with all its essence, audio, touch, smell, even with my hair and soles of my feet. In this aspect I love more the peace of the soil and its growths, more than water. Meanwhile, I have inherited from father a passion to walk barefoot, it is a pleasure of mine.

At some time in the past as an adolescent, I loved the city, but now I have long lost a taste for it and horribly am tormented without nature, and this contact with it is only possible for me presently occasionally. To the extent that I do not understand the enticement of winter, since I cannot tolerate cold, and the only beauty I see in winter is maybe frost, to the same extent I love the heat, to the point I forget about myself as I wander through forests, the forest streams and evenings, nights at a campfire, viewing the horizon from hills, the distance. Without this I am totally unable to live.

I want to share some landmarks with you that will disclose to you my personal tastes and inclinations, sympathies and antipathies. This will in part help you to divine my inner world.

I love:
The orient more than the occident.
The history of the west of the 12th and 13th centuries.
The music of Bach, Wagner, [Modest] Mussorgsky. But expecially Wagner.
[Sandro] Botticelli, Fra Angelico, but the one with the first place is Giotto.
Vrubel. Tutchev.
Don Quiote. *Peer Gynt*
With the exceptions of [Gustave] Flaubert, [Guy de] Maupassant, [Paul] Verlaine, and some of Hugo's dramas, French literature is foreign to me. I extremely dislike France, except for 2 or 3 items. I do not understand the enthusiasm over Henri de Régnier and I was bored reading him, likewise, alas, Stendhal. I found Théophile Gautier to be repulsive and everything that he had to do with art.
The *Pickwick Papers* I re-read almost each year.
I exalt Lermontov and Dostoyevski above them all.
Of the ancient cultures to which I sense a great attraction in general, I especially love and I do not cease to be amazed by Egypt, and respectfully.
After literature, architecture stands next in place. The styles I like most are those of Egypt, and especially the 13th dynasty, Gothic, Arabic architecture, and the southern Indian of the 17th to the 18th centuries.
Of the sciences, I am talentless, and I cannot get any further than the times tables. At one time I was enthused with astronomy, but any further serious study was halted by my absence of mathematical skills and my repulsion toward mathematics. This also shuttered me away from the path of architecture.
Sadly I also possess no talent or ability in any physical trades, or for that matter, even public speaking. I have a difficult time in addressing an audience. Some of my negative character traits of laziness, conceit, being

quick-tempered, and having a tendency to be a couch potato. As a result, I love to spend the long winter nights in a quiet room with books and paper.

I love the sun more than the moon, but the evening more than the morning.

In a subsequent letter I will continue what I have started in this vein about my tastes, likes, character traits. You also continue. I do not know how you feel about this, but for me this is very important and a surprising joy.

This self-analysis in the letters may have helped Daniel to overcome his bouts of despair and melancholy. A nostalgia is noticeable toward brother Vadim, since at the time Daniel wrote this letter, they had not seen each other some 20 years.

1936

Daniel departed to Trubchevsk at the beginning of July 1936, even though earlier he thought he would be unable to do so. Over the 3 years he had not been there, the small city changed little, which provided him joy, especially with the many changes occurring in Moscow. He wrote to brother Vadim in Paris regarding this latest excursion to the wilderness:

> You can only envy me. It has already been 2 weeks since those repulsive appurtenances called shoes have touched my feet or a hat to my head. The touch of these vile objects are replaced by the caress of a warm, soft atmosphere and the mother-earth. The amazing, mesmerizing, softly-enveloping heat, the rare storms, with almost no cloudy days the entire summer. This summer was beautiful.
> Twice I spent nights on the banks of the Nerussa River in the forest. This is a medium size river that can be crossed at a few shallow spots. It flows through virgin

forests, where a person can roam for entire days on end and not meet anybody, filled with gigantic oaks, colossal ash and maple, whose roots penetrate under the swift flowing waters that are so transparent, so clean that the entire world of fish and plants beneath the surface are clear and accessible. Just a few times a year, people gather here and go swimming. These are the days when the hay is mowed, and then it is desolate again.

None of my Moscow acquaintance are presently with me, none of them have the same love of nature and roaming as I do. As a result this year especially I wander alone. I now continually dream about next year, when I will again wander along these places sacred for me.

After a few more days, when the full-moon night begins, I will depart for an entire week into the forest at the junction of the Nerussa and Navla. Using a good atlas you can find these places. It is south of Bryansk, between Bryansk and Novgorod-Severski. I do not know if maybe from my end it is not good for me to write to you such. It will just all the more draw you here. But my soul is exceptionally full, so yes, I can share some of this with you.

It seems that Daniel also had some divine experiences during this torpid summer of 1936, during his forest roams in the region. In *Rose of the World* he describes another mystical experience.

In the following years I spent the summer for the most part in the regions of the Bryansk forests and much occurred to me there, which recollection comprises the delight of my life. But I especially love to recollect my meetings with the *stikhials* of *Liurna*, those which I thoughtfully at the time named – souls of the rivers.

Once I took the initiative for a individual excursion, over the course of a week roaming the Bryansk forests. It was very dry. Strands of dark blue gloom extended the plumes of the forest fires, while white smoke-filled clouds slowly moving rose often over the massive pine groves. In the interval of several hours, I had to wander down a hot dusty road, not noticing a fountain or a stream. The intense heat, suffocating, as though in a greenhouse, caused me intense thirst. I did have a detailed map of the area, and I knew that soon I should come across a small stream, and one so small that on my map it did not even have a name. And so it was: the character of the forest began to change, the pines gave way to maple and alderwood. All of a sudden the red-hot road burning the soles of my feet turned downward, and in front of me was a green marsh of tall grass. I ran out of the grove and saw about 20 feet ahead of me the long-awaited river curving. The road crossed at this ford. What a pearl of the universe! What a charming child of God that was able to meet me here! It was only a few footsteps wide, covered entirely with low-laying branches of ancient willows and alders. It meandered following a exact course along a green depression.

Throwing my heavy knapsack on the grass and removing all my outer clothing, I entered the water to the chest. And when my warm body was immersed into this cool pool, and the ripples of the shade and sunlight shined on my shoulders and face, I suddenly felt some kind of invisible entity grabbing my soul with such an immaculate joy, and from where I could not ascertain. But it was with such amusing happiness, that as though it loved me already for a long while and was waiting for me for a long while. It was entirely as though the most subtle soul of this river. All meandering, all vibrating, all lightheartedly, all consisting of coolness and light, worry free laughter and kindness, evolving from joy and love. And when, after my soul's long stay in its soul, and my body in its body, I lied down on the bank under the shade of overhanging branches and closed my eyes. I felt that my heart was so freshened, so washed, so cleansed, so blessed, as much as it could possibly be since the first days of creation, at the dawn of time. And I understood that what occurred with me at this time was not a normal bath, but a genuine bath in the supreme sense of this word.

Back to reality, when Daniel returned to Moscow from the thick forests of Trubchevsk, its streets were hot and dusty. The political processes and the political struggle that began to unfold one after the other after the Kirov's murder and affected the conspirators, but all of this did not interest Daniel. The next victim was Trotsky, the primary enemy of Stalin's dictatorship. The trial for the revolutionary activities of the Trotsky-ites were held August 19-24, 1936. No less than 30 were found guilty and sentenced at the trials, and they all felt victim to Stalin's ruthless authority. Even Trotsky, who fled to Mexico, was tracked and assassinated.

On the night of December 31, 1936, Nikolai Muraviov died, an old and respected friend of the Dobrovs and whom Daniel knew from childhood. The incident also delivered Nikolai from arrest and subsequent incarceration and death in some concentration camp. Alla Andreeva recalls what Daniel related to her about the wake a couple of nights after his death:

> Daniel read the Gospels the entire night at his coffin. He always read the Gospels over the coffin of his deceased friends, instead of the Psalter. It was exactly at this time that men entered the room with an arrest warrant for the deceased and a search warrant for the apartment. The coffin with the body of the deceased set on a desk. Daniel continued to read, not stopping even for a minute, while those who arrived opened the desk drawers with all their contents, and took away all the papers.

1937-1938

This was a horrifying year, but the horror became commonplace as it seemed to many that the Soviet government's repression would not affect them as they were innocent of everything. During the days they counted who was arrested that night. The agencies did their best to carry out the arrests with the least amount of attention. They executed by shooting in secret, while not telling the relatives of their fate, but instead telling them that they received a sentence of so many years and without communication, which left the relatives bewildered. Little information was published in the newspapers about trials and arrests, and the population did not know what to believe.

At the beginning of 1937, one of Daniel's closest friends, Sergei Nikolaievich Ivashev-Musatov, married Alla Bruzhes, an artist, a beautiful woman, and 15 years Sergei's junior, she was born in 1915. Sergei had been married once before to a woman named Natasha. Alla was the daughter of a physiologist, professor Aleksandr Petrovich Bruzhes, a very prominent person from St Petersburg, and her mother was Yulia Gavrilovna Nikitina from Novgorod. They hoped their daughter Alla would become an actress, but ended up as an artist. She entered art school in 1935.

Alla talks about her family and early years in her memoirs:

We returned to Moscow during the winter of 1920/21 from Oryol Province, to a impoverished, snow-covered post-revolutionary city, right in the middle of the era of war communism. Soviet authority already started to show its ugly face: the execution of priests, nobility and former officers; the devastation of the [Orthodox] Church consisting of pillaging the churches of all their sacred objects, the implementation of communal apartments. This was all the work of the devil through the Bolsheviks.

We were assigned 2 rooms in a communal apartment. When my brother was born in 1922, he and his nurse lived in a room behind the kitchen. Other than the 4 of us in our rooms, there were 2 other families in the other rooms, and we all shared the same kitchen.

My father was Aleksandr Petrovich Bruzhes, he was half Dane and half Lithuanian, and from St Petersburg. My mother was Russian and with some gypsy blood somewhere in the lineage, Yulia Gavrilovna Nikitina. Her family originally descended from Novgorod. When they married, my parents came to Moscow, and then moved to Oryol, and now we are back in Moscow.

My father was a typical intellectual atheist from the beginning of his life, and many intellectuals were the same way. But still, I never in my life met a person who possessed more Christian attributes and more honor than this unbelieving physiologist. He was a marvelous person. And why did he survive all these years, and even with the later repercussions? One reason: he never noticed what the Soviet government was doing. He saw it but pretended like he never noticed. He was never a member of the [Communist] Party, and had no intentions of ever joining. He was plain and simple an honorable person. He would not allow anybody to get to know him personally or his views or convictions, and he was not about to be labeled anti-Soviet. He realized that if he would let matters bother him, this would be the end of his life.

Father was very musically inclined. He first studied at the St Petersburg Conservatory under Nikolai Andreyevich Rimsky-Korsakov, and for a long while oscillated between science and music, and then selected science. My mother had a naturally beautiful voice, she was a soprano. As a result our home was always filled with music.

Father then attended and graduated from Petersburg University in biological studies and then entered the Military-Medical Academy. Due to upheavals that occurred in the school in the pre-revolution era, my father left the school and he and mother moved to Moscow, where I was born. My mother completely disagreed with the move to Moscow, as it banished all opportunity for her to become a singer in Petersburg. In Moscow, she could not get a foothold in the music theater and by now the revolution was on the horizon. My mother was a lively, happy, very good person, although sometimes temperamental and fiery. She never did one drop of harm to anybody.

Returning from Oryol, my father went to work at the Obuv Institute of Professional Diseases in Moscow, and part of his time was spent in local hospitals. He did renovation work at one of the hospitals at the beginning of World War 2, so they could treat wounded soldiers efficiently.

I married Sergei Ivashev-Musatov in February 1937. I was 22 years of age and he was 15 years my senior. He was originally a mathematician by education, but he discarded this in favor of art. He was a very talented and interesting person and we had much in common.

The first thing that Sergei did was introduce Daniel to his new wife. As Alla recollected in later years:

He [Sergei] wanted to show me to him, as his deliverance. This is what occurred. Sergei called him and asked him to come out on the street. It was the beginning of March. It was already dark, the snow was still falling and in clumps. The winter weather was overwhelming, and not yet thawing to disperse the frost.

So we arrived at Mali Levshinski corner where this ugly small house stood, and the door exited directly onto the street. Daniel was always precisely on time. So when we arrived at the house at the designated time, the door opened and this well-built, tall person walked out.

Now 60 years have passed. And I remember his hand, Daniel's warm hand, his handshake. I remember his very polite and joyful facial expression, and his unusual brisk stroll. He was happy for Sergei. So under this soft falling snow began our friendship that would last our entire life. That is all I remember of that evening.

So Sergei Ivashev-Musatov and his wife now regularly made a appearance at the Dobrovs, although more often they were with the Kovalenskis. Alla also recollected this period:

The Dobrovs always had many other guests. At table the conversations dealt with many interesting topics, and of which many I had never heard earlier. You name it: philosophy, Orthodoxy, Catholicism, Beethoven. I cannot remember if there were any direct anti-Soviet statements, but this atmosphere seemed to prevail. I immersed myself into this atmosphere, truly, but only with my ears due to some anxiety, if I can express it in this manner, because I only listened and I was otherwise silent. And I felt that this was my sphere.

One of the characteristics of the era was that not too many people would gather together. With Dobrovs it was different. Many would fill the room on Easter and Christmas. Moving the dinner table to the side, about 20 persons fit comfortably. The door into the dining room was always open whenever guests where there, just in case the secret police decided to attend, and already one of the neighbors received an arrest warrant. From the moment of my acquaintance with the Dobrov family, many of their friends were arrested. But it is hard for people to break old habits, and so at the dining table they could continue to speak their minds, regardless of who might be standing at the front door.

But Daniel was tormented with personal problems that spring, of which he wrote in another letter to brother Vadim:

The previous months have been exceptionally difficult for me, one of the most difficult in my life. It is a pity that I cannot describe what is torment it has been for me. An ugly, barbaric interlace of events that I have tolerated an entire year, and which in the recent months has reached to the size of Herculean pillars of torture and ugliness. This of course pertains solely to the sphere of my personal life, and to describe the history would take a complete volume. But at this time, thank God, the worst is behind me.

The household has little happiness, and uncle Aleksandr is ill and ready to retire and go on pension. The attitude between certain members of the household could use considerable improvement. In short, our old home is also passing through a sufficiently difficult phase.

Daniel was working at the time as a graphics artist at home and had to finish a project by July, so he could go on a planned vacation to a small city along the Oka River, and then to the Crimea and return to Moscow by September 1. Some plans changed although he did travel to Sudak on the Crimean Peninsula at the beginning of July. He took Maria Pavlovna Gonta with him to help him with his depression and upsets.

Maria Gonta was earlier married to the poet Dmitri Petrovski, and they divorced in 1929, the marriage did not last long, and especially that Dmitri was 20 years her senior. Maria was very attractive, and she was very admiring of herself. After her divorce from Dmitri, she had a short-lived affair with another Soviet poet, Boris Pasternak. Her romance with Daniel began in May or June of 1927, and was a passing infatuation, even though some suspected it was an attempt to escape the repercussions from the failed romance with Pasternak.

Daniel wrote a short verse in regard to the short romance with Maria in his poem *Yantar*:

I loved these child-like lips.
The brilliant speech and softness of her face.
You, the sunshine, the young, healing the wounds.
My first change and first spring.
To an incomparable paradise,
You lowered the ancient mountain,
Even my soul was affected.

Although they spent most of the time in Sudak, they traveled the entire peninsula together. They also visited Evgenia Repman, whom he had not seen in 3 years, and who was now invalid. Returning to Moscow, the romance dissipated, and Maria returned to her melancholy state, her memory still focused on Pasternak.

The arrests continued. People just disappeared from sight one after another. Daniel at nights would be writing his poetry and hear a car stop, doors open and then close, and the car speeding away with the gas peddle to the floor. It would also disrupt his thinking, wondering. In the neighboring houses along Mali Levshinski, Valpishevski was arrested, he was a truck mechanic; Borsov, a supervision at a local bakery; Gutman, a power plant operator; Efimov, a director at a local bank; Trofinuk, an superintendent at a school; Belov, a supervisor at a local clothing manufacturer. All of them were declared guilty of participation in some terrorist organization, all were shot, some at Butovo, some at Kommunark, others at Donskoi Monastery now closed and converted for Soviet state use. A female neighbor, Lomakina, was exiled from Moscow because her husband was arrested as an enemy of the people. Daniel heard of them as gossip was circulated in the neighborhood upon his return from Sudak. But the majority attempted to live as though nothing horrible was occurring, and if the terror did not affect them directly, they quickly forgot about what they did hear.

Alla Andreeva narrated what occurred at an intimidating assembly at the institute where she was studying.

They gathered us all and closed the door. They read to us the result of some investigation and inquisition. Then they proposed to everybody to agree to capital punishment. All of us picked up our hands. But I can in no way understand why this is all I remember. Once I asked a friend, "Do you remember this?" She said, "Not entirely." And when they were reading the request for a consensus, they watched who raised their hand and who did not. It was only obvious why, otherwise that night they would end up in Lubyanka.

Beginning about this time, Daniel was under administrative surveillance just before the Soviet holidays of May 1, and November 7, and he was arrested that year and each year until he was conscripted into the military, but his jail time was short. He was included in the list of the undesirables. Kovalenski would warn Daniel that one day this will end poorly.

The concept of Daniel's novel *Night Wanderers* arose from a combination of persons and events and some of it is autobiographical. He actually started writing shortly after his return from Sudak. The protagonists are persons much like Daniel himself in different phases of his character, including the troubled self, the seeker, the mystic, and the nature lover. The events are based on his own life, his travels, his visions and mystic experiences, and especially the conditions of the time in Soviet Russia with the Stalinist government's oppression, which have a direct impact on the characters of the novel. Daniel's goal for the novel was a improvement of life in Soviet Russia for the future, based on contemporary events and characters. It was the era that composed the novel. Only the first chapter rewritten by Daniel when he was in prison based on his memory of it, with a few fragments, have survived, the balance is pieced together by interviews with his readers, and especially Alla. As he would complete the chapters he would rush to his friends and read it to them line by line. He never suspected, and neither did anyone else that 10 years later this volume would be the reason for his arrest and incarceration of the best 10 years of his life, and 9 years of Alla's life, and the many years of all those who either read the book, or knew of it, or were somehow affiliated or associated with the Andreevs.

The heroes of the novel are inwardly tortured as is the author, seeking and waiting for responses or discoveries, aspiring for activity, but doomed to a purposeless ruin. The primary characters are the 3 Grobov brothers: Adrian Vladimirovich, the eldest, and the next Aleksandr, and the youngest Oleg. In some respects they reflect Dostoyevski's 3 Karamazov brothers. The 3 Gorbovs become the alter-ego and mouth-piece of Daniel's philosophy of culture, history, polity, society, religion and the search for a meaning of life in general, within the setting of Stalin's Soviet Russia.

Adrian in the first chapter is a professor of astronomy and a mystic searching the star-filled skies for other worlds hoping to one day touch the presence of cosmic comprehension. In his personal life he is laconic and dry and lives day to day in a mechanical manner with his cold character. The next chapter describes his brother Aleksandr, an archeologist, in love with Russian antiquity, for which reason he visits the ruins of Trubchevsk, and with nature also. He is mesmerized by trees, the star-filled sky, rivers, and nature in general. For some reason he likes cottage cheese, just as does Daniel, considering it the basic food substance, along with honey. Aleksandr is a man of exertion, decision and inspiration, just as is his wife, Tatyana. Then we have Oleg, the poet, religiously inclined, an artist with a dual personality. He has a steady job as an artist, just as Daniel. Oleg most reflects Daniel with his roaming and aspirations. Oleg's goal is to marry Irina Glinskaya, but a spiritual marriage or platonic relationship. According to Alla Andreeva, Irina bore a strikling resemblance to Akedsandra Dobrova.

The Gorbovs had a cousin, Venechka Lestovi, who was for the most part a truck driver or chauffeur. He was a secondary character in the novel. Venechka was a comic character, full of laughter and almost pathetic, a joke, and full of absurdities, a genuine anachronism. When he discussed religion he seemed to be heretic. So perhaps Venechka was the personification of that something Daniel felt was missing from his own life.

Another secondary character is the young architect Evgeni Morgenstern, and it is anybody's guess why Daniel assigned him a German name. He loved architecture and had fantasies about contructing large cathedrals dedicated to various deities.

One other character is the brother of Irina Glinskaya, Leonid Feodorovich Glinski, a self-taught scholar who would regularly pray for the redemption of Russia. He was the organizer of a secret mystic brotherhood, similar to a Masonic or Rosicrucian Lodge, of which all the main characters of *Night Wanderers* are members, except for Adrian Gorbov. When the novel begins, Leonid is arrested one night for refusing to voice his consensus for the capital punishment of some accused person after he was cvonvicted of some political crime. Now he is incarcerated in some common prison, along with a Hindu, an Orthodox priest and an Islamic mullah, and they also eventually pray with him, taking turns, for the redemption of Russia.

Another character to be mentioned, but appearing later in the text and who is apart from its mystic vein, is Aleksei Yuryevich Serpukhov, a participant of a group that is organizing terrorist plans and who is connected with a foreign spy ring.

Scenes in the novel occurred at night. The first night connects the events in the world with those in outer space, somewhere in the great nebula Andromeda, which the eldest Gorbov brother watches at his observatory. There is no doubt that Daniel derived his information from the recently read book noted above by James Jeans, where photographs of spiral nebulas are included. The chapter continues with a mystic meaning of the event, and twice does Daniel reference the American astronomer Edwin Hubble. The selected colors of red and light blue also evolve from Daniel's astronomical studies.

The main contents of *Night Wanderers* are the fantasies, spiritually guided but often painful, of the Gorbov brothers, their mystic searches, and the thoughts of Glinski and his colleagues during the horrifying nights of the Stalinist era.

Irina Yusova recollected her memories of the content of *Night Wanderers*. She and her sisters became friends with Daniel sometime in 1937, but it was a couple of years later that they become closer and she heard from others about the novel's subject matter.

> Autumn of 1937, we accidentally found out that the son of Leonid Andreev lives in Moscow, that he is more talented than his father, that he is a poet, but he has never been published. This interested me, that he has never been published. So how can we meet him? This is impossible! Then something occurred, or maybe it was fate. He at the time was working on his novel *Night Wanderers*, where the scenes occur in an astronomical observatory, and he wanted to look at the constellation Andromeda. We have a friend who has a telescope at his house, and we made arrangements to get together. My sister and I then were at his shed where he kept his telescope at the time Daniel was to arrive.
>
> Daniel was impressive: he had a tall, slender figure, a very pale and dark face like a malnourished Indian, a large forehead with his hair thrown back, a nice but thin nose, easily drawn lips and 2 long dimples at the edges of his gaunt cheeks. His eyes were brown, not large and not pretty, but containing some type of meaning. He was emaciated, introverted and austere, not once did he smile. Invited into the house for a glass of hot tea, he flatly refused. Tatyana offered to translate his poetry into English, but the conversation never went any further.

The younger sister, Irina Vladimirovna Yusova, worked as a microbiologist in a laboratory. The older, Tatyana, began as an English translator, but then ended as a science researcher in a geological institute. The sisters did not actually get along and had completely different characters. As Irina recollected:

When Daniel finally visited our home, both mother and us were impressed. He did not often drop by here, once every 3 weeks or so, but each time spent the entire evening reading his poetry to us, and initially these were neutral poems – about nature, walking barefoot. But some of the poems included some statement or passage that would be unacceptable to Soviet censurers and so unfit for publication.

With each visit he become more open about himself to us and then began to read the poems reflecting his psychological experiences. So then our friendship became more solid. Then he opened his other and inner world to us and this world was so extraordinary.

When the Yusovs moved to a closer residence on Stanislavski St, Daniel would visit more often. The mother and 2 sisters had 1-1/2 rooms assigned to them in a communal apartment, the total living space was about a 15 foot square. But then this is how just about everybody lived in Moscow at the time.

Making a living seemed to be the furthest think from Daniel's mind, and he only engaged in it to the extent necessary to earn a living, while the balance of the time was spent in the deep nights composing his novel.

Daniel received a letter from brother Vadim in May 1938, and responded quickly with just a short note. This was the last correspondence between the brothers until after World War 2.

1939-1940

In the summer of 1939, a month was spent with Tatyana Yusova and another friend Maria Vasilyevna at the city Malo Yaroslavetz, about halfway between Moscow and Kaluga, along the Luzhi River, a branch of the Oka River. The site was famous for a battle against Napoleon in 1812 and included several museums and the battlefield site memorial. Tatyana Yusov was convinced by now that she would become Daniel's wife shortly.

That year Daniel became friends with Rostislav Mitrofanovich Malutin. One day Rostislav dropped by the Dobrov apartment at Mali Levshinski and informed him that he was an associate at the Literary Museum in Moscow. He had some biographical information he wanted to share with Daniel regarding his father. Gradually the formal attitude of the 2 dissipated, and they met several times in the future, since both were very literature oriented, as well as discussing political issues. Daniel did visit Rostislav's apartment, where he met his wife Vera Feodorovna and her parents. They all lived together. At the same time, both were very careful as to what they communicated to each other. The era was still to dangerous to be too open with someone a person hardly knew.

Daniel had by now long abandoned his dream of actually traveling to India. So with thoughts of spiritual experiences, in the spring of 1940, he again spent time at Trubchevsk, and this was his final visit. This is only known to us from the memoirs of Alla Andreeva, but Daniel did not leave any notes or records of his visit.

This was a difficult year for Daniel, apart from working as a graphics artist, the balance of his spare time was dedicated to *Night Wanderers*.

Daniel hardly made his presence known in public during 1939 and 1940, and until the German invasion. He worked during the days and wrote at night. In addition to *Night Wanderers*, Daniel completed an autobiography titled *Childhood and Adolescence, 1909-1940*, and a continuation of his *Catacombs*, that he started in 1928.

THE YEARS OF WORLD WAR TWO

1941

Dr Philipp Aleksandrovich Dobrov died April 20, 1941, at the beginning of Easter week, of an unexpected heart attack. He had just seen patients at his home and escorted them to the door, and went to wash his hands. The family took him into Daniel's room where he passed away.

On June 22, 1941, the Germans crossed into Russia. Even though a peace with Germany existed for a long while, since the end of World War I, and recently with Adolf Hitler's new reich, few considered it valid. So when the news of the invasion was announced, it effected everybody, even those who expected it.

The opinion of some Russians can be concluded from the interview that Daniel had during his inquisition in regard to Rostislav Malutin.

> On one of the initial days of the war, Malutin unexpectedly came to my house one day and began a rather open conversation with me regarding the current events. It consisted of our common anti-Soviet views and

then he stated that it was time to put our words into action. He then informed me that he considers the fascists of Germany to be summoned to appear as a historical weapon whose purpose is to liquidate Soviet authority in Russia, and the result would be the transfer of authority into the hands of anti-Soviet underground groups, whose intent is to install in the country a parliamentary procedure. This is the reason he [Malutin] stood for the defeat of the Soviet Union in the war with fascist Germany. I told him of my doubts that Germany can secure the creation of a parliamentary procedure in Russia.

I had a negative attitude toward his propositions. I informed Malutin that I have no experience for such activity, nor any inclination, nor any ability. I let him know that I counted myself a writer and wanted to remain such in the future. Other than this I expressed to Malutin my doubts that the victory of fascist Germany will cause a positive factor to materialize in Russia.

At the beginning of the war, Daniel started to write his poem *The Germans*. He was attracted to them due to the positive influence from van Goethe and Wagner. But when Hitler's armies invaded Russia, the German genius was transformed into a mortal and ruthless squall. Irina Yusova listened to Daniel reciting the poem and recollected:

> It was composed at the very beginning of the war, when the news of fascist bestiality still did not reach us. Regarding Hitler, Daniel only knew that he was a mystic, a vegetarian, that he conducted some kinds of mystical séances where he would communicate with the geniuses of the German race. This sentimentally interested him. The poem started with a list of all the beautiful contributions that this diverse nation provided: the Bayreuth Festival Theatre, for example, the

Chrismas plays, Wagner's *Lohengrin*. Once the war started the attitude changed.

The poem itself was a masterpiece, and consisted of distinct parts, each one consuming a page. The length of each line and the rhythm alternated compatible with its content. The conclusion of the poems was composed after the ruthless conduct of the fascists was circulated and the barbarity and cruelty were likewise included. Daniel attributed a demonic mind to Hitler.

The poem was eventually lost, although some fragments of it were transferred into *Russian Gods*, and subsequently into *Leningradski Apocalypse*.

There is no basis to suppose at either before the war or at its beginning that Daniel hoped the German would liberate Soviet Russia from the Stalinist regime, even though he was, like all the others, unable to fathom the amount of damage that the war would cause to Russia. In the diary that he kept in 1943, while at a military hospital, Daniel openly recorded his attitude toward the war and Soviet authority:

> It is clear that I cannot view German fascism as anything else other than a reactionary power, infringing on the very existence of Russian culture, on the independence and integrity of the Russian nation, a living entity that I sense as part of myself and which I love. I deeply love the ancient culture of Germany and Italy, German music and poetry, Italian art and architecture. This is why this malignant tumor that has appeared in the body of these cultures seems terrifying to me, and to remove it requires the most serious of surgical procedures. This is why I feel there is no other manner of ending this progressing war except for the complete and terminal liquidation of the fascist regime that has caused so much desolation and catastrophe, which the entire history of the world has not known to this time.

On the night of June 25, 1941, Moscow tested its sirens, but it was obvious that the Germans and the war approached Moscow. Pskov fell on July 9, Smolensk on July 16, Novgorod on August 15, Dneprpetrovsk on August 25. On September 8, a German blockade surrounded Leningrad, and in the meanwhile their front moved toward Moscow. The first bombers reached Moscow on the night of July 22, but Daniel survived since he just arrived in Peredelkino, south-west of Moscow, where he went to stay with Yusovs who had rented a house before the war. Irina Yusova recollected the time.

> About a month after the war started, Daniel arrived here to spend a few nights with us, and it was that very day, once darkness fell, that the first air attack came on Moscow, the German bombers. The rays of a number of searchlights glared into the night sky moving from side to side, but as soon as a searchlight caught a bomber, it would not lose it, but followed it, and then other searchlights joined to create a lighted cross with the bomber in the center. The scene was mesmerizing. Very close to our home, but hidden in the forest, was an anti-aircraft gun battery. But the bombs did not reach it, but shards of the bombs did hit the corrugated steel roof of our house. Daniel was horribly upset and nervous. His friends and family were in Moscow, but he could not travel there, and now that it was dark the trains were no longer running.
>
> But there in the distance in the direction of Moscow, in one place we could see a light and it was just getting bigger – the glow of a fire! Looks like a bomber did reach Moscow and bombed it. Daniel's alarm got worse. He tried to figure on which part of Moscow the bomb dropped. He almost did not sleep that night and as soon as day broke he took the first train and returned to Moscow. Returning home he guarded it, just as did

everybody else their home, just in case the Germans would drop incendiary bombs.

At nights the searchlights flooded the sky, and during the day the Germans bombed Moscow. With Daniel and his mystical other-world attributes, the war more than just agitated and perplexed him, it was difficult to identify with one group of people causing such devastation to another group, and without cause or remorse, and it seemed like without culpability. It was more difficult for the Dobrov household, now all of then having aged and Dr Aleksandr now gone, upon whom the livelihood of the family depended. Life became bitter and complex for Daniel, with people's lives dissolving around him. Kovalenski had his illness, his aunt Elizaveta who raised him and whom he considered his mother, as well as aunt Ekaterina, were by now semi-invalid and aged, and it seemed all of this occurred all at once, and so the impact of such speedy events tormented Daniel. Kiev fell to the Germans on September 19. By autumn, Moscow was a besieged city, emptied of a good part of its population.

Vyazma was taken on October, 2, Oryol on October 3, and Tule right after, Bryansk on October 6, and then they entered Trubchevsk on October 12. The Soviet government proposed the evacuation of all the members of the Union of Writers on October 15, but Daniel Andreev and Aleksandr Kovalenski were not included. Moscow was in the process of evacuation beginning October 16, and even Stalin was gathering to relocate to Kuibishev.

The day of October 16, 1941, was permanently engraved into Alla's memory.

> Everyone is fleeing Moscow, every person afraid of remaining. The Germans reached the heart of Russia. We hear on the radio what we have become accustomed to hearing, "Our army is deserting, deserting, deserting." By the morning of October 16, the only ones remaining in Moscow were those who had nowhere to go or no reason

to flee. We decided not to leave and endeavored to hold together.

Moscow was officially under siege on October 19, and the city was encased. Every person was allotted only a half-pound of bread per day. Stalin entrusted the military leadership to Georgi Zkukov. Wood was likewise in desperate demand to keep the remaining residents warm, and they turned to burning furniture in their stoves and fireplaces.

How Daniel was able to survive these months is known from Irina Yusova's recollections:

> Daniel to begin with was a very impractical person, as it seems was the entire Dobrov clan. They had no food stored away, none at all, or even other items they could use as barter, and very soon he began to suffer from hunger. We tried to the best we could to feed him more. Yet I do not remember when the time started that he would come to our home regularly twice a week for a late dinner, after Tatyana would return home from work. Time went by so fast. I think that Daniel was only filled with food the times he left our table. And just as regular, twice a week, he would sit on our sofa and read to us what he composed since his previous visit. Initially it was his poems, *Yantari* and *The Germans*, and then it was his novel, and up to the time that he left for the front. When he was ill, either Tatyana or I would admonish him and go to his house with food for him. But Tatyana would get angry at me for doing this without her. Even though she was glad and it was important for her that Daniel eat, she had the feeling that she was responsible for his nourishment, and not me!
>
> Central heating in our building during the war did not function, and it seems that slowly all the regions of the city lost heat and were disconnected. In any case, due to the extreme cold outside, Daniel spent the night with us in a small room. At night after dinner, he would retire

there, and we would close the door and try not to make any noise. He was also working on his poem *The Germans*, at the time. But I do not remember how late he would write and finally go to sleep. He would rise several hours after we did and then read to us what he wrote during that sitting. This was more than 80 beautiful lines when completed.

Electrical service took a while to return to normal, and so when I received at work an electric heater for my personal use, I immediately took it to Daniel. I do not remember the words he used to thank me for it, or maybe there just were not any. But I well remember his profound gaze of gratitude. Then his mother entered,[30] who already knew what I brought, and she silently but enthusiastically gave me a big hug, but then told Daniel that I always brought satisfaction into her life.

1942

Either at the end of January or beginning of February 1942, Daniel found out that Malutin was wounded and was recovering in a Moscow hospital. It was Malutin's wife, Vera Feodorevna who informed him, and Daniel visited him.

Also at the beginning of 1942, Kovalenski along with Leonid Ivanovich Timofeev received a contract to publish books titled *Khudozhestvenaya Literatura* (*Fictional Literature*) for the distribution of native compositions for patriotic purposes. The first volume would especially include a Russian translation of the works of Maria Konopnicka, a Polish writer. Daniel help to select poems for the anthology, worked as a typesetter, and prepared the manuscripts. For a short while during early 1942, Daniel was ill with paratyphoid fever.

One woman helped with the work and this was Tatyana Morozova, whose husband was in Leningrad. While working on

---

[30] Referring to Aunt Elizaveta Dobrova.

the book, Tatyana received word that her husband died of malnutrition in Leningrad on January 7. Tatyana's life was also quite difficult. She was ill with the remaining effects of encephalitis, from which she almost died. She came to Moscow before the war hoping for work and money, since she and her 2 daughters were not used to village life and laboring on a collective farm, while her husband went to Leningrad. In Moscow she had a few friends and relatives.

In June 1942, Daniel's foster mother, his aunt Elizaveta Dobrova, died after a 4-month prolonged illness. With her death, and that of Dr Dobrov a few months earlier, Daniel was now alienated from the balance of the family since they were no longer close to him, as he was an Andreev and the balance of his family was in France.

Irina Yusova described the period:

When his mother was bedridden due to illness, he often went to the market and would buy for her a jar of strawberries for 20 or 30 rubles. He told me that she did not seriously understand her situation, and she became capricious and demanding, so unlike her daily character.

The Kovalenski clan separated themselves and would eat by themselves. This disintegration of the family over food now occurred very often. Often even the husband and wife would eat separately. Except for the 2 times a week when he was with us, Daniel was constantly hungry. Even his cousin,[31] it seemed to me, always acted like she was in a panic. The one time that I saw her, still before the war, when I was at Daniel's home, she flatly did not like me. She was amazingly in disaccord with the general style of the household: she wore bright make-up, had large protracting lips, long earrings down to the shoulders, and one shoulder – they were white as marble – was always exposed, even though it was winter, to give the appearance she was somewhat voluptuous. When we

---

[31] Aleksandra (Shura) Dobrova who was Kovalenski's wife.

had a cup of hot tea, I do not remember what we spoke about, but I remember that she had exceptional poise and shallowness.

Even though he was 36 years of age by now, with the Dobrov household disruption and his guardian parents both gone, Daniel again felt like an orphan, and this brought him closer to the Yusov household. Sister Tatyana still carried the hope she would become Daniel's wife and was persistent in her endeavor.

There was no time and no strength for any out of town trips that 1942 summer. Daniel and the 2 sisters only had a short 2 day trip outside of Moscow, and which was even perilous with the siege.

In October 1942, Daniel was conscripted into the army. Before leaving for boot camp, Daniel went to the home of Sophia Aleksandrovna, the sister of Dr Dobrov, who lived in a Moscow suburb called Valentinovka. His intent was to bury his handwritten manuscript of *Night Wanderers* in her garden.

Daniel was conscripted as a non-combatant due to his spinal deformity and was mobilized not far outside of Moscow, at the Kubink train station. He wrote about this experience in his diary:

> Myself, I personally consider this a duty and obligation, for me to be included in our common struggle for liberation. The inflammation of nerve roots in my spine, which is called spondyloarthrosis, prohibits me from active military service. For several years I wore a metal corset and removed it not long before the mobilization. I received this exemption from marching and physical labor by the medical commission. But I do not sense I will be moving about much or working hard, as in the actual army. My place will be right here.
>
> Some moral issues that I have adopted since childhood and which have been inculcated within me permanently, dictate to me to not flee dangers or open

battle, but at the same time, they hinder me from participating in anything that contains an element of deceit, although this is very allowed during conditions of war. For example, I would not want to be a scout. I have no doubt that I would find it difficult to justify this position and defend it logically, but what is ingrained into my senses is stronger and more of an imperative, than any logic, and it is not subject to any reconsideration.

At Kubink, overflowing with a reorganization of persons, registration took its time for Daniel. He did little while there since he was assigned as a non-combatant.

1943

Daniel did get a 2-day leave for New Years Day and he returned to the Dobrov household. There he celebrated with the Yusov sisters and the Kovalenski's, and Alla and Sergei Musatov also came for the evening. Beginning this evening, Daniel began to distance himself from Tatyana, while drawing closer to Alla. However, rumors spread that Daniel and Tatyana married before he left for the front.

Daniel was somehow able to travel to Dr Dobrov's sister's house to bury his manuscript of *Night Wanderers*, now leaving for the front and wondering if he will return. Daniel left another copy with the Yusov sisters, along with other compositions of his.

In January 1943, the Soviet army prepared a penetration through the German's Leningrad blockade. Daniel was mobilized as part of it as part of the 196th infantry division, although Daniel was at the rear with the supply train. The object was to march across the frozen Lake Ladoga (Ladozhskoe Ozero) and attack from the east. From the point of mobilization, it took 2 days to march across the lake.

The Soviets attacked the German blockage of Leningrad on January 12, and on the 18th, the blockade was broken and Soviet troops entered entered the city. It was late at night when Daniel entered the devastated city with its empty streets and filled with snow. The January frost was overwhelming, the temperature was 30 degrees below freezing point. Daniel described the event in *Rose of the World*:

> As we walked through dark and evacuated streets to the area of troop disposition, I relived an experience that I had a long while ago as an adolescent, but not embellished at all as was the other. I was as though thrust through specific stations of the front line at night, first viewing through them as though they were transparent, and then consuming it, the dry and gloomy. Within it the contradictory irreconcilable principles became dark and barely glittered, while their stunning scale and inspired horrible terror as a great demonic entity stood behind them. I saw the 3rd *yuitzraor* clearer than ever before. It was only due to the vague brightness of its enemy approaching me that preserved my mind from irreparable rupture. This was our hope, our joy, our defense, the great spirit, the national guide of our native land.

The 3rd *yuitzraor* is the demonic personification of Stalin's despotism, while the spirit as the national leader, and the enemy of *yuitzraor*, was Yarosvet. Such experiences are unfolded in Daniel's poem *Leningradski Apocalypse*. The night that is mentioned in this poem is not one of the nights of the blockade, but a ferocious mystical night of a great battle of the 2 most powerful dragons of global history – the *yuitzraors*, with their demonic hordes. As *Rose of the World* narrates:

> Deep night has arrived. The powers of light turned themselves to a temporary benevolent inactivity, the monster is finally caught. Only the peripeteia of this

capture were visible to all on earth. Precisely did spiritual paralysis shackle the higher capabilities of people and barely was the most intense of meditation and transcending creative ascension able to raise on occasion the human soul over the impenetrable cover of darkness.

This decisive capture of the city's German defense was not only Stalin's triumph, but Daniel likewise depicted Russia filled with Hitler's soldiers, as he saw it that January night. Food was sparse in Leningrad, but documents indicate that Daniel shared his with hungry children.

About this time Daniel received news that the last of his aunts – his mother's sisters – died, Ekaterina Mikhailovna Mitrofana.

In April 1943, Daniel was transferred to the funeral command of the 196th Red Army Infantry Division. His duty was to record the remains, if identifiable, of the dead and bury them in the field, in unmarked graves. They would gather any documents or valuables from the bodies and record them, and if there was a manner of identifying the dead, then such items would be returned to an address identified with the dead. Not only Russians were buried, but any Germans. The work and difficult and horrifying. Stomachs were severed open with intestines on the ground, or a torso with a hand, arm, foot, leg missing. The stench of decomposing flesh was unbearable. Many of the dead had been lying in the snow frozen for several months and now with the spring they were thawing, and with the weather warmer the bodies were putrifying. They were gathered and piled on carts, covered with canvas and hauled to some open pit just dug. Daniel stared at the horror of war before his very eyes and all of this left its indelible impression on his psyche. The scene of massive death and the job of disposing bodies as objects, objects that were once living humans just like himself, molded his attitude toward war and military service, making it repulsive and objectionable. In *Rose of the World*, the concept of war or a military would no longer exist, and Daniel's previous conviction of objection to war was further confirmed with this scenario of gathering bodies and parts of bodies and disposing of them in unmarked graves, or just holes, and many of them not identified.

One soldier in the infantry, Feodor Khorkov, recollected his experience with Daniel. Their division was camped along the Neva River, opposite Shlisselburg Prison, and they were living in adjoining dugouts.

> Every spare minute Daniel would run to me and share with me his impressions. He recollected his father, relatives, his life. Then I first realized that his brother, Vadim Leonidovich, lived somewhere in France, and due to the war he was sorrowful that all communication ceased. We were all very hungry, but if some of the higher-ups left the camp, we were able to have their share of buckwheat porridge and cabbage soup.
>
> Daniel, slender as he was, lost weight and became thinner. Every day he saw dismembered and putrefied corpses, piled on wagons and hauled to large pits. On occasion I would walk up to him, and he would raise one of the tarps on the wagon and I saw a blue colored corpse. The soldiers name was inked on his stomach. Then he asked me to go away and shouted, "I cannot take this any more. Go away!"
>
> Our 196th Infantry Division moved place to place: to Karelia, to Kolpino, then to Leningrad. Then they transferred us to a location along the Neva River. I worked as a secretary for the military division and lived in a dugout. Daniel would bury the dead and during his spare time would dine with me. We ate watery soup from the same pot.

Daniel's service in the funeral command exhausted him physically and devastated him psychologically. If it was a woman, Daniel tried to always place some flowers on the grave.

Daniel also suffered a bout with malaria, as he wrote to Valentina Mindovskaya on July 21, 1943:

> So what is the purpose of the life of a human soul? True, I have still not had the opportunity to encounter the most horrifying and cruel incidences of war, but nonetheless I saw much difficult and indescribable sorrow. And disregarding this, the joy of life has not died in my soul, or hope or the thirst for creativity or belief. On the contrary, they are more fervent now than they were at any time earlier.
>
> The external circumstances of my life flow along this channel into which it fell about a month back, but, obviously, it will again follow changes, although it is still not clear to me what direction it will be.
>
> Silence for a long time reigned around me and is now replaced by noise, but this is at a great distance from us, several kilometers away across a flat, calm field. The weather is better but it still rains every day, but at least it is warn. Physically I feel myself far from being healthy, likewise in my psychological state. But I think after this month is over, the general condition of myself as a human will improve.
>
> My malaria has also recently subsided with the quinacrine provided.

Daniel was awarded a medal for the defense of Leningrad.

August 24, 1943, the 196th Division joined with the Baltic front, and was moved to Pskov province, to the region between Velikie Luki and Nevel, then Daniel ended in the hospital, this was the 595th Surgical Field Hospital. Khorkov recollected the event:

> The constant hunger and endurance heavily took a toll on his health. He did not complain, bore all the burdens, and then he collapsed. He was diagnosed with split sacral vertebrae (spina bifida) that caused him horrible

torment. In August 1943, he was taken to a hospital. He wrote to me from there, that he was getting well and even helping in the surgery room, but it was difficult to endure the sight of human blood.

The aggravation of his longtime pain in the vertebrae occurred as a result of being overworked with moving artillery shells when he was part of the supply command earlier. Due to his many years of exposure to the medical field as a result of his exposure to uncle Dr Dobrov and his treating patients at the house, once Daniel was on his feet his status changed from being an invalid patient to being a hospital attendant, and then a registration attendant. Daniel adapted easily to the hospital environment and the work was light. The opportunity also arrived for Daniel to correspond with remaining friends in Moscow, his future wife Alla and also Valentina Mindovskaya. Daniel also kept a diary at this time and where he also included autobiographical information.

1944

A new campaign, the Riga operation, began early summer 1944, the field hospital relocated to the region of Rezekne, in the eastern part of Latvia. The area was artistic, green hills, pine forests, lakes, and the Latvian summer was refreshing.

Daniel was desperate to return home, his inability to write tormented him. But here in Rezekne he was able to supplement *Night Wanderers* with a few lines. He also wrote to friends in Moscow, also to Valentina Mindovskaya:

> Every moment of my free time is dedicated to writing. I live rather well, to the extent I can in my situation. I am preparing for a business trip to Moscow sometime the second half of June, but it will be short. With bitterness I think that I will not succeed in seeing anybody at all, since my work is up to my neck.

> Here I have hills, forests, lakes, and twice I have gone on hikes, strolling through the forest, bathing and enjoying. I have no place and no time to read, but *Night Wanderers* is still moving forward, although slowly. Without my initial manuscripts, that I left in Moscow, any large work to continue is impossible. Once I return I can again dedicate myself entirely.

Daniel arrived in Moscow June 14, and stayed at his home for a week. During the 1-1/2 years of his absence, Kovalenski was occupied with his translations from the Polish. But the conversation was little about Kovalenski's work, as Daniel was agitated over the condition of Sasha Dobrov, his cousin. Before the war he suffered a relapse of encephalitis, and now he was back in the hospital due to depression caused from the narcotics he was taking. Daniel did have a chance to visit him.

For his future wife Alla, these few days shined with a summer sun, being special and having a direct affect on their destiny. When Daniel met her, she thrust herself into his arms without reservation. She later recollected:

> I returned home from some place. Sergei sat with a ice cold expression on his face, one to which I was accustomed. I entered the room. He raised his head and said, "Daniel is here on a business trip. He is at the house on Mali Levshinski." Silently I turned around and ran. I ran the way a 12 year-old girl would, not stopping even for a second, straight through the entire Arbat, and along Plotnikov Lane, to Mali Levshinski. I ran the route with which I was familiar, as I did during my school years, but not quite like a careless foul that only wanted to run with no purpose. Now I ran – literally – to meet my destiny, and while running I dropped or threw everything I was holding, anything that held me back or served as an hindrance or slowed me.
>
> I ran as if I knew what my destiny was, and the choice I made was obvious: an implicit subjection to my

destiny. So I ran like a teenage to meet love, and not to mention prison and concentration camp, but the most primary was the greatest happiness in the world, closeness to the creativity of a genius. Maybe this is also the closest I would ever get unhindered to these other worlds. But I did not know this at the time. In fact, I knew nothing of any of this.

I ran. I rang the doorbell. One of the neighbors opened it. I flew up the stairs, ran through the front room and threw myself straight towards Daniel's room. I opened the door but the room was empty. I turned around and ran back through the front room and entered Kovalenski's room. Daniel stood there with his back to me while conversing with Kovalenski who was sitting on a sofa. Hearing the door open, Daniel turned around, saw me, and abruptly stopped his conversation and walked up to me. We took each other by the hand and silently walked through the front room, and silently entered his room. We sat on a sofa, holding each other's hand. We were together.

Our road was now the 2 of us to move forward and encounter whatever we would encounter, and we did encounter much, and terrible things and immense happiness, and only the type of happiness that occurs with people who actually understand that they must share with each other all that life will provide them.

Then Daniel returned to the front.

Sergei very difficultly endured me leaving him, but he did not seem to consider that he did the same to his first wife Natasha. He ended up at a psychiatric clinic, and Natasha and I visited him regularly.

That day, June 21, 1944, was the brightest day for Daniel and Alla that year. For Sergei Ivashev-Musatov it was a blow, while for Tatyana Yusova, now 40 years old and who was convinced she would become Daniel's wife, it was a catastrophe. This was not the first occasion for Sergei to land in a psychiatric hospital, he had bouts with depression regularly in the past, and the relationship with Alla disintegrated. Daniel's occasional correspondence with Alla from the front would cheer her, and she would write back and inform Daniel of her dissatisfaction and desire to leave. Alla eventually realized that her marriage to Sergei was a mistake, and he watched its gradual dissolution.

Daniel left Moscow and returned to his service at the field hospital. At the beginning of autumn, the field hospital received a notice of redeployment. The army moved forward into Czechoslovakia, Hungary, and Austria, while the hospital was at its tail. In October 1944, Daniel received a commission to participate in an exposition in Moscow, at a new museum to triumph the victories of the Red Army. Alla spoke of his return:

> Early that morning I heard the doorbell. I always knew his ring. So I jumped out of bed, ran and opened, but nothing of the sort. I got a chill. I sat on the sofa and froze, and I did not even have the strength to shiver. But then he walked up the stairs and came in through the door. He look horrible. A pathetic picture of a disheveled soldier: his jacket no longer looked like a jacket, it was in tatters.
>
> Somehow we had to rebuild his life, and I thought the museum connection would help. Daniel was supposed to work at the military museum as a professional artist, but this was not his type of work.
>
> I went to the museum and talked to the director. I told him that Daniel would work at home and I would go back and forth between him and the museum. It worked out.

What did not help any with Daniel's return was that the manuscript of *Night Wanderers* that he left with Tatyana Yusova was discarded, and the only other copy was the one he buried at an aunt's house and which by now disintegrated. As a result Daniel had to start from scratch, from the first line all over again. In one respect it was not so bad, since Daniel gained much experience with the war, and further developed his understanding of people and events. All of this he would incorporate into the new version.

Writing defined Daniel's life and it likewise became primary for Alla, whom Daniel considered his wife, although they were not legally married, and would not be for a few more years. They lived together at the Dobrov home, although by now the apartment was vacant of any Dobrovs, yet Aleksandr Kovalenski and his wife Shura still lived there. With a decisiveness and prudence Alla started to build a mutual life for themselves, and at the same time protecting her husband's compositions. She also quickly changed the submissive attitude Daniel had toward Kovalenski, and curbed the procession of uninvited friends circulating in and out. The atmosphere of the home changed for the better.

Daniel's room was medium size of about 10 feet by 15 feet. It contained a small dining table and sofa, a bed, and one cupboard for dishes and personal belongings. A small table in a corner with his father's old typewriter served as Daniel's study. There were 2 windows overlooking the courtyard, and the space between the windows was filled with photographs, all about the size of a postcard, of people who were close to Daniel's heart: Tolstoy, Vl. Solovyov, Dostoyevski, Tutchev, Lermontov, Hugo, Ibsen, Chopin, Shubert, Schumann, Wagner, Beethoven, Bach, Mozart, Borodin, Korsakov, Mussorgsky. On the other side of one window was a larger portrait of *Dante and Beatrice* by Henry Holiday, and also one by Dante Rossetti, along with the *Mona Lisa*. Daniel always had a photograph of his father, Leonid Andreev, somewhere in his room and another photograph of Alla as a 3-year-old girl. On another wall was the icon of the Theotokos of Vladimir. In between were bookshelves and books all the way to the ceiling. There was no ceiling light, and only a few lamps in the corners of the room, and since Daniel did not like entering a dark room, one lamp was always on in their absence. They never locked the door to their room. Their entire wardrobe hung on a few nails on the door. They had no dresser, and it would have been empty anyway.

This room became Daniel and Alla's home. Daniel was 38 years of age and Alla was 30. Dinner was still cooked in the dining room shared by the residents, and over a kerosene stove, and they either ate in their rooms or at the ancient dining table. A boiler in the cellar provided heat to the rooms, but it had to be lit every day by someone and with wood that was still difficult to come by.

1945

The war continued and the Red Army penetrated further into Europe with the Prussian campaign and hecatombs of sacrifices. Daniel wrote about Stalin in *Rose of the World*, that he, "with his ice cold callousness was forcing millions of Russians into a meat grinder," while Hitler, "was grinding his teeth, foaming at his mouth, throwing himself on the floor and gnawing at the carpet in anger, vexation and grief at so many of his compatriots perishing, but he continued to force them into battle."

It was only after Daniel's return to Moscow that he began to feel the repercussions of the war years. Gradually illnesses surfaced, new ones as well as old. He was not able to get adjusted to civilian life again or remove the impact and impression that the war events psychologically left on him: the daily injury and death and dying, watching the suffering, and expecially the devastating effect that being part of the funeral command had on him. Daniel reflected on much of it in *Rose of the World*, about the war being nourished and sustained by demonic powers. He felt that during his military service he was just a mechanism in the ruthless war machine, not having any actual control over himself day or night during the 2 years on the front. Alla noticed this about Daniel:

> Somehow he tried to explain that a person cannot return from war an undamaged person. He will definitely be wounded either physically or psychologically or morally. So he will return affected by war and very deeply. It was

not without good reason that when, several years later, he began to write *Rose of the World,* his thinking was agitated and overwhelmed with what he considered the 2 primary dangers that threatened humanity: worldwide tyranny and global war.

Not yet officially discharged, Daniel wore his military uniform through the winter and spring of 1945. His work at home on behalf of the Military Museum continued, and he received a regular check, although later he spent time there. Alla was also receiving a check for her work at the Moscow Region Union of Artists.

On May 12, 1945, Daniel wrote to his friend Mitrofan:

My unforgivable prolonged silence, or better said, disappearance, was caused entirely due to a barbaric and barely tolerable winter: illnesses and bouts of extreme workload at some fervent speed. Right now I continue to rise at 6 AM, and return home by 10 PM, and then I collapse into bed. But the opening of the museum, where I am working, must be ready in just a few days, and then calm will return. But my health is nasty and I need to take measures to take care of myself.

THE POST-WAR YEARS

1945 – Continued

On June 25, 1945, sometime after the opening of the museum, Daniel was formally released from military service with an honorable discharge, and was recognized as a permanently-disabled veteran of the war. As a result, he received a pension of 300 rubles a month. Daniel was diagnosed with manic-depressive psychosis of an atypical form.[32] Now he was able to remove his military uniform and not worry about the patrols who watched for military personnel not wearing proper uniforms. He could also return to his writing and have some rest. Of course, he still had to make a living, since his pension was hardly enough for himself and Alla, even with her income. But Daniel's type of writing did not meet the criteria for Soviet press, which lesson he learned earlier, so he decided to take the example of Aleksandr Kovalenski.

During the war, Kovalenski was translating Polish novels into Russian, rather innocuous works, and he also composed a few short stories of the Soviet style, but none met with success. After the war, Kovalenski was translating the Norwegian Henrik Ibsen, a favorite author of his, from Danish into Russian, and

---

[32] Today this is known as Post Traumatic Stress Disorder.

figured it would be accepted by Soviet censurers. *Brand* was completed in 1946 and was accepted for publication. Later that year *Peer Gynt* was published, and the play was performed March 6, that year.

Daniel could not compromise or capitulate to Soviet censurers to have his compositions accepted for publication, so he gradually but persistently continued on *Night Wanderers*, now essentially starting from scratch, but expanded with Daniel able to contribute more due to his war-years experiences. His characters likewise encountered the effects of war and Oleg Gorbov returned from war, blind. Daniel wrote in a contemporary style about the Stalinist terror and difficulties of Soviet life, his fears of the era, and his benevolent suggestions of improving the situation. The book was the materialization of Daniel's philosophy, ideology, and view of Soviet life, all combined into one volume. Alla later recollected:

> But Daniel sensed obviously that everything that dealt one way or the other with the manner the novel displays the tie of the reality of life with his fatal logic.
>
> He wrote every night. I would go to bed, fall asleep, while Daniel sat at the desk behind the typewriter and page after page, chapter after chapter recreated the entire novel. Regardless of the immense depth of ideas, thoughts, beautiful images that he developed, Moscow is portrayed completely marvelously in the novel, it is so vivid, real. Every evening he reads to me a chapter of the novel, what he wrote the previous night. And he did not just plainly read it, but we lived every line together.
>
> This is when my strange capacity for empathy came into usefulness. Often Daniel would turn to me, explain some situation that was occurring in the novel, and would ask me my opinion. Of course, this pertained more often about female characters. "Tell me, how is the story moving along? Should I include more emphasis in the way she is speaking?" And I strived to identify with the

character of the heroine, to place myself in her spot and guess how she would conduct herself.

So did we live as though within the envelop of the novel, and its heroes surrounded us as though they were actually alive.

Night was the state of the environment, absent of light, while *Wanderers* referred to their search for the light in their personal life. The novel unfolded together with the destinies of the heroes who entered the mystical fraternity, concentrating on and surrounding Leonid Glinski. Not because Leonid found what he was looking for and dedicated himself to it, but that he was most reflective of Daniel. Character Leonid also had terminal tuberculosis, to be identified with Daniel's spinal disorder and constant pain. Moscow did have its mystic fraternities at the time, even in Stalin's era, including Masons and Rosicrucians. But Leonid did not share Helena Blavatzki's Theosophic doctrine, and because neither did Daniel. He sought some personal mystic truth, a personal revelation. Leonid was present during each of the wanderer's nights, a seeker of higher truths and light. Daniel's hero during the summer of 1937 was unexpectedly arrested and confined in an overcrowded cell, and which foretold unconsciously Daniel's own eventual fate. Daniel as a poet was depicted in Oleg Gorbov.

Although no copy of *Night Wanderers* survived, Alla recorded some notes from her reading regarding the episode of Leonid's incarceration.

> The inquisitions were endless and almost always at night. A completely diverse category of people were among those crowded in the cell, with an Orthodox priest and [Islamic] mullah. The 2 of them and Glinski understood each other without even talking, like a 3-cornered shield. In turn, one of them would silently pray for all those in the cell. When that person was summoned for an interrogation, or gets exhausted, using a gesture he would pass his prayer-turn to the other.

One chapter was dedicated to an eye to eye confrontation with one of Glinski's colleagues who was earlier arrested. This chapter is titled, *Remnants of a Person*, and which essentially was Glinski's state and subsequently the termination of the life of this hero.

When Glinski's turn comes for his interrogation, he discards every evasion and begin to frankly speak: not of his company, not of people, and he does not mention even one name. The interrogators are dumbfounded with Glinski speaking without them providing him questions, and he tells them what he thinks of Soviet authority, of Russia ruined, of that monster Stalin, about the entire terrible, armed political machine, against which he stands alone, ill and defenseless. He speaks all the clearer and fervently, gradually understanding that his entire life was lived only to culminate at this minute, in this torture chamber, in order to announce to these executioners and murderers that they are executioners and murderers, just henchmen of evil

Under the conditions of Soviet efficiency, this address was supposed to end with Glinski's execution by shooting, but his end occurs in a different manner: with a strong surge of blood gushing from this throat, beginning here in the interrogation room. Then they carry him to the prison hospital where he quickly dies.

Rest for Daniel was now needed and at the beginning of July they traveled to Filipovski, a local village north of Moscow, about 100 miles. It was Daniel and Alla, and Galina Rusakova with her husband. Tatyana Morozova was living there with her daughters, and she invited the 2 couples. The village was surrounded by virgin forests, meadows, fields and ponds. Alla recollected the vacation in later years:

> We had a very good time the 1-1/2 months we spent there. All of us hiked together or else just the 2 of us,

myself and Daniel. Exactly while we were there, August 6, the Americans dropped the atomic bomb on Hiroshima. Daniel tolerated the event horribly. Nothing in all the world was so valuable to him as culture, and so he concluded the accomplished devastation as the possible beginning of the destruction of global culture. I lived through the event differently, more from a female perspective, but for him it was very tragic and profound. Humorously and wildly we discussed having Daniel attempt to place an atomic bomb under Red Square.

We hiked together much. It seems that all the villages just laughed at us, because they could not understand the type of people we were: we did not gather mushrooms, and in general did nothing, but as the villagers expressed it, "Roaming and roaming." Yes, we walked, walked through the forest, along the roads. And praise God.

Much as with his hikes at Trubchevsk, they walked miles in every direction, carefree. Rain started the beginning of August, which forced them indoors for a while, and then intense heat caused mosquitoes to swarm the area. The 4 guests left Filipovski for Moscow on August 19.

Immediately after arriving in Moscow, the Andreevs departed for Izmailovo, a Moscow suburb east of the city, to visit Valentina Mindovskaya. Her husband was still not released from the military. Near her was the residence of 2 other women who were also friends of Daniel: Ekaterina Alekseevna Balmont, wife of the late-poet, and her close friend, Olga Nikolaevna Annenkova, and whom they visited.

The 2 female friends were convicted anthroposophists. Both of them from an early age sought the resolution of the riddle of the mystery of existence according to Rudolf Steiner. Annenkova at one time listened to Steiner's lectures and participated in building the Goetheanum, and even received from Steiner the right of acceptance into his School of Spiritual Science. In 1931 she was arrested due to her effort with organizing an anthroposophic group, and so was sentenced to 3 years exile in Oryol, central Russia.

The 2 friends were attempting to lure Daniel into their anthroposophist convictions. Books of Anne Besant, Rudolf Steiner, as well as Andrei Bely's biography of Steiner, were at their home. However, their effort failed in convincing Daniel to join.

While at Izmailovo, the Andreevs likewise strolled through the forests and visited the ancient sites and palaces of earlier centuries. Daniel and Alla returned to Moscow at the beginning of September.

Daniel returned to his novel at nights, but it seems that everything would interfere. It was difficult to find food, he would have bouts of depression, running errands all day on mundane and trivial matters seemed to never end. The daily grind was more difficult for Daniel if he was not writing. Alla would comfort him with periods of relaxation when she would sew and he would read to her his latest chapter. He would also read aloud Dostoyevski, Merezhkovski, *Tristan and Iseult*, some of his father's plays and poetry. The 2 would attend the theater and listen to Wagner, Beethovan, and other orchestra music conducted by Yevgeny Mravinsky. Consumed by his novel, Daniel wrote less poetry.

Alla recollected the difficulty of the era:

So did our life begin. We were very poor. At this time I was already a member of the Moscow Region Union of Artists, but there was still little money. This is the reason we could not formally marry, we had no money to buy rings. The formality of my divorce went easily. I did not want to further injure Sergei, and so took a document testifying to his commitment to the psychiatric hospital to court and used this as my reason for a divorce, and they granted it to me. Daniel and I legally registered as a couple on November 4, 1945. What was important was that we were together and, of course, we thought at the time that it would just be a while longer before we could have a formal wedding ceremony. But it was not for another 12 years.

1946

Alla recollected the beginning of the new year:

> On Christmas Eve of 1946,[33] the Lord gave us the opportunity to together listen to the church bells of the Novo-Devichi Monastery. We walked to the Novo-Devichi cemetery to the grave of Daniel's mother.

After Christmas they again traveled to Izmailovo. Valentina Mindovskaya's husband, Lev Mikhailovich Tarasov, was discharged from military service in December 1945, and due to injuries he sustained in his back, his shoulders bent forward and inward. As with Daniel, Lev worked in the hospital ward and as a result returned psychologically devastated and with a nervous disorder, along with regular depression. He was always agitated, silent, and smoked a lot. Their friendship developed to the point that they were as though family.

They returned to Moscow and on February 26, the Soviet government reduced the price on all essential products by 50%. This included bread, pasta, canned goods, and even cigarettes, which made life easier, but neither of them had a steady job. Shortly after, Alla went to work at the Tretyakovski art gallery creating posters.

On May 2, after Easter, the Andreevs traveled to Izmailovo for the final time. The region was just turning green with the spring weather and warm sum. On that same day, Alla's brother Yuri married at the Tarasov home, and all enjoyed the festive occasion. They strolled through the park after and had a dinner at the house.

---

[33] Orthodox Christmas is celebrated January 6.

It was particularly here in Izmailovo that Daniel went to visit Nikolai Pavlovich Amurov. They became friends while in the hospital corps and spent time reminiscing the period. As life normalized, wartime associates began to funnel through the house at Mali Levshinski.

Daniel's love of geography resurrected with his discharge from the military and the end of the war. As a result Daniel became closely associated with Sergei Nikolaievich Matveev, who worked at the Institute of Geography of the Academy of Sciences. He traveled central Russia considerably and created an immense pile of notes and comments. This attracted Daniel and who decided that a book of Russian travelers to the region would be a means of income. Matveev provided Daniel with all his information along with other resources from his library, and Daniel wrote a small book: a biography of Russian researchers of the mountains of central Asia. The book's authors were both Daniel and Sergei, because Daniel was still unknown, and the book was published in September. A second book was already in progress about Russian researchers, but now Daniel was sole author and was able to get a contract in advance for publication. Sergei was excited that he was able to help Daniel in his endeavor as a successful writer.

But their friendship also backfired, as Sergei Matveev would also be arrested in the matter of *Night Wanderers*, even though he had nothing at all to do with it. It was solely due to association with Daniel and with no other basis.

The Stalinist regime continued to be inhumane and Soviet writers were likewise oppressed. The Andrei Zhdanov affair in July caused the denunciation of satirist Mikhail Zoshshenko and he was isolated from society and lived the balance of his life in poverty. Zhdanov likewise had the popular poet Anna Akhmatova expelled from the Union of Soviet Writers.

In July, the Andreevs along with the Bruzhes family departed for a vacation in Zadonsk, in south-central Russia. Few people still lived in the city who remember the regular pilgrimages to the famous residence of St Tikhon of Zadonsk, but now the facility lay in ruins. The famous Rozhgestvo-Bogoroditzki (Birth of Theotokos) Monastery was vacant of its original Orthodox clergy and was transformed into a factory for the processing of local vegetables. The Vladimirski Cathedral survived. Daniel wrote to friends about his Zadonsk vacation:

> Before my eyes were the following: an opened window with geraniums, further was the street and gardens, and even further was the Don River and its villages and forests. The forests are inaccessible and we were hardly able to make even one decent hike. This was all the more vexing because the weather was so pleasant and with much sunshine. The result was that for 3 weeks all we did was look at the local region: the interesting half-destroyed monastery, the shores of the river, the tree-covered hills with its picturesque background. We bathed in the river's shallow water and strolled through town in the evenings with the Bruzhes.
>
> I was able to sleep the entire night without waking. I wonder how I will be able to return to my books on geography after here meditating on more important tasks, those only known to God. At times the region seems to laugh at us and this scares me.
>
> We eat well, sleep well, but spent most of the time wandering about local gardens.

Returning to Moscow, Daniel received a postcard from his brother Vadim in Paris at the beginning of September. Daniel immediately replied with a letter, the first correspondence with him in 8 years.

> My dear, kind, natural brother!
> Finally, I can be assured that you are all alive and well! Eight years I have not received from you even one piece of news. And although the belief that you are alive never left me, but this was not sufficient a reason not to

be worried over you and your family. Joyfully did I find out about your partisan work behind the German lines. So did we together fight the same enemy, but from opposite ends of Europe.

First of all, I must inform you of sad news: in 1941, just at the start of the war, uncle Philipp died unexpectedly of a brain aneurysm. The following year, while also in difficult circumstances, my mother died after a painful illness that lasted 4 months, and then 6 months later, aunt Katya followed her.[34] Our family has dissolved and the old Dobrov home has ceased to exist. Sasha for a long while now lives separately with his wife. Shura and her husband still live in our apartment, but the cooking and life in general is completely separate from ours, and when I says ours, I mean myself and my wife Alla. We have been married 2 years; we married in very strange conditions, completely, its seems, inappropriate for the era, during my short leave from the front in Moscow.[35] Our meeting, love and cohabitation is the greatest happiness that I have known in my life. Alla is an artist, landscape painter, and portrait painter. Both of us work at home and we are never apart from one another more than 2-3 hours at a time.

I was on the front for a long while, participated in the defense of Moscow and Leningrad. I was in Leningrad during the blockade, arriving there solely by one route: across the ice of the Ladozhskoe Ozero. Then I was discarded to the regions of Veliki Luk and Nevel, and finally, Latvia. The war severely devastated my health, both physically and mentally. Before the end of the war I was removed from active service and placed in a hospital. But I am incapable of complete recovery. Now I am among the number of the category of invalids of the Fatherland War.

---

[34] This was Aunt Ekaterina.
[35] Although Daniel calls it marriage, he alters the actual circumstances for his brother.

My capacity to hold a regular job is greatly reduced, I am also very limited in my ability to move about. Tied with this was my need to have to change vocations. I wrote a small book on a geographic theme, and people liked it. Within a few days it will appear in public, and I have received an order for a second, on the topic of geographic research, which is where my time is present spent.

Recently we both returned from the small city of Zadonsk, where we spent our summer vacation; we refreshed ourselves there and I even gained some weight. Our life is very quiet, and on occasion we will attend a concert, and on a rare occasion even the theater. Of course, I wish matters would be better.

We love you and are lonesome for you, and your family means a lot to me, and I would like to hug Olechka and Sasha and kiss Olya. I cannot find words to describe how I feel. I embrace you tightly, tightly, my brother.

Once settled back in the apartment in Moscow after the Zadonsk vacation, they sat in their room without money and both became sick. Somehow they had to get well and get out of poverty. Daniel spent much of his time at the main Moscow library with his research for his next book, and then in bed all night with a fever. His next book was titled, *Russian Researchers of the African Continent*.

Daniel continued to read Dostoyevski in the evenings alone to Alla, and now was able to get a copy of Leonid Grossman's biography of Dostoyevski. Although *Night Wanderers* was not the critical item on Daniel's agenda, he hoped to apply what he read from Dostoyevski to his own novel. Leonid Grossman lived also on Mali Levshinski, with whom Daniel would converse regularly, but now after reading the Dostoyevski biography, Daniel paid a special visit to speak with him.

DANIEL ANDREEV – ARREST AND INTERROGATIONS

1947

Alla later wrote of the months before the arrest in her memoirs:

> Our destiny was already determined. What was strange was that we completely turned no attention of ours to so many things, although knowing about all of this, what was occurring around us. Truly though, I do not think that anything would have helped much. All of a sudden some unknown person came along, and for what reason, and appeared in our presence, and began to convince us to change our apartment to another on the corner of Ostozhenka. Then down in the cellar, in the former Dobrov kitchen, noise and knocking began. They said that the room was being converted into a shoe and boot workshop. But of course, no workshop ever started. It was plainly obvious that in the floor of our apartment a listening device was installed. Then without any invitation the telephone repairman came and announced that he had to repair our telephone. But our telephone was working just fine, and there was no reason to fix it, but the eyes of this so-called repairman had a strange ice-cold appearance that caused shivers to run down my spine, and I still remember it right now.

After everything was said and done, Daniel and Alla were amazed at their own inattentiveness, carelessness. While Alla was working at the Tretyakovski gallery, suddenly a young man with a camera approached her and asked permission to photograph. Another occasion a neighbor noticed that someone climbed into the attic and was doing something with the louvers or shutters leading into their apartment.

All of these were investigative procedures of the MGB.[36]

The Andreevs started to be more careful. One of the neighbors knew an informer tied with the agencies. Annoying premonitions began to affect them about this time. Alla recollected the era:

> I remember the feeling that as if an immense snake wrapped himself like a ring around our house, sometimes closer, sometimes further. And there was another strange thing. At night I lie on the sofa. Daniel sits at the typewriter, we are literally next to each other. But in the very middle of the night I hear the doorbell and then I think, "They have come." I freeze. But no one walks in. Then I would experience this again.

Daniel's work continued on his book on African researches until it was finished and accepted for publication, and then every minute of time was dedicated to *Night Wanderers*. Every evening he read what he completed the previous evening to Alla, and the closer he came to completing the novel the more he wanted people to read it. Daniel lent a chapter or 2 to friends to read or the entire manuscript to the extent it was completed. At the same time, Daniel needed some constructive criticism or comments.

The revised novel begins with the characters in an observatory looking at the stars of the nighttime sky through a telescope and ends the next morning as the morning star rises. All the heroes circulate through a series of scenes that night, and

---

[36] Ministry of State Security, also known as KGB, Committee of State Security.

many of which are recollections. Daniel himself was regularly interjected into the characters and his personal experiences were likewise reflected in theirs, although subtly.

Daniel gave the 2nd part of the novel to Irina Armand to read. She returned it after a few days with a comment about enjoying the fiery attitude the author had toward life. While the manuscript was in Irina's possession, she showed it to her mother, Tamara Arkadevna, who also read some of it, and then went hysterical and this led to a heart attack. Tamara was on the edge of a nervous breakdown herself due to the recent arrests in her area. She was convinced that because of the book's contents, the secret police were sure to show at their apartment, and so she started to imagine footsteps on the staircase. In case this should happen, Tamara decided to tell them that she found the manuscript in the subway, and then demanded that Irina return it the next morning. Tamara's words were eventually self-fulfilling prophecy.

The Avsuki couple visited the Kovalenskis on the evening of April 20, along with the Andreevs. The conversation varied on different topics including the condition of Soviet Russia. Daniel made a statement to the effect that it would be to the benefit of the USSR to be defeated in a future war with America. But Margarita Avsuka reprimanded Daniel telling him, "Is it not shameful for you, a Russian person, to curse your homeland with such a calamity." Later, during the arrests and interrogations, Daniel's statement would be to his detriment, but Margarita's statement would rescue her from her imprisonment. But Aleksandr Kovalenski would not be so fortunate; he continued working at the Soviet Union of Writers, without any knowledge of what was soon to occur to him or his wife Shura.

Informers continued to intervene into the Andreevs' life, as Alla later recollected:

> We became acquainted with one poet, or more precisely, a poet and actor of the Vakhtangov State Theater. The person was interesting and somewhat possibly of use to Daniel. I could only admire and be happy as the 2 of

them conversed and understood each other with just a few words, as if they found each other as very compatible close friends. But I did not know the rest of the matter, whether he worked directly for the KGB, or he was an informer, or they just interrogated him about us, but he betrayed us in any case. And likewise my school friend from earlier years betrayed us, but in her case, I think they required it of her. Hardly would she have done this on her own, but if they did summon her presence, they scared her and threatened her and she of course told them of the novel *Night Wanderers*, and of my anti-Soviet views.

The poet and actor was Nikolai Vladimirovich Stefanovich, formerly of the Vakhtangov Theater, but he was now invalid as a result of injuries he suffered during the war. Stefanovich was now indirectly involved with the theater, but because he was still a good actor he became connected with Soviet agencies as a front with the betrayal of other suspected anti-Soviet writers. He lived not far from Mali Levshinski and near the theater.

Stefanovich regularly visited their home with many conversations, and eventually Daniel gave him a copy of the manuscript of *Night Wanderers* to read.

On the day after Daniel's arrest, when Alla was still unaware of it, Stefanovich called her and asked, "So how is Daniel Leonidovich? So what is going on with him?" Of course, she told him that all was well, and she was happy that he would call to check on him. Stefanovich then offered to return the manuscript, although Alla said she did not need it at the time with Daniel away.

Stefanovich also played an important part in the arrest of the Kovalenskis.

Alla's school girlfriend, to whom she refers, was Galina Khizhnyakova; the 2 were close friends from early school days. Apparently, the State agency summoned her presence and forced information out of her, sufficient for an arrest. The documents pertaining to Andreevs arrests stated:

Facts of the dissemination of illegal anti-Soviet literature were confirmed by testimony provided by G.V. Khizhnyakova.

But there were others who either capitulated to Soviet intimidation or were direct Soviet informers that provided information on the Andreevs. Victor Semeonovich Abakumov, formerly deputy minister of the National Ministry of Internal Affairs, was assigned personally by Stalin in May 1946, as Minister of the Ministry of State Security, MGB. He summarized the initial results of the first stage of the investigation of the Andreevs and his circle in his report to Stalin:

> In the process of secret-service intelligence, information was acquired that D.L. Andreev and A.A. Andreeva surrounded themselves with people of a hostile attitude and they had malicious anti-Soviet conversations among them, disseminating slander and intentions against Soviet authority.
>
> Other than this, through the secret-service there was also confirmed that Andreev wrote a series of anti-Soviet compositions and read them to his close hostile circle.
>
> The MGB USSR was secretly informed of the anti-Soviet compositions of Andreev under the title of *Night Wanderers*, in 4 parts. In one of the chapters Andreev summoned an active struggle against Soviet authority using means of terror against the leaders of Soviet leadership.[37]

While Daniel was at Vladimir prison he wrote to Alla that he felt both Stefanovich and Khizhnyakova were planning something against him, but at the time he just could not admit to himself that any such thing would occur.

---

[37] Interesting that Abakumov was himself executed as a traitor to the USSR in 1954.

Alla recollected the event of April 21, 1947, the day of Daniel's arrest:

> When Daniel wrote his book about the Russian travelers in Africa, it was already submitted for publication and was supposed to soon be released. Suddenly he received a telephone call with an invitation to fly to Kharkov and deliver a lecture on the topic. Daniel was very surprised, but why not, he thought. Very early that morning an automobile drove up to our house. I walked outside and accompanied Daniel. I remember the last words of my husband, "It is so good that all the difficulty we have lived through is past, as I do not have the strength to live through it all a second time."
>
> He sat in the car and it drove away. As the vehicle was driving away, Daniel looked at me through the back window.

Other than the driver, there were 2 other persons sitting in the vehicle. They drove to a Moscow airport, but there Daniel was removed from his vehicle and placed in another. Now he realized that he was arrested, and he watched the regular landmarks as the 2nd vehicle returned to central Moscow.

Daniel's traveling papers issued by the ministry of higher education were dated April 22. The edit for his arrest was signed by Major Kuligin that same day, and the next day the papers were countersigned by General-Lieutenant Ogoltsov of the MGB USSR, and also by the prosecutor. The orders along with the procedure for his incarceration were issued April 23. It is odd though that Daniel was arrested and then the official documents for his arrest were issued after his arrival at Lubyanka.

Arriving at Lubyanka, Daniel was placed in a box: a cell with no windows and without a bed. Then the regular prison introduction routine: shower, search, fingerprints, photographs. The prison attendants operated silently, procedurally, mechanically. Every inmate, unexpectedly extracted from mundane life, encountered the prison environment in their own way. From Daniel, his passport, pension document, traveling papers to Kharkov for his lecture, 2 letters, 2 pocket diaries, one with addresses and telephone numbers, a notebook with sketches, 3 books, including an English-Russian dictionary, and a map of Africa, were confiscated. Since Daniel did not have a suit, he borrowed one from his father-in-law, and it was also confiscated. Likewise, 2 small icons of Orthodox saints.

The following morning, Alla received a telegram supposedly from Daniel in Kharkov, and he informs her that he arrived and all was well. Alla did not suspect anything. Stefanovich later came and returned the manuscript, giving it to Alla at the door and immediately leaving. Late that night, April 23, MGB agents came for Alla.

The 1-1/2 years of interrogation now started for Daniel. The first inquiry began at 11 AM, April 22, the morning after his arrest. It lasted an hour and was conducted by Major Ivan Feodorovich Kuligin, Deputy Minister of the Second Department "T" (for terror). He, as usual, began with a standard questionnaire, those which dealt with relatives, and especially any that lived outside Soviet Russia.

After an hour's interval from the first inquiry, another deputy minister along with Kuligin led the 2nd inquiry, Mikhail Adrianovich Zhukov. They began with excerpts from a letter to Tatyana Yusova and then maneuvered to the subject of his novel.

Question: What literary composition is the subject of the discussion in this letter?
Answer: While I was in the army, I sent to Yusova in Moscow a letter, where I wrote making her the executor of my estate and entrusting her to publish any of my literary compositions that are in her possession after my death.
Question: What literary compositions did you leave in the care of Yusova?

Answer: Leaving to the front in 1942, I left with Yusova a collection of my lyric poetry, the poem *Monsalvat*, and it was unfinished, and *Krimgilda*, and *The Forest of Eternal Rest*. The title of the final poem was later, after my return from the army, I changed it from *Nemerecha*, which in the Bryansk dialect means – impassible thick forest. I also left with Yusova the novel that I just started, *Efemera*.

Question: What other compositions did you leave with Yusova?

Answer: I did not leave anything more with Yusova.

Question: Is this correct?

Answer: Yes. Completely correct.

Question: Is there any reason why these compositions – based on their content – should not be published in the Soviet Union?

Answer: There is nothing in any of the compositions that I just mentioned that would be considered anti-Soviet.

The poems *Monsalvat* and *Nemerecha* have shades of mysticism. The same type of shades of mysticism are also in my other poetry. These compositions, of course, cannot be published right now.

Question: You affirm that you have not written anti-Soviet literature?

Answer: Yes, I affirm this.

Question: Let me quote to you one place from a letter that follows the vein at the beginning of the interrogation, "Such a fire cannot be touched by anyone form the outside, as with Irina Feodorevna." Who is this Irina Feodoronva?

Answer: I do not know of an Irina Feodorovna. I suppose that the topic deals with Mansurova, who it seems was called Maria Feodorovna. I as if explained to Yusova that Mansurova was like an example of the trustworthiness of a beloved friend.

Question: You are lying. You distinctly know whom you had in mind, Yusova, remembering the name Irina Feodorevna. I ask you to speak the truth.

Answer: I reply, that I do not know Irina Feodorevna.

Question: And the heroes described in your compositions, did you not give one of them the name – Irina Feodorevna.

Answer: No, I did not.

Question: Stop your obduracy. Through our inquiry we precisely know that Irina Feodorevna was a heroine of one of your composition. Now speak the truth.

Answer: I will stop being obdurate. Irina Feodorevna is definitely the name of a heroine of my one novel.

Question: Which one?

Answer: The novel is called *Night Wanderers*.

Question: Did you also leave this novel with Yusova?

Answer: Yes, I left it.

Question: Listing what you left with Yusova, why did not you name this novel?

Answer: Because this novel contains a criticism of Soviet activity, which could be interpreted in the end as having anti-Soviet statements.

Question: So what other composition did you write that contain anti-Soviet views?

Answer: There are outlines of my poem *The Germans*, which I wrote in 1942, and also a few more rhyming verses.

Question: Are these compositions also in the possession of Yusova?

Answer: No, these compositions I left in my apartment.

Question: Specify to us where these anti-Soviet compositions you wrote are to be found.

Answer: I will not say during this interrogation.

Question: Why not?

Answer: I worked 10 years on the novel *Night Wanderers*. This work is very valuable to me, and I cannot consciously doom it to annihilation. My other anti-Soviet compositions are hidden together with this novel. As a result, I cannot reveal to you their whereabouts.

Question: This means you refuse to surrender your anti-Soviet works?

Answer: Yes, I refuse. In any case, right now I will not tell you this.

Question: The interrogation regards this as a continuation of your struggle against Soviet authority. Take note of this.

All of the MGB officials involved knew about *Night Wanderers*, but in accord with methods of inquest, the person being interrogated had to admit that nothing can be hidden from them or should be hidden from them, as they will find out one way or the other anyway. Other than this, Zhukov also asked question about Kovalenski's compositions and gave Daniel the impression that he also knew about them in detail.

The 3rd interrogation the following day began 10:30 PM. It continued almost the entire night, ending about a quarter to 4 AM. Two officials were questioning: deputy Ivanov who replaced the exhausted Kuligin, and Zhukov. The subject matter was the same, Daniel's compositions having an anti-Soviet content. They impressed on Daniel that his obstinacy is futile. Eventually Daniel responded,

Answer: I understand this. I have decided to let you know the place where my anti-Soviet compositions are located. They can be found in my apartment, where I live. When you enter the apartment there is a front room, and there is a staircase of 7 steps. Alongside this staircase is a banister. On the left side of the banister at one spot is a collection of items for our domestic use. If you remove them,

> you can lift up the board and then you will find a hidden compartment. This is particularly where all of my anti-Soviet compositions are contained, except for those that are lying around the room.

After this, Tatyana Yusova was interrogated. She was brought there the same day with Daniel's confiscated manuscripts. She was interrogated 5 hours in one sitting, and then she was temporarily released. Tatyana immediately let her sister Irina know what occurred.

The matter regarding Daniel Andreev, beginning with his arrest, was handled by Department T. The 2 men at the top with the responsibility for the interrogation was Major-General Aleksandr Giorgievich Leonov and deputy Vladimir Ivanovich Komarov. At one point Leonov told Daniel, "You have no idea, Andreev, the special knife we will use to extract your intestines from you. And literally!"

What was an absolute necessity were facts dealing with the work of an organized and hostile underground group, and one that did not just plainly occupy itself with only anti-Soviet agitation and propaganda, distributing personal writings, but that they were preparing a defined and premeditated terrorist act against the head of the Soviet government, Stalin. If not this, at least the MGB felt they had sufficient material to find Daniel guilty of at least agitation and propaganda.

With the need of evidence of intended terrorism, the agents depended on their method of interrogation: late at night, sleep deprived, intimidation, threats on family, informing that family was already arrested and already confessed to the same, and of course blatantly lying of their release should they confess to the accusations, no matter how false or incredible or impossible as they may be. With some self-accusation, the agent's goal will have been accomplished. The agents were able to apply some of the fictional events in the novel *Night Wanderers* to intended terrorism on the part of Daniel Andreev. In one of the chapters, an attempt on the life of Stalin is described in precise detail. The

Soviet agents were relieved when they read this passage, since in their interpretation this was not a fictional composition, but instructions for action.

The anti-Soviet underground was depicted in *Night Wanderers* as the Glinski group, a gathering of adherents whose common identity was their dislike of all that was imposed upon their country: communism, socialism, atheism, all of which was leading the nation to a spiritual ruin. The novel likewise defined the group's task, as the proceedings recorded the following passage as incriminating:

> Night over Russia will inevitably end with a new dawn, and this dawn will display the extreme stage of the spiritual destitution of the people, and those who understand this must be prepared to start to fulfill the demand of resolving the destitution.

It was easy for the agents to interpret the above statements as anti-Soviet propaganda and agitation and preparations for terrorist action, even though the characters were fictional. During one interrogation, the agents actually read from the novel specific passages that they considered to be sedition, and felt the attempt to call the work fictional was just a maneuver to cover its intended purpose. The interrogation records noted:

> The first is an very careful masquerade. A denial of any kind of unified anti-Soviet display, in order not to expose himself. The second is an active underground effort.

The accused themselves did not know who of them were involved or arrested in the matter of Daniel Andreev. They never saw each other in the interrogation rooms, or in the jails, and the agents never informed any of them of any of the others, except in the case of having to tell them that such and such already confessed. The accused would often deny knowledge of another to protect that person, but the agents already knew the entire circle of Daniel's associates, even though some did not know the others.

At one of the initial interrogations, the agent proposed the question, "And who read this novel of yours, *Night Wanderers?*" Daniel then listed them, not realizing that he was now placing every one of them in jeopardy as being an accomplice, and many of them would not have been arrested unless they were mentioned by Daniel. Daniel provided them the following names:

1. Yusova, Tatyana Vladimirovna;
2. her mother, Yusova, Maria Vasilyevna;
3. Ivashev-Musatov, Sergei Nikolaievich;
4. his wife, Musatova, Natalia Vasilyevna;[38]
5. Khizhnyakova, Galina Vasilyevna;
6. Armand, Tamara Arkadievna;
7. her daughter, Armand, Irina Lvovna;
8. my wife, Andreeva, Alla Aleksandrovna;
9. Stefanovich, Nikolai Vladimirovich;
10. Dobrov, Aleksandr Philippovich;
11. Malakhieva-Mirovich, Varvara Grigorevna;
12. Bruzhes, Aleksandr Petrovich;
13. his son, Bruzhes, Yuri Aleksandrovich;
14. Kaletzkaya, Maria Samoilovna.

Along with them, those who read the novel *Night Wanderers*, are the following persons who have since died:
15. Dobrov, Philipp Aleksandrovich;
16. Dobrova, Elizaveta Mikhailovna;
17. Mitrofanova, Ekaterina Mikhailovna;
18. Finkilshein, Varvara Dmitrievna.

Individual chapters from the novel I read to Ivanovski, Aleksandr Mikhailovich, and his wife Maria Vladimirovna. These were chapters from the very earliest version of the book. I think it was about 1937 that I read some of it to Ivanovski.

---

[38] This was Natasha, Sergei's first wife.

Individual sections I also read to Vasilenko, Victor Mikhailovich. Persons did know of the book's existence, such as Khandozhevskaya-Dobrova, Galina Yuryevna; Kovalenski, Aleksandr Victorovich; and likewise his wife, Dobrova, Aleksandra Philippovna; and Matveev, Sergei Nikolaievich.

At this interrogation, the question whether Daniel missed any person that read it or knew about its existence, Daniel replied, "As far as I know, I have named them all. If I remember another, I will let you know." Galina Khandozhevskaya was Daniel's cousin Aleksandr Dobrov's 3rd wife.

They were not in a hurry to arrest all whose names were provided. Even then, the agents at Lubyanka laughed, that all the suspects lived in a series of houses on Arbat Street, so it would be easy to gather them. Agents were assigned to keep them all under surveillance, and each one was arrested in a predetermined sequence. Some were retained in confinement after their interrogation. As Alla later recollected:

> My parents survived, since they did not read and did not know of Daniel's compositions. Also Galina Rusakova survived, a very close and beloved friend of Daniel, although she did read the novel. In the course of events, they arrested persons who solely had an indirect relationship with us.

The final list of people arrested numbered 36, although the total that were suspected of being accomplices reached 200 before the matter was concluded. Lev Tarasov was arrested; Galina Rusakova mentioned above with her husband; the 73-year old mother of Sergei Musatov; the aged mother of Tamara Armand; the other Yusova sister, Irina; and the grandmother Ivasheva-Musatova; and even Stefanovich, although he was the informer. It never entered into Daniel's mind that the names he related to the interrogators would be accused of crimes against the state.

On July 16, Aleksei Pavlovich Shelyakin was arrested. He and Daniel were both in the military and became acquainted since both enjoyed literature. The agents found his name in Daniel's correspondence, and a search of his home provided a stack of letters from Daniel and a diary that contained personal information about their activities together. Of those in the entire list of suspects, Shelyakin did not know any, not one of them, however he was there somewhere when Daniel read excepts of his novel and including the chapters that dealt with the subject crimes against the state, and this was noted in one of the letters from Daniel. At the same time, agents found passages in his diary that were considered anti-Soviet, and all of this was sufficient to land Shelyakin a 25-year sentence.

In August, Tatyana Yusova was arrested. Two men arrived, one in uniform, one in civilian clothes, in late evening to their apartment on Stanislavski Street. Tatyana at the time was living at their summer house, but her sister and her husband, Vasili Vasilyevich Nalimov, were staying there. However they searched the apartment and confiscated all documents and correspondence they could find, especially letters she received from Daniel along with photographs.

But it was 3 years since Daniel and Tatyana saw each other, but this made no difference, and she was apprehended and arrested and taken to Lubyanka. Sister Irina heard of commotion regarding Daniel's arrest and she departed from Moscow earlier, and the agents did not bother to further locate Irina. The incident devastated their mother, Maria Vasilyevna, and she died before the investigation of her daughters was over.

On August 24, they arrested Sergei Ivashev-Musatov and Victor Vasilenko. The former was arrested at his home, while the latter was at the railway station on his return from a vacation in Baku.

The Dobrov family for a long while was already under surveillance by MGB agents due to their knowledge of Dr Philipp being a "monarchist." With further interrogations of the persons on the original list provided by Daniel, they likewise would mention other persons that agents would add to the circle of Daniel Andreev. So the conspiracy expanded and inflated.

During his interrogations, Daniel had to answer questions on his anti-Soviet activity. He informed them that this began back in 1928, when he recognized his negative attitude toward Soviet authority, noticed its persecution of the Russian Orthodox Church, the absence of a free press, collectivization. But his opinions he only expressed in the privacy of his family at home. Of course, there was no way to get Dr Dobrov and his wife or other members as witnesses since they had died, but then all living members of the extended family became suspects.

Further interrogation of Daniel extended to Aleksandr Kovalenski and his wife Shura. The following exaggerated confession of Daniel is recorded in the interrogation proceedings:

> Kovalenski was especially vexed at Stalin. In 1934, after the murder of Kirov, he revealed that the attempt on Kirov did not provided tangible results and could not summon any changes in the country. If a person wanted to sacrifice himself, Kovalenski stated, he should have shot at Stalin. Kovalenski subsequently several times told me of his terrorist mood and said that he was personally ready to kill the head of Soviet government. Dobrova, Kovalenski's wife, shared her husband's terrorist intentions, and not just once in conversations with my wife Andreeva and I, she explained the necessity of using violence to estrange Stalin.

The Kovalenski couple were now doomed. Even though they were both seriously ill, this did not affect their role in Daniel's terrorist circle. Kovalenski wore a plaster corset due to spondylitis, while Shura barely had the strength to leave her room, and seldom did she even leave the apartment.

Vadim Safonov, hearing that his friend Daniel was arrested, went with his wife to their apartment to get some details from Kovalenski. But Safonov was not aware that his name was later added to the list of suspects. When Kovalenski opened the door, he did not invite the Safonovs in, but just told them, "If you enter, you may also get arrested." They left. Other friends of Daniel arrived and he told them the same, aridly and without further explanation. Then MGB agents came for the Kovalenskis.

With the arrest of Aleksandr Kovalenski and his wife Aleksandra (Shura) Dobrova, the MGB agents nailed closed the door to Dobrov's apartment and this was the end of the family's residence there for over 30 years. The Lomakin neighbors walked out to bid Shura good-bye, as they did when Alla was arrested, and she was flooded with tears. They would never see her again, since she would die in a concentration camp.

The Kovalenski couple were arrested October 1. Somehow the process of Aleksandr's application for the Soviet Union of Writers was still active, even when he was in prison, so on October 24, the application was approved. But he would not know about it until 9 years later when he was released from concentration camp.

Shura's brother Aleksandr (Sasha) Dobrov and his wife Irina were arrested on November 2. Later the Zhalabovskis were arrested. Their name was acquired via Kovalenski, and when their apartment was searched they found some of Kovalenski's poetry manuscripts, and this was sufficient for them.

The biologist Dmitri Romashov likewise was taken to Lubyanka. He was in the same classes at school with Musatov, and apparently also friends with Daniel. Somewhere along the line, Dmitri was at someone's house and there listened to Daniel's poetry, and his name was somehow retained.

Another incidental person caught in the web of suspects was Nina Ivanovna Gagen-Torn. She was arrested once already in 1940 for anti-Soviet agitation and was confined to prison until 1945. Now she was again arrested, in 1948, as an accomplice in the matter of Daniel Andreev and again imprisoned, now until 1953.

The arrest of the Andreevs was a precisely and carefully planned operation, in complete conformance with the practice as defined by the MGB regarding "spies, saboteurs, terrorists, and participants in the anti-Soviet underground." In a special correspondence to Stalin of July 17, 1947, in regard to the arrest of the "terrorist" Andreev, Abakumov reported the following:

1. Before the arrest the criminal was investigated using defined measures, in order to accomplish the arrest suddenly and without interference, with the following goals.
   a. Avoiding escape or suicide;
   b. Inability to attempt to inform other confederates;
   c. Prevention of any destruction of subject evidence.

During the arrest of this important state criminal, when it was impossible to hide his arrest from his surrounding associates, or impossible to simultaneously execute an arrest of his confederates, and in order not to scare them and not give them any possibility to squeeze from their crime or destroy subject evidence, the secret arrest occurred directly on the street in the presence of other special pre-arranged circumstances.

The goal of the interrogator at the initial interrogations is to have the inmate openly admit to all of the crimes he committed against Soviet authority and betray all of those who are tied to his crimes, without the interrogator making the slightest impression that he personally is interested in the proceedings or the material that he is acquiring from the inmate.

During this process, the interrogator learns of the inmate's character, and presents from the first approach: promises of amelioration of prison regimen, allowing goods to be delivered to him from relatives; permission to read books, longer strolls with free time, and etc.

If this fails, then the 2nd approach: increase the pressure on the inmate with threats of severe retribution for the crimes he committed in case he should refuse acknowledging his guilt, and etc.

If this fails then the 3rd approach: apply a method of persuasion by utilizing the inmate's religious convictions, his family and personal ties, conceit, ambition, and etc.

Often in order to successfully manipulate the inmate and make the impression on him that the departments of the MGB know everything there is to know about him, the interrogator reminds the inmate of individual intimate details of his personal life, vices, which he has hidden from associates and others.

The acquired evidence to organize the interrogations, as a rule, should enter the questioning gradually, with the intent that the inmate will not have the possibility to know the full extent of information that the MGB possesses about the activities of the inmate's crimes.

In dealing with inmates who stubbornly refuse to submit to the demands of the interrogations, who conduct themselves provocatively, and who use every means to prolong the inquest or try to evade the matter or force the subject to a tangent, austere measures allowed by regulations must be applied. These measures include:

a) Transfer to a prison having more cruel regulations, where time allowed for sleep will be curbed, and food will be reduced, and the inmate's cell will be bare, and the deprivation of other daily needs;
b) Solitary isolation;
c) Deprivation of strolls, gifts from relatives or friends, and the right to read books;
d) Assignment to a punishment cell for a period up to 20 days.

Note: while in the punishment cell, other than a stool bolted to the floor and a cot without blankets or linen, no other appurtenances are permitted. The cot for sleeping will only be provided for 6 hours a day. The inmate held in the punishment cell will only be provided 300 grams of bread a day,[39] and hot water once a day, and hot food once every 3 days. Smoking in the punishment cell is prohibited.

Not only these stipulated measures applied in the matter of Daniel Andreev, there also existed unwritten rules, further developed bestial methods. To break an arm of a suspect that was refusing cooperation often occurred.

1948

Daniel mentioned the following in one letter after his release from prison:

> The most difficult period of my life was the year 1948, the time of the initial interrogations, which proceeded in terrifying circumstances and led me to a state of deep depression. I would not allow God to even impose something similar to this on my worst enemy.

Not understanding fully what would occur to him should he not speak the complete truth, Daniel was literally tortured by the interrogators. But what could he say that they did not know? Now the topic turned to confirming the guilt of the listed suspects. Eventually, Daniel was forced to admit that he organized a terrorist group. So when the proceedings finally defined the members of Daniel Andreev's group, the interrogators began to siphon more concrete evidence: when and about what he spoke with his confederates. The minutes of the proceedings were recorded by the interrogators, but is easy to ascertain how much of this was fabricated by the interrogators

---

[39] About 10-1/2 oz.

for the official record, inserting blatantly fallacious and self-incriminating statements to indict Daniel further:

Question: So to what period did your terrorist inclinations apply to Ivashev-Musatov and Vasilenko?
Answer: With Ivashev-Musatov I discussed the question of terror in 1929, at his apartment in Moscow, it was on Yulanski Lane, No. 12. I said to him that a violence estrangement of Stalin from his leadership of the country will make our struggle against Soviet authority easier.

Specific to my question proposed to him, whether he shares the use of terror against the leadership of Soviet government, Ivashev-Musatov answered that he would be well pleased should a terrorist act occur against Stalin.

As far as Vasilenko is concerned, well, I began to tap his conviction regarding the use of terror back in 1937, when I became close to him and developed a trusting relationship. In conversations with Vasilenko, I informed him that I personally will not raise my hand against Stalin to kill him, and Vasilenko, noting my words, then said that he himself is prepared to execute some terrorist act against him.

Question: Now let us know about the terrorist inclinations of your wife Andreeva.
Answer: From the beginning of the interrogation I understood that Andreeva told the examiners of our mutual hostile attitude. I had a much closer personal relationship with Andreeva, and I shared with her all of my most secret thoughts. She knew of my hate of the leadership of the Soviet government, and she fully shared my terrorist intentions, and she surfaced as my closest and active ally in committing some hostile act against Soviet authority.

> Constantly influencing Andreeva, I was successful in molding her hate toward Stalin and to prepare her ahead of time for some decisive actions.
>
> In conversations with me and other participants of our anti-Soviet group, Andreeva more than once announced that she was herself prepared to commit some terrorist act against the head of the Soviet government.

For Daniel the proceeding became a horrible experience, not just due to the nighttime exhaustive interrogations and beatings, but because he also had to subscribe to records containing monstrous and unbelievable accusations against his closest of associates. Alla recollected in later years the situation with Daniel:

> He was severely beaten by the interrogator at one of the inquests. So Daniel Leonidovich, once back in his cell, asked for paper and wrote a protest to the public prosecutor in regard to the illegal means of the inquest process: beating and humiliation. Some time passed and he is again summoned to examination. In the cabinet, other than the interrogator, sat some unidentifiable general. He says, "I am the public prosecutor. Your complaint was delivered to me, and it seems to indicate that possibly unlawful methods are being utilized by our interrogator. I need you to explain to me if this is really the case." Then the interrogator stood and walked up to Andreev and said, "Where did you get this notion that we utilize unlawful methods?" And he used his boot to kick Daniel Leonidovich's leg with it, and says to him, "None of our inmates is ever beaten." And then he kicks his leg again with his boot. "Does this mean that instead of repenting, you are discrediting the Soviet departments of investigation?" And then he kicks him again.
>
> It was obvious he was hitting him right in front of the eyes of this general, but after all was finished, then the

general said, "I am convinced that the investigation is being conducted by lawful methods, and you, Andreev, are slandering our Soviet penal institutions."

It was only reading in his cell that brought Daniel any respite from such maltreatment. One book in his possession at the time was Ivan Alekseevich Novikov's *Pushkin at Mikhailovskoe*, which he read in his cell.[40] Later Daniel wrote about the consolation provided by the book.

> This was a window leading to fresh air from the stench of the punishment cell, exactly a breeze of soft and pure wind saturated with fragrances of watered meadows. Returning from nighttime interrogations tortured to my limit and knowing that I have no one to whom to turn for a sincere and uplifting word, I was comforted with the thought of this book that waits for me, as a consoling friend, and which will motivate me with some encouraging memories.

The investigation was also able to uncover Daniel's visits at the apartment of the Kemnitz couple and with Evgeni Beloyusov and others, and this was back in 1935. During Daniel's inquisition at Lefortovo, they were able to procure his signature on a falsified document that stated:

> Taking a second look at the Beloyusov circle of associates, I was quickly convinced that there was a hostile mood against Soviet authority tied with them. These common anti-Soviet views united us, and so I succeeded to create one more anti-Soviet group that consisted of Beloyusov and his wife Lisitzina, Dobrovolski, Trishatov, Kemnitz and his wife Skorodumova.

---

[40] Aleksandr Pushkin was exiled to Mikhailovskoe, near Pskov, the years 1824-1826, due to his clash with the Imperial government of Russia. It was there that Pushkin wrote about 100 of his popular compositions.

I must add that along with this that the more intimate association that I had developed with Skorodumova-Kemnitz, the more I shared with her my terrorist intentions against Stalin.

Victor Kemnitz and his wife Anna Skorodumova were arrested in Penza, February 10, 1948. Then February 12, Evgeni Beloyusov was arrested in Kamensk-Uralsk at the factory where he worked.

Also the following confession was recorded as part of the investigation of Daniel:

In our regular conversations we discussed the condition of our country, slandered our political party and the Soviet government, and spoke of the inevitability of war against the USSR, and stated our assurance of the hope that Soviet authority would be defeated.

Skorodumova and her husband Kemnitz, a German by nationality, ecstatically recollected the social order in Germany, exalted Hitler and his fascist political party and confirmed that particularly Germany will surface as the liberator of Russia from the Bolsheviks. Skorodumova declared that when Germany attacks the USSR, then that will be the end of Soviet authority.

Other than details of terrorist intentions, and which was primary in the matter, the investigation diligently also concentrated on getting Daniel to admit to pro-German opinions and desire for Russia's defeat in the war. The proceedings record the following falsified conversation:

Question: And so, when Germany attacked the Soviet Union, did you start to quickly prepare your confederates to migrate to Geman military service?
Answer: Yes, all the participants of our anti-Soviet group greeted the invasion of the fascist army into the

Soviet Union with great joy, and with the hope for a soon defeat of Soviet authority.

Not doubting in the victory of the German army, I rejoiced that my long-awaited dreams will happen, when I will be able to accept a direct participation in the overthrow of Soviet authority, and then to create a new system of government together with the German occupation.

The initial military successes of Hilter's army literally overwhelmed us and we, day to day, waited for them in Moscow. At our assemblies we already openly deliberated on the question, what will we take with us when we migrate to the Germans when they occupy Moscow, and what will our role be in the installation of a new government in Russia after Hilter's victory. We all came to the common conclusion that we can count on the loyalty of the fascist authorities, that they would be behind us to continue this hostile work against Soviet authority.

With Kovalenski, Vasilenko, Ivashev-Musatov and Yusova, we agreed to migrate to the occupation authorities after the defeat of Moscow by the Germans, and we would offer them our services.

Question: What activities of betrayal did you intent to commit on behalf of the Germans?

Answer: We figured that the Germans would utilize us in the sphere of propaganda, where we are able to carry on a struggle against Soviet ideology and direct new views to the population, views that were in line with the German occupation. Our views and the views of the German occupation, as we figured, were the same.

Personally I was ready to be hired at the directive of the Germans to any post and accomplish whatever they assign me. In order to please Hitler's devotees and condescend to acquire their trust, I prepared my anti-Soviet poem *The Germans*, especially dedicated to the Germans, and I intensely worked on finishing my anti-Soviet novel *Night Wanderers*, with the purpose of publishing these compositions coincident with their arrival in Moscow.

However our hopes for the arrival of the Germans into Moscow was not justified, which caused us considerable grief. But another opportunity for success surfaced and other possible methods for struggle against Soviet authority when I was conscripted into the army in 1942 and placed at the front.

Question: Where did you continue to propagate your hostile activity?

Answer: No, during the period of my service in the Soviet army I was not able to do anything in this direction. Although I completed my service working in the rear, and was not on the front lines, still, finding myself in the conditions of serious war conditions, I understood that with any indication of the slightest hostility on my part against Soviet authority, I would be executed by shooting. I had no success in recruiting persons in whom I could trust because I was frequently moved from one command to another.

Remaining an irreconciled enemy of Soviet authority, for some interval I pretended to be patriotic, but I did not sever the tie with my confederates in Moscow, expecting to return to Moscow and renew my hostile activities.

Question: Did the opportunity present itself to do this?

Answer: Yes. Discharged from the army in the summer of 1945, due to illness and returning to Moscow, I again organized ties with the participants of our anti-Soviet group, with Kovalenski, Dobrov,

Dobrova, Vasilenko. Ivashev-Musatov, Matveev, Dobrovolski-Trishatov, and Ivanovski.

Because he was German, Kemnitz was exiled from Moscow with his wife and lived in Penza during the war. Beloyusov and wife were part of the evacuation to the Urals. But the investigation still concluded that they continued to, "remain active enemies of Soviet authority, with the difference that, after the defeat of Germany, they reoriented themselves as Anglo-Americans."

The record of the investigation indicated that Daniel recognized this new attitude in them, and again under pressure subscribed to the following record:

> At the gatherings that I renewed at our apartment, Kovalenski, Vasilenko and others admitted that England and the USA will force Soviet leadership to take a route of integral transformation entirely, with the introduction of private property, freedom of business, dismantle of the collective farms, and the creation of a multi-party democratic government.
>
> They confirmed that the Soviet Union exited the war with Germany so economically weak and disabled, demoralized, and defenseless in military fortitude, that they would not be able to oppose any of the demands of the Americans.
>
> I held to another opinion and proved to them that the Soviet leadership will not yield to any concessions, and that it had to be overthrown with the use of violence, and this is why England and the USA will be compelled to begin another war and against the Soviet Union.

The investigation diligently also concentrated on confirming the existence of a serious and multi-year hostile underground, and especially one connected with countries outside the Soviet Union. The interrogation continued, and Daniel purported to state to the following:

In a conversation with my wife Andreeva at the end of 1946, I informed her that if upheavals begin at the time of war between the USA and USSR, then the first thing I would do is sneak into the Kremlin and kill Stalin. Andreeva supported me and declared that she is ready to act with me.

However, I need to admit that recently I began to rethink the matter, that perhaps I would be presented with better opportunities for hostile activities again the Soviet Union if working outside our country. I was convinced that I would be able to publish my anti-Soviet compositions there, those on which I worked over the course of many years, and so I could actively commence with such propaganda against the Soviet Union.

But this sham statement seemed insufficient for the interrogators, and Daniel was forced to confess more, and the record stated the following:

Question: So you did not just mentally intend to flee out of the country, but actually made plans to do so? Please explain further.

Answer: This is true. At the end of 1946, I intended, and together with my wife Andreeva, to go to the American consulate in Moscow, and pass myself off as a dissident suppressed by the USSR government, and ask for asylum in America, and so use this means to go abroad.

Deliberating in detail our intention, I and Andreeva came to the conclusion that it would be difficult to materialize such a thing, since we would eventually be discovered and arrested as a result.

Rejecting this plan of action, we decided to flee across the Caucasus Mountains and then across the border into Turkey, and from there somehow manage to make our way to Paris. In order to implement our plan to flee abroad, Andreeva and I sought support from Matveev, a member of our anti-Soviet group, who was familiar with geography and knew the Soviet-Turkey border well.

Otherwise, we would go to Batum or locally and acquire the assistance of smugglers to get to Turkey.

Question: So why particularly did you want to flee to Paris.

Answer: My brother the writer, Vadim Leonidovich Andreev, resides in Paris. During the Russian Civil War he fled there with remnants of the White Army.

With the help of my brother I would renew ties with necessary associates, publish my anti-Soviet compositions and continue an active struggle against the Soviet Union.

This is all that I have to say about my hostile activity.

Question: No, this is not all. You have not yet informed us of your ties with foreign informants and not told us their names, those whom you felt would work with your hostile activity. We plan to continue the interrogation until all information on this matter is gathered.

The examiners quickly brought Daniel's attention to people whom he should have mentioned earlier: Aleksandr Aleksandrovich Yugrimov and his wife Irina Nikolaievna, the eldest daughter of Muraviov. At the end of 1947, Yugrimov, a participant of the Opposition, the Soviet-patriotic block, was exiled from France back to Russia. On June 15, 1948, Yugrimov was arrested in Odessa. His wife and mother-in-law were at their summer home and arrested there, while in Moscow a sister was also arrested. Somehow the examiners discovered that this family had associated with Daniel's brother Vadim in Paris, and subsequently Daniel had corresponded with them, but not of matters pertaining to the issue at hand, although the examiners modified the correspondence to appear such.

Yugrimov spent a short while in Lubyanka, and then was transferred to Lefortovo Prison. There he understood what the interrogators expected of him as far as cooperation was concerned. Later, Yugrimov recorded what he finally confessed under pressure:

> In 2 words, this can be summarized in the following: Daniel Andreev here is an incorrigible terrorist. Vadim Andreev there is an incorrigible agent of American and English informers. And I am likewise an agent who came in order to connect ties between them, and so I was sent back to the USSR under the guise of exile for this goal.

The interrogation at Lefortovo was directed by a person named Ivan Aleksandrovich Sedov, who accused Yugrimov of "espionage and diversionary tactics." The inquests occurred almost daily, and on one occasion during an interrogation, he ruthlessly and maliciously beat Yugrimov on the back with a flexible stick so bad, that when he was returned to his cell in the morning, it was black and blue and blood-soaked. Yugrimov could only lay on his stomach in his cell.

Another person from abroad with whom the examiners attempted to create a connection was Fatyukov, who arrived in the USSR from France in 1945, having in his possession a letter from Vadim Andreev that he delivered to Daniel. But no matter how hard the examiners tried, the evidence to create a connected with a conspiracy abroad, based on Daniel's association with his brother and a few friends, did not succeed.

Sedov reported to Stalin, "Abakumov on his rise is ready to destroy anything interfering him." As a result the matter of Daniel Andreev at Lubyanka was assigned a special significance and no effort was to be spared. After the initial interrogation of all the suspected conspirators at Lubyanka, Abakumov had them all transferred to Lefortovo Prison, also in Moscow.

Abakumov sent a special report to Stalin regarding the matter of Daniel Andreev:

> To Comrade J.V. Stalin:
> Regarding the arrest in Moscow of the terrorist D.L. Andreev and the liquidation of the anti-Soviet group that he headed that had terrorist intentions. In all, 16 persons were arrested so far.

Regarding the Intention of an Attempt at Stalin's Summer House

Regarding this, Andreev confessed:

> Not just once did I think about various means of materializing my terrorist inclinations against the head of the Soviet government. In part, I had the intention of figuring a possible manner of accomplishing an attempt on the head of the Soviet government at his summer house in Zubalova outside of Moscow.

At the Bolshoi Theater

Regarding this, Andreev confessed:

> Not just once did I meditate on the possibility of materializing my terrorist intents against the head of the Soviet government during some festive assembly or some spectacle at the Bolshoi Theater, but I then came to the conclusion that the tactic was unfeasible, and because during the time of some festive event there would be too much light and in the theater there would be no light, and so in either case it would be difficult to aim and shoot and escape, and I would end up as a senseless sacrifice. So I just had to contemplate on the manner of shooting more.

Besides this, Andreev during this period often walked along the Arbat, spying on the routes of the vehicles carrying J.V. Stalin.

Stalin was not interested in the balance of details and this was a sufficiently detailed report. It is difficult to ascertain whether Stalin knew or suspected that the entire report was falsified by the interrogators and Abakumov to provide something to Stalin that did not exist and to justify their jobs.

Daniel was moved to Lefortovo prison and the examination there was as if right from the start, the majority of questions were repeats, dramatically arranged to depict a structure of an anti-Soviet underground with branches extending in every direction and carefully organized for its terrorist tactics, just as it was reported to Stalin.

Daniel's interrogation of July 28, was conducted by lieutenant colonel Sorokin, in the presence of the deputy minister, major-general Leonov. During the course of the interrogation, Leonov initially sat and listened to Sorokin's questions and Daniel's answers, and then began to inset his own questions, sometimes loudly and monotone, and often walking about the room. The proceedings record Daniel confessing the following:

Question: You appear as an active enemy. You have contemplated many vile plans of struggle against the Soviet people. Tell us about this.

Answer: I did not want to speak of my more serious crimes, but realized that hiding them will do me no good.

All of my hate was turned against Stalin, in whose person I saw the personification of Soviet authority, the strong leader of the Soviet government. For this reason, beginning from this time, I set the killing of Stalin as my target. I was convinced that the death of Stalin will initiate a disorganization in the Soviet government, activate hostile influences in the country, and speed the fall of Soviet authority.

Preparing myself for terror, I read and reread much literature regarding terrorism, and became enthused over their content. Then I began to search for the opportune time to materialize my terrorist act against the head of the Soviet government.

The interrogators utilized Daniel's friendship with Gavriel Andreevich Volkov and his wife to justify Daniel's intent to kill Stalin at his summer house at Zubalovo, because Volkovs lived at Nikolina Gora, just a few miles from Zubalovo, and also near to Muraviovs, also friends of Daniel. Gavriel died in a Soviet prison in 1943, but his wife was still alive.

Question: Did Volkova know the reason you were visiting her at their summer house?
Answer: I did not discuss my intentions directly with Volkova, but she knew of my hostile attitude toward the leader of the party and Soviet government.
Question: What information did Volkova furnish you, so you could materialize your hostile tactic?
Answer: Volkova and her husband and I took strolls in the region of the village of Nikolina Gora. After I became acquainted with the region I came to the conclusion that, utilizing the natural conditions, it was possible under cover of the forest and growth to penetrate directly to Stalin's summer house, and then while he was taking a stroll I could perform my terrorist act.

But when the Volkovs informed me that the entrance to the summer house was securely guarded, while the summer house itself was

	surrounded by a high stone wall, and then figuring that there were probably alarms in the area, I realized that I would be unsuccessful in stealthily reaching the summer house.
Question:	So it is a known fact that you continued to visit Volkov's summer house even later on.
Answer:	I never abandoned an attempt on Stalin. In 1938, I again visited Volkova at her summer house at Nikolina Gora and was finally convinced in the insurmountable obstacles to the materialization of my intentions, so I decided to route my tactic to another place.
Question:	Where?

A dentist named Amalie Yakovlevich Rabinovich lived in a apartment along Arbat Blvd. He was a close friend and patient of Dr Dobrov, as well as being the dentist for the entire Dobrov family. During the summer of 1939, Daniel went to Dr Rabinovich for dental work. The interrogators utilized these visits as the background for their fabrication of an organized tactic for Stalin's assassination.

| Answer: | Earlier I likewise visited Rabinovich and knew that the window of his apartment overlooked Arbat Blvd. I intended to utilize this location in order to shoot out the window at Stalin's vehicle as it would drive along Arbat. I did not share my intentions with Rabinovich. I went there 3 or 4 times under the pretence of needing dental work. While at Rabinovich's apartment I ascertained which window would be best to shoot from, and the best manner of escaping after my attempt.

  In addition to this, I especially strolled along Arbat Blvd, and followed Stalin's route, and several times was I successful at seeing how his vehicle did not quite reach the building where Rabinovich lived, since it would turn right onto |
|---|---|

Bolshoi Afanasyevski corner and drive along Mali Afanasyevski, bypassing the Gogol monument, and the off into another direction to the Kremlin. Based on my observation, I concluded that Rabinovich's apartment could not be utilized for the materialization of my plan.

Now the question arose regarding a weapon.

Question: What weapon did you have in your possession as you were stalking the vehicle of the head of the Soviet government?

Answer: Fearing the possibility of arrest by his guards, I did not have a weapon in my possession when I would survey the movement of Stalin's vehicle. I intended to acquire a weapon somewhere after I finalized selecting a spot to commit my terrorist act.

Question: You are lying. The interrogation clearly states that you earlier looked for a weapon and you trained to be an accurate shooter. Speak the truth.

Answer: Having firmly decided that I would commit my terrorist act against Stalin by shooting from a pistol, in order not to miss my target, and be able to act effectively, I began to train to shoot accurately.

To accomplish this, I visited and joined a shooting club, part of a larger sports organizations that was meeting at a shooting gallery near Nogin Square. I seriously practiced over the course of several months and learned how to handle a gun and shoot accurately.

While at the shooting gallery, I also ascertained the best means of acquiring a gun, but for some reason I was not successful.

The topics of interrogation now shifted to the Bolshoi Theater, supposedly concocted in 1940, and then to a parade and celebration at the Kremlin.

Answer: Knowing the arrangement of the Bolshoi Theater, I mediated on the means I could there carry out the assassination, but then likewise there were just too many obstacles and interferences.

 Subsequently my hate toward Soviet authority and personally toward Stalin grew more and amore, and I continued to figure some means to materialize my terrorist intention that I had long planned.

 During that same year of 1940, I decided to somehow take advantage of one of the state holidays that occur at Red Square and figure some means of committing my attempt against Stalin there, maybe during one of the celebrations. I waited for the celebration of the October Revolution held on November 7, 1940. I participated in the celebration along with a group of working Moscow artists and painters.

Question: What column did you walk in?
Answer: In the column of the Kuibeshevski region.
Question: Where was your place in the column?
Answer: I stood on the right flank and passed through Red Square about 70 or 80 feet from the Mausoleum.

 With our movement across Red Square I felt a tremendous compaction of the ranks against each other, and under such conditions it was very difficult for me to shoot. Other than this, I noticed that the entire wall of the Kremlin was lined with guards and that the entire square was surrounded by soldiers.

 Any further preparations to commit a terrorist act against Stalin were interrupted when in 1942, I was conscripted into the Soviet army and left Moscow.

Beginning with Daniel's arrest, the first stage of proceedings extended for 13 months. During this period, the compositions of alleged groups were defined and the scenes of activities. To conclude the investigation, several of Daniel's confessions had to be presented in a concrete form, his terrorist intentions had to be verified, and of course they had to find a weapon. Each of the alleged suspects also faced an interrogation once transferred to Lefortovo prison.

Vasilenko was also transferred to Lefortovo and he explained his experience during interrogation:

> Two men held me from under my arms and with all their strength they threw me from the doors forward and down flat on the stone floor of the interrogation room. The first time they forced this upon me I was seriously injured. Then I decided to prepare myself for such heaves. Then the interrogator laughed, "Did you learn your lesson?" And then he added more, but what he said is unfit for print. This vocabulary seemed to be the fashion there.
>
> Then again more interrogations, they beat me, threw me on the floor. One of my ribs were broken, and beginning at the end of 1948, I could no longer sleep in prison on my right side.
>
> The criminal code statute was terror and they wanted to execute all of us by shooting. I just waited to be shot. For 14 days I sat in solitary confinement, waiting. The interrogator said, "You will be shot."
>
> And when they came for me, they entered my cell at night, it was frightening. Very frightening. Three of them entered, and then a 4th, and ordered, "Get up!" And I jumped. "Turn around!" And silently they stood behind me. I knew that they shoot in the back of the neck. I had

strange sensations. So this is how Dostoyevski felt when he stood on the scaffold. True, one time he did. And myself? Well, I was an ordinary person. I stood and whispered, "Lord God, have mercy on me."

Then they quietly walked away.

Nahum Korzhavin was in the same cell as Vasilenko at Lubyanka, and he recollected him as being a soft, intelligent, slender, good-natured, and defenseless person. The examiner soon ascertained this about Vasilenko and took advantage of his weakness. After the interrogation, Vasilenko subscribed to all that was recorded, most of it falsified, of course. He was placed in the punishment cell and had ice cold water dripping on him from the ceiling. He was only able to survive by placing a couple of handkerchiefs over his shoulders. Vasilenko received a 25 year sentence for his suspected role in the matter.

1949

As a witness, Galina Rusakova was summoned for interrogation in January. As Daniel recollected the event:

> This was an earth-shaking incident that occurs once in a lifetime, but with her noble character she was able to protect herself from self-incrimination while summoned in the capacity of a witness.

But the witnesses that were summoned knew nothing special or else could not know anything anyway. Other than conversations that they heard from others, and not themselves personally, that Daniel Andreev had written a novel of some sort, was all they could offer. Sometimes they mentioned an accidental or off-the-cuff criticism of Soviet authority, but nothing of any substance. They knew nothing of what was in *Night Wanderers*, or of any underground, or attempts on Stalin, or any weapons in his home. Gradually everybody that was not previously arrested was brought into Lefortovo prison for interrogation, every person suspected of association with Andreevs.

On June 5, Irina Armand, Aleksandr Ivanovski and Sergei Matveev were arrested, all old friends of Daniel.

On June 15, Tatyana Nikolaievna Volkova was arrested. She was confined to solitary confinement the entirety of 6 months before she was sentenced. She was able to smuggle a letter through a friend named Fadeeva, who tucked it under her scarf, and she recorded the following:

> They interrogated me 49 times. I was not allowed to sleep for an entire month, because they would interrogate me during the night, while during the day I was not allowed to even lean against the cell wall. After a month of sleeplessness, I no longer comprehended who I was and lost touch with reality. The interrogator, Major Novikov, incessantly terrified me, threatening to kill me. Noticing and paying serious attention to those horrors that were occurring at night in the adjoining cells and interrogation rooms of Lefortovo prison, my fear was fully realizable.

On June 19, Dobrovolski was arrested. After a special report that was submitted to Stalin on June 23, Elena Lisitzina, the wife of Evgeni Beloyusov, was arrested.

Over the course of 6 months, Volkova was interrogated 49 times; Alla Andreeva – 195; Kovalenski – 173; Vasilenko – 126; Ivashev-Musatov – 123. It was a conveyer belt of routine nightly tortures and terrifying experiences. No matter what was stated at the interrogation, any word in a response, was manipulated and could lead to some threatening accusation.

Daniel continued to be interrogated, following the interrogations of the others, at Lefortovo. The documents recorded his confessions and the monotone structure of the conventional questions and answers is obvious:

Question: Continue explaining your new organization and its intents.
Answer: I continued to expand the circle of my connections and recruit new adherents, counting on creating an organization for active struggle against Soviet authority. I acted cautiously, carefully did I approach people whom I felt I could recruit.

During the final period I worked in attracting into our anti-Soviet group: Aleksei Pavlovich Shelyakin, an architect, who was a student along with me at school, and Irina Lvovna Armand, an instructor of English language at the Moscow State University, with who I was friends since 1938 due to our similar involvements in literary activities.

At this time Kovalenski was successful in attracting the attorney Sergei Dmitriyevich Shepelev into our anti-Soviet group, and Ivashev-Musatov was able to get the artist Natalia Vasilyevna Kuznitzova, and whom he later married.

I placed before the participants of the anti-Soviet group that I headed the task of the hostile work to which they would be committed. The more active of them continued to work in the direction of somehow implementing our intended terror.

Question: Why did you especially write an entire chapter dedicated to terror in your anti-Soviet book?
Answer: Yes, at this time I completed my novel, *Night Wanderers*, where I dedicated a large section to the terrorist struggle against the leadership of the Soviet government. As in the past, I considered terror the best means of active struggle. I would read the chapter on terrorism to my adherents, and convince them that Stalin's

murder would speed the war of the USA and England against the Soviet Union.

The following is what Daniel heard from an incessantly wailing and tearful Vera Malutin in regard to the treatment of her husband Rostislav, who was also arrested as a confederate in the alleged conspiracy due to his friendship with Daniel.

> The beatings took a bestial character. He was continually beaten on the legs up to his kneecaps, and his knees turned into irrecoverable sores. The interrogators wrenched from him a list of friends and demanded to know all of the new conspirators.
>
> Then they put him into a punishment cell: a rock-walled, ice-cold pit, filled with water about 12 inches deep. They placed a short board at the bottom between the 2 opposing walls, with the top just above water level. The poet sat naked on this board so not to fall into the water, but the board was too short and narrow for him to lay on, and so he was unable to sleep.
>
> In order to acquire a confession, he was tortured not only with interrogations, but with beatings and the punishment cell.

Dobrovolski wrote about his experience of the interrogations:

> The interrogation eventually ended. I was completely exhausted and I signed every document they gave me and without even looking at it. The interrogator gave me one more piece of paper with the words, "Sign this one also." I picked up a pen. The interrogator said, "Not yet. You did not read it. Read it first and then sign it." The paper talked of my agreement that all that was confiscated from me, personal documents and papers, books, diaries, fragments of my compositions, handwritten notes, and all the manuscripts of my completed stories, were all to be cremated.

I signed it, but no doubt my face showed my anxiety and torment.

"What is the problem?" The interrogator asked, "Why are you in anguish?"

I said, "And you do not expect a mother to suffer when she signs the sentence for all of her children to be executed?"

"Well, well," said the interrogator. "Even Gogol burned his manuscripts. So it is all the same to us, should we burn yours. Nobody needs them anyway. So we are making this easier on you by doing this ourselves."

My entire life was now at its end, and all I possessed would now be ashes.

In addition to Dobrovolski, they likewise cremated all the manuscripts and personal documents of Beloyusov, Vasilenko, Kovalenski, Lisitzina, Shelyakin, all collected correspondence, and even the letters of Leonid Andreev. Alla later recollected the tragedy:

> They even burned the letter of Leonid Nikolaievich regarding the death of Daniel's mother, soaked with tears now dry. His final letter which we considered so tremendous that we read it several times over. It was somehow smuggled into Russia, since a letter of this type at that time would never have arrived by regular means. The letter also spoke of the revolution, and I can only compare it to the final diaries of Leonid Nikolaievich, which he recorded before he died, when he understood all that occurred in Russia.

All of Daniel's confiscated compositions were also burned: poems and verses, autobiographical notes, personal letters and documents, diaries, and especially the manuscript of *Night Wanderers*. Daniel protested to the burning of his literary efforts and his father's items. He begged them to commit his father's and great-grandfather's letters to a literary museum. But his plea was futile and all was cremated. Many of those sitting in Lubyanka recollected the caustic smell of burning paper.

Was this a malicious joke? No, it was an arranged incident to finally break the will of the accused, tortured in every other way over many months of interrogation. But they could not have executed anybody. On May 26, 1947, an Edit was published, *About the Termination of Capital Punishment*. It was exchanged for a 25-year prison term, and because the nation was no longer at war.

On October 30, 1948, all the conspirators of the group of Daniel Andreev received their sentences. Daniel's sentence read:

> Andreev, Daniel Leonidovich, for participation in an anti-Soviet group, anti-Soviet agitation and terrorist intentions, to be incarcerated in prison for a term of 25 years, the term beginning April 23, 1947. All possessions to be confiscated.

Along with Daniel, 19 other people, relatives and friends, were also sentenced. Daniel alone was assigned to a prison, the others went to labor camps. A 25-year sentence was handed to Alla Andreeva, Victor Vasilenko, Aleksandr Dobrov, Aleksandra (Kovalenskaya) Dobrova, Sergei Ivashev-Musatov, Aleksandr Kovalenski, Anna Skorodumova-Kemnitz, Alexsei Shelyakin. A 10-year sentence was handed to Tamara Armand, Evgeni Beloyusov, Tatyana Volkova, Aleksandr Dobrovolski, Aleksandr Ivanovski, Victor Kemnitz, Elena Lisitzina, Sergei Matveev, Tatyana Yusova, Galina Khandozhevskaya, and Sergei Shepelev. They were all guilty of participating in an anti-Soviet terrorist group, created and headed by Daniel Andreev, and participating in gatherings that he conducted, as the sentence read:

> Where they declared their hostile attitude toward Soviet authority and the leadership of the Soviet government;

expanded their malicious slander regarding Soviet activities; exerted effort against the provisions of the Communist Party of the USSR and Soviet government; and organized hostile agitation within their surroundings.

Each guilty person was brought one by one into a room and there each heard their sentence. They did not necessarily know each other, and none knew how many were actually tried and sentenced. In addition to the above were some of Daniel's associates from the time he worked in the hospitable during the war: Aleksandr Petrovich Tzaplin and Nikolai Pavlovich Amurov. Likewise old friends of the Dobrovs: Feodor Konstantinovich Konstantinov, and the couple Ignat Aleksandrovich and Maria Aleksandrovna Zhelabovski, who both received a 8-year sentence. Natalia Vasilyevna Kuznetzova, the first wife of Ivashev-Musatov, was assigned to a psychiatric hospital in Kazan.

Each of the sentenced was assigned their labor camp: Alla Andreeva, Aleksandr Dobrov, the Kovalenski couple, Tamara Armand, Aleksandr Dobrovolski, Aleksandr Ivanovski, were transferred to Dubrovflag labor camp in the city Yavas, at the northwest region of Mordovia Semi-Autonomous Republic. Victor Vasilenko and Alexsei Shelyakin went to Inta, Komi Province, where they finally met each other, and Tatyana Volkova was also assigned there. Elena Lisitzina and Tatyana Yusova went to Taishetski labor camp in Irkutsk Province, Siberia, not far from Lake Baikal (they were exiled the furthest). Anna Skorodumova-Kemnitz to Kengir, in the geographic center of Kazakhstan. While her husband Victor Kemnitz, Evgeni Beloyusov, and Sergei Ivashev-Musatov landed in Marfinski Sharashka, in the Marfino suburb of Moscow. Of course, none knew where the others were assigned, unless they happened to met at the same camp; they were distributed all over the USSR.

Alla sorrowfully recollected in her memoirs another dismal event:

> Sergei Matveev was one of those whose death I feel we caused. There was no basis at all for his arrest. He received a prison sentence and died at some transfer station on the route to Siberia from internal bleeding due to a perforated ulcer. Once he indicated symptoms of severe internal pain, they moved him to a local hospital where he died. I still remember his beautiful face.

Alla Andreeva – Arrest and Interrogations[41]

1947

Alla was arrested at their apartment on Novi Levshinski on April 23, 1947, 2 days after Daniel left with the MGB agents in their vehicle. She recollects the event:

> Three men entered. The captain who headed the visit conducted himself very professionally. As far as he was concerned the search of our apartment was routine and a daily exercise: it lasted 14 hours. They searched every page, book by book, in our entire immense library. But it was obvious that they knew what they were looking for: Daniel's novel and poems. Finally, the captain asked, "So how much longer do we still need to search? Give us the manuscript."
>
> I stretched my hand to an opening in the wall and then set *Night Wanderers* down. They were not leaving without the novel, and I am sure the search would have continued not 14 hours, but double that, to find the novel.

---

[41] Much of the following are selections of Alla Andreeva's book *Sailing to the Heavenly Russia* (Плаванье к Небесной России), translated by the author.

No one slept in our apartment and my father was calling the entire time. All night. He, of course, understood. Regularly we would call each other, just to hear the other's voice and be assured that all was fine. And so father called late at night. One of them grabbed the receiver and in an official manner responded, "She is not here." And so did he respond until morning. All was clear as to what was occurring.

They would not let me out of the room. Once they allowed me to go to the toilet and a soldier accompanied me. While leaving the room I was able to grab my thin diary. At one time when Daniel read it, he said humorously, "You know, your diary is not much different than *Wanderers*." I remembered what he said, so I clandestinely took it to dump it in the toilet.

I wanted to sleep, to plainly not feel anything at all. I did not cry, but just answered their questions, whatever they were.

Went we entered the front room, the entire apartment was silent. One neighbor accompanied me out. She gave me a piece of black bread and a few lumps of sugar. I thanked her and then said in response, "Anna Sergeevna, here are my kerosene coupons. Take them." At least the coupons will be put to a good use.

A passenger car pulled up for me, not a black one, but a beige color. I had a new and very pretty coat that I was able to take with me and wear on the trip to Lubyanka. My mother sewed it for me. The books and correspondence they confiscated they took separately.

So did my journey begin through prisons and labor camps.

The first stage was Lubyanka. It was a fortress located in the very center of Moscow, and its 4 huge buildings forms a rectangle saturated with prisons inside. I was placed in the first building, the one that overlooked Lubyanksi Square. Obviously the office windows faced the street, but the cell windows were facing the inside square. But not having been there before, we really did not know what we were looking at. That the building was very old was apparent due to its high ceilings and the design of the high windows. Very little light penetrated into the room due to the iron grating over the window.

At Lubyanka they took me direct to the bottom, to the cellar, and I was convinced they were leading me to torture and to execute me by shooting. Here suddenly my torpid quietude ended, of course, completely abnormal for me, and I started to wail. My escorts laughed at me. It was obvious they were accustomed to such a reaction from those they were dragging to the cellar, expecting to be tortured and executed, but simply to be finger-printed. I was completely devastated and flooded with tears, I wailed frantically. I was convinced that Daniel was already shot, and from that day I cried non-stop for several months. Even unconsciously tears were plainly flowing all the while.

They said that I even cried in my sleep. When at the first interrogation, the interrogator asked me something, I made the sign of the cross, thinking that all had ended with Daniel and that that the same would happen to me. But the torture was not actually that long.

Fortunately, I was never beaten, and I think the reason was because the interrogator quickly realized that he would be more successful by just manipulating and intimidating me, and so I would tell him all he wants. And he was right because these men were trained to be very professional in their vocation as interrogators. In any case, if he was to use force, then the malice would only increase. My interrogator at Lubyanka, unconditionally, was a professional in his field, now that I recollect his tactics. When I was first brought to be questioned, I thought that Daniel was already gone and that the same would occur to me that day or the next and this would be the end of me also. They asked me, "Do you know your husband's disposition? You are aware of his attitude toward Soviet authority?"

I replied, "Yes, yes, yes. All how he thinks, I also think! All that occurs to him, let it occur to me." I consider myself just as responsible in these proceedings as Daniel. True, that at the end when I subscribed to Section 206, which is my familiarity with all the protocols, I did not see any special difference between my testimonies and all the others. I see 2 basic reasons for this. Fear that penetrated our entire life and which from an early time gnawed at our will, creating antagonism, and especially antagonism against the agencies. But even then, we were never political activists. During these years, when a person was arrested, he was gone forever. An arrest was gloom, silence and torment, and to think about a close associate in such a predicament caused a 10-fold despair in yourself.

They read to me the list of persons that were previously decided to be arrested as a result of their connection with us. Among the number, for example, were women who only came to our apartment to help with the housekeeping. One name was a shoemaker, to whom we gave our shoes for repair. Finally, Daniel's nursemaid when he was a child, but by now this woman was 60 years old. The list seemed immense. It literally contained every person who ever entered our home or called us on the phone.

I told them, "These were just ordinary people that we knew. If we needed something and asked for it, they would bring it."

"Alla Aleksandrovna," the interrogator replied, "Tell us please, truly, so we do not arrest those we do not need."

And I suddenly developed this horror at the thought that they would just as well bury this shoemaker and this woman, and whose name I do not even remember, and mama and papa and brother and all of Daniel's acquaintances, those who never heard one line of the novel, and no matter what the truth was anyway.

Of course, it was best for me to say less. All that occurred with the interrogation was the result of us just not being prepared for it or its ramifications. Although we were inherently opposed to Soviet authority, in reality we never did anything. We never planned any assassination of Stalin, which they then ascribed to us; we did not assemble to overthrow the government, and which we considered to be unassailable anyway. We were only privately opposed to the contemporary polity and mainly due to our weakness and helplessness to do anything anyway. Those such as ourselves numbered in the tens of millions, and the fear of these people before those who sat in the Kremlin was just the same as the mystic subconscious fear of the Kremlin residents before us. Stalin suffered with a mania of persecution which was imposed on him by the manipulation of documents. And now he had good reason to fear, and it was the insane number of persons who were arrested, killed, tortured and who all at the same time developed a fear of his political machine.

It was easier to gather additional incriminating testimony from Alla, who in her naivety blared out rumors and personal information, and became the person most responsible for including the most number of people into the interrogation as suspects, although she had no clue as to what she was doing. Alla later wrote about it, regretting what she did:

The interrogator called me by my first name and patronymic, and he read to me verses. He said, "Alla Aleksandrovna, please, tell us, how such people, just like yourself, like these and others, who were just now arrested, how you, Russian people, were able to attain such malice toward the form of our country, toward the manner that our Homeland lives. We want to understand what the intelligentsia thinks, we want to be together with you, but it seems that all avoids us. No one tells us anything."

And I was so stupid and told him everything. For over a year. And this is what was also important. I could not forget that in front of me was a Russian person just like me who sat and led the interrogation. They took advantage of my feelings, and it was a trap. The interrogator was very calm, he recorded all that I said: his questions, my answers. Then he allowed me to read the pages. I read them, was surprised at what I read and asked, "This is not what I said. You have recorded something else other than what I said."

But he replied, "Alla Aleksandrovna, understand, these are, if I can say it, standard statements. I am obligated to record our conversation in a legal form."

This interrogator was Ivan Feodorovich Kuligin. He cheerfully related the circumstances how he, a student at the forestry institute in Siberia, was summoned by the Komsomol and directed to work at this state agency. He could not refuse. Ivan Feodorovich seemed to have a blank stare, as though always gazing, and was aloof with a shade of intellectualism. He was able to quote literature. He conversed calmly, cheerfully smiled, spoke about his small daughter, but was impersonal.

In later memoirs, Alla admitted how foolishly she conducted herself at the interrogations, and decided to act infantile to somehow avoid further admissions of people's involvement or Daniel's writings. With information gathered from Alla, the interrogators treated Daniel ruthlessly and cruelly. As Alla recollected:

Because I was not able to distinguish between *us* and *them*, I later understood what an intolerable mistake I made. We were separate parts of one huge national tragedy of Russia. And this is how I was able to completely openly and precisely explain to the interrogator all that I personally, and not just I, but others also, had against Soviet authority, communism, and what it caused to Russia.

They said to me, "So this is what it is! How interesting! No one else has ever told us this. This is why it is so exceptionally important to know this and so resolve it. We need to understand one another."

And I fell right into their trap. Then they asked me, "So this is your opinion in simple terms? This is how you consider things?"

I replied, "This is how every normal and honorable person considers things. A respectable person can only conclude that Soviet authority is an evil; the kolkhozes[42] are the ruin of Russia's peasantry; and what was done to the church was criminal. What is especially criminal is the number of people killed behind your walls during a peaceful era."

"So this means that not only you consider it this way?"

"Of course, not just myself. How can you think otherwise?"

So did they gradually lead me to disclosing my opinion of Stalin, which is not at the head of my crimes against the state. In addition to this were all the items that occurred since the revolution: the ruin of Russian culture, the church, Russian nobility, peasantry and Russia as a country in general. If I was to have said that this was just my opinion, I would only be charged under Section 58-10, anti-Soviet agitation. But that I said that all respectable persons feel the same, then now Section 58-11, anti-Soviet group, applied to me. When my proceedings reached Stalin, all of it was arranged under Section 58-8, which was under the heading of

---

[42] Collective farms.

"Preparation of a Terrorist Act – the Assassination of Comrade Stalin." The interrogator was very calm.

One time they brought me for interrogation during the day, which occurred seldom. The interrogator stood holding a newspaper in his hands, "So matters have turned for the better for you: the death penalty has been abolished."

And I am thinking, "Why am I even here? Why would the death penalty even apply to me to begin with?" But it did have a direct relationship to me. The prosecutor was dissatisfied with the proceedings. Even though my interrogator was promoted shortly after due to his supposed success in these proceedings, he was not able to reach a crime that capital punishment would apply. I remember during one interrogation with the prosecutor, he said, "We could just about arrest everybody along Arbat Street in order, one house after another."

That day I had to sign something else, and which I did, and then I asked, "Is this all?"

The interrogator looked at me and replied, "For now that is all."

They then transferred me to Lefortovo. Now I know that it was due to the personal order of the Minister of Internal Affairs, Abakumov, that I was transferred there.

Alla recollected Lefortovo as a nightmare of horror:

A terrifying, monstrous place. The cells were small, no more than 3 persons could fit in one and then uncomfortably. The gray cement floor, the brown walls and black ceiling, iron doors. The toilet bowl in the cell, alongside was the wash sink, both all black. The ceilings were high with a window opposite the door. My bunk was directly below it, but even if I were to stand on my bunk, I could not reach the window. The window was covered with a grate anyway. Hardly any light at all penetrated into our cell from the outside, but we did have a light, and it was a bare bulb that was on around the clock.

As a person arrived at the prison, they would pass an old garden and an embellished façade of the building from the era of Empress Catherine the Great, with large columns, but it was all just a façade.

There was also something else about Lefortovo which remained secretive to me. On Saturdays and Sundays a roar enveloped the entire prison. Every person who stayed these years in Lefortovo, remembers the noise. Shivers ran through us when we heard this sound, because we knew that once the roar started this meant the torture started, and the roar was meant to drown out the screams. Some people that I considered level headed explained to me that alongside Lefortovo was the TsAGI,[43] and this roar was the aerodynamic tunnel.[44] But if this was the tunnel, then why was it particularly operating on Saturdays and Sundays, and even then, not every week?

Alla recollected her experience during interrogations:

The initial 3 weeks I was held for interrogations every night, and they occurred during July. The guard would open the window in the door and I would hear the beating and screams of the men. This was sufficient for me. All the women in the prison heard this and, of course, each voice seemed to them to be their husband or son.

No one read verses to me. No one called me by Alla Aleksandrovna. They did not give me to sleep for the 3 weeks. No doubt this was a system intricately developed by doctors: sleep was only allowed one hour a day and

---

[43] Central Aerohydrodynamic Institute
[44] However, the Institute was moved from this building in 1935.

one night in a week. And so a person would go out of their mind, but not totally. It was definitely possible for a person to completely lose their mental faculties, but the guards would not allow this, but at least to be halfway insane when brought for interrogation. I was summoned for interrogation every night. And so I will never forget one unusually episode that was important to me. Once, and I do not know the reason for this, they released me somewhat earlier than normal.

I was walking to my cell happy. And my head only entertained one thought, "Sleep. I will now get to sleep an entire hour." And so as I walked along the outdoor passage from the interrogation wing to the prison, along an iron fenced walkway, and with the bright morning sun shining on me, then I suddenly understood: If all of a sudden the corpses of the 2 most beloved people of my life were laying on the ground – Daniel and my father – I would step over them and go into my cell to sleep! I will never forget this. An angel approached me and his silent voice vibrated in my soul and said to me, "Remember this! Remember! A person cannot descend lower than a condition such as yours. Remember this and when you decide to accuse somebody of something, remember this." And I recollect this, knowing that this is one of the most important memories of my life. Due to this I seldom criticize anybody who is not able to survive the interrogations.

By the time this was over, I told them all I had to say and was sucking on my fingers so bad, nothing was left. During these nighttime interrogations I would plead with them, "Please give me a clean sheet of paper, I will sign it, and then you write whatever you want, because I can no longer stand any of this anymore."

Then when I returned to my cell, then sleep was not sleep but a delirium. I collapsed somewhere in a corridor and then the interrogator began to shove into my mouth pieces of human flesh. And then an entire day without sleep, the entire time they shine a light and stare into my eyes, and it is impossible to even recline. And it is night again and another interrogation.

The interrogator continually prodded me, wanting to know if we had any weapons, and finally he said, "You are lying. You do have a weapon."

"No, not at all."

"Your husband testified. There was a weapon."

I thought to myself, "God, poor Daniel! This means we did have a weapon, and he must have hide it from me. He was plainly protecting me, not wanting me to know."

"So did you have a weapon?"

I answered, "If my husband said so, then this means, we did."

"Where is it?"

"I do not know. I never saw it."

Then a second search was made of our apartment. They knocked against all the walls hoping to find a secret compartment. What they found was a window long plastered over, and they were overjoyed when they found it, and threw down all the books on the shelves to access the area. Sometime in the past, the Dobrovs did not want another window and so plastered it, and no one seemed to remember it. Anyway, they found nothing at all in the wall when the plaster was removed.

Then I supposed that the weapon was kept in the woodshed, because my husband would go there regularly to get wood. They also searched the woodshed. I was in terror because I imagined how difficult it was now for Daniel, because he hid from me the location of this weapon. He is probably thinking that they are torturing me for no reason. It would have been simpler if I knew where it was so I could just tell them.

That morning I began to wail out loud, all that I thought about the interrogator, Stalin, Lenin, Soviet authority. Statute 58-10 definitely applied to me the manner matters were progressing.⁴⁵ Then the interrogator said, "Will you stop this. All you do is wail and you are not aware of what you are saying. And not once did you blurt out the hiding place of the weapon."

This is why they imposed on me such a disheveled mental state. As I said earlier, they did not give me sleep for 3 weeks. It was obvious that I was in such a physical state that when I set my bare feet on the cement floor, it seemed warm, meaning, my feet were ice cold. I do not knew if they mixed anything into my food or drink, but it was possible. I then imagined a horrible thing: during the 19 months of interrogation I only once asked to use the toilet. This was strange, since the interrogation would last entire nights. I had an escort accompany me to the toilet. He stood at the door, and this was the first time after all of 19 months incarceration that I saw myself in a mirror. I well remember the face, and it was difficult for me to claim it as my own. This was an emaciated white mask with large black eyes. But my eyes were never large and they were blue. And my eyes stared at me from the mirror, and they seemed to be a different set of eyes. About this time I realized that my vision was damaged, now at the present I am seriously affected with glaucoma and partial blindness.⁴⁶

It began this way. When my turn came I was taken for interrogation. It occurred in a large room. Along one wall behind a desk sat the interrogator, along another wall was a stool for me. The room was illuminated from a bright light, so I could not either close my eyes, and there was no way for me to lean on anything. When I first walked into the room it seemed gloomy, as though only a table lamp was on. But when I sat, here was this bright light directed right at me. I understood that something was occurring with my eyes, but this did not last long.

---

[45] Article 58-10 of the RSFSR Penal Code: Anti-soviet Agitation and Propaganda, punishable with a minimum of 6 months in prison.
[46] Alla was about 85 during this interview by a Russian journalist.

There was nobody to talk to about this and no reason why anyway. Then I knew that the light was causing my mental faculty to malfunction and I would strongly agitate. This is what caused my illness. Toward the end of the interrogation, they would make a spectacle of me,

Once I heard that the minister was going to personally interrogate me. "Glory to God, maybe he will be reasonable and understand." They stared at me so strangely.

Minister Abakumov arrived at Lefortovo. They brought me to him, and along the route to the cabinet, there was a soldier every 5 feet or so. They bring me into the room and there sits my interrogator, and the department head, and with them is a fat, distinguished man with oriental features in a black suit. He begins to interrogate me, "You have a weapon. Why did you not tell us where it is?"

"Because I do not know," I answer.

"Then, you do have a weapon?"

"Well, if you, minister, say that I have a weapon, this means that one exists. But I have never seen it." Never in all the years I have lived under Soviet authority did I ever think that a minister could lie.

He came close to me and stared at me and said, "You are so young. How did you get stuck in this?"

When I was given all the volumes of documents of the proceedings to read, it appeared that it involved over 20 persons and over the course of 19 months, and not once did any of them see each other, and most did not know others, and each one was interrogated individually. No actually courtroom proceeding occurred or anything near to a trial, and of course, none of it could have. The Special Commission – OSO – sentenced us.[47]

---

[47] Special Council of the National Committee of Internal Affairs, this was also headed by Beria.

Alla felt that she was the sole responsible party for all the interrogation and sufferings of Rostislav Malutin, and his wife Vera's sufferings, for being an informer. She personally did not even know him and only mentioned his name as an associate of Daniel's due to pressure during one of the interrogations. Later Alla wrote to Daniel in prison about this:

> It was particularly me that belongs the statement that he made to you, to propose to you, for you to become part of some kind of organization, and you rejected his offer, saying, that all you wanted to is write and nothing more. I knew absolutely nothing about this, what he was talking about, and I definitely knew that he said something ambiguous to you, and that you did not even know what he meant. Of course, I said this as a result of some psychological ideal, what some stupid people would call integrity, but particularly residing in idiots. However this is something we need to talk about and not write, but it seems to me that particularly whatever this connection is with Malutin, and whether any such participation in regard to anything all was serious, we do not know anymore, but it just seems to have resurrected its ugly head. This incident of stupidity, as with so much else, I consider myself to be the most responsible.

On September 3, Galina Khandozhevskaya was arrested. This was the only occasion during all the interrogations that Alla was face to face with another person accused in the conspiracy. A friend of Alla's later recorded the event as she explained to him what occurred:

> She told Galina, "Yes, I was the one who wanted to hit Stalin with a stool. It was not you, but I. You did not even pay attention to any of my words."

Later the interrogator read to Alla the accusations, among which was Article 58-9, regarding terror. Alla asked, "Why is this?"

"Because you said, you wanted to injure him with a stool."

"Yes, I said that I would be greatly satisfied should I bounce a stool off his head because of what he did to Russia."

"So, Alla Aleksandrovna, is not this a preparation to commit a terrorist act?"

"You tell me, Mikhail Feodorovich, what kind of terrorist act would this be? Where is the stool? Where is Stalin?"

"We will deal with this matter later. You do understand, that a standard legal form does exist? This is what you said. I am the examiner. I have recorded this. I am not writing a novella and not a novel. I am recording the proceedings of the inquest."

And he convinced me. I then signed all of the pages of the proceedings, not even reading them.

What helped me to psychologically live through the horror of Soviet prisons and the labor camp? What within me was able to resist the general and individual effect all of this had on me? Yes, of course, it was faith. Belief in God applies to those who believe, but such are few in Moscow prisons. But there is no need to think regarding me, a believer, that I prayed, read the ecclesiastical rules, observed at least some type of a rhythmic religious life. None of this occurred. No matter how hard I try to recollect what was occurring within myself during the period of the interrogation, I cannot remember any of this having occurred. Only perhaps at an accidental moment or some specific situation.

I remember one conversation with the interrogator. His question, of course, was in a humorous manner. "You are a believer, of course, and do you pray for this interrogation to be honest?"

"I do not see any need to pray for such a thing."

He was surprised. "Why is that?"

"Because we should not ask of God something that is concrete. I can only ask for Him not to abandon me and Daniel."

But I never petitioned for this aloud. Rather, more correctly stated, I grabbed faith without words, like a child grabbing the edge of a skirt, or a shadow, or veneration of an icon, with a despairing soundless petition, but its contents still vague. It seems to me that I can also say that there occurred an inner and, more precisely, subconscious effort of my soul's preparation of this frightening road imposed by God upon us. Not a test, not a punishment. I do not believe in a punishing God. I believe He sends us what we are to accept, to proceed with what He entrusts us. There was no logic of any type, no deliberation of any type, regarding this. I fear that I do not possess these qualities. Yet something was materializing within an oppressed soul, gathering strength to renew it.

And there was something of a purely female character that provided additional means to resist the horror of prison, at which a male would laugh. For example, we would still devise head coverings, and how we did this I do not remember, with scraps of cloth or even paper and wherever we could find them. The sentries would take them away, but we would still find pieces, and we always combed our hair, and figure a way for curls, and even had manicures. Of course, it was all very plain. All it took was some of the whitewash on the prison walls. We would wipe the corridor walls with our prison uniform and transfer it to our fingernails for them to shine, since we had no lacquer. The interrogator would go insane from malice when we entered his office with a manicure and brushed hair.

And even after the monstrous nighttime interrogations at Lefortovo, I would rise and do some physical exercises, and ones that I never in my life did willingly. These were certain purely female attempts of a despairing nature to resist going out of my mind. Whether all of this superficial embellishment helped, I cannot say, but I was able to resist insanity. Even though I appeared at the interrogations with a gray-green face and huge bulging eyes, but I was still manicured and brushed.

So this is how the Lord collects a person. Why? I do not know, but He collects. Arriving at the labor camp I was entirely different than the young woman that arrived at Lubyanka. I did not become hard, but just changed. When one of those at the labor camp told me that all the women there swear, I calmly replied that never in my life have I used profanity and I will not swear here either.

In response she laughed, "Just wait and see how you will swear in the labor camp."

I expressed myself again, "Not in the labor camp, nowhere, never, will I use such language." And so it was.

During the course of the proceedings [at Lefortovo] I repeatedly saw many women. Were there any genuine criminals among those I met or perhaps sleeping on the next cot? Yes, I did meet 2 criminals. One was named Maria Aleksandrovna, she was from Crimea and she said she was at one time a member of a monarchist organization. Later she worked with the Germans and betrayed communists or Jews to them. She was paid 1,000 rubles for each person clandestinely delivered to them. It is obvious she was very pretty as a young woman and no doubt took much advantage of this. She was married several times, also living with Czechs, living with Germans. Once she returned from an interrogation completely disheveled and agitated. This is what occurred: Persons who were executed by shooting were exhumed, their photographs were taken, and a stack of these photographs were given to here and they said, "Now show us the ones that you betrayed." And for several hours she sat with these photographs and pointed to her sacrifices. She got the same sentence as I did: 25 years. We later met each other at the train station near Mordovia labor camp.

The 2nd criminal was a very young nurse. She was called Anichka. I do not know how her proceedings concluded and why she was arrested. But she did tell us willingly, and laughing over it, how she killed wounded Germans in a hospital. She would inject something fatal into them and watch them suffer and die. She laughed exuberantly as she related this to us. But I do not think she was arrested for killing wounded military captives. It was obviously for something else.

Then there were these completely different figures. A Hungarian, Anna Bainberger. She was a wife of a Jew, and when Budapest was occupied by the Nazis, she went to work for the Germans at some government office. She was able to save her husband this way. This is all I know. She was brought from the labor camp to Lubyanka, and I do not know what then happened to her. She was a marvelous and immaculate person, but already very ill.

I remember another woman, she was a domestic worker, and it seems, at the home of a scholar, it seems, a professor. She related to agencies that the professor and some associates of his were members of some anti-Soviet organization. She was arrested and incarcerated likewise.

One very believing elderly woman was incarcerated only because she was a member of the True Orthodox Church. She did not commit any other crime except that she was a member of this catacomb church, which did not recognize Soviet authority or the official [Orthodox] Church. Initially we had a good relationship since she considered me a believer. But then she found out that Daniel and I were living together, only calling ourselves husband and wife, but never actually married. Then she started to call me an unwedded [*not fit for print*] and refused to further associate with me in prison.

There was Shura Yui Ninkhyan, and her husband was Chinese, so she took his name. It was only because of her Chinese name that she was arrested.

Alla later recollected receiving her sentence:

They read the sentence. There were 3 reactions. I saw how Daniel's cousin started to wail, hearing the sentence of 25 years. I could not in any way understand. Then it was my turn and some type of disreputable and repulsive scum read the sentence to me. Initially I could not figure the reason for the statement, "Do I hear this right?"

He stated quickly, "You heard it right." And he then said it again syllable by syllable, "25 years in a labor camp and 5 years of exile."

Then I said, "Repeat it one more time." And he did.

Later, Daniel told me how he reacted, and I know exactly. He laughed and thought to himself, "They imagine they will hold me 25 years?" And somehow he was right, but for the most part, he seemed to always be right. But with God, our time does not pertain.

I, naturally, so much wanted a child, to have a son from the person I loved. I knew how much Daniel loved children and how much he wanted to have a son. There, while at Lefortovo, I conclusively realized that our separation would be for a long while and that we would never have a child. While sitting on my prison cot, I fantasized carrying him in my arms, holding a small child in my hands, touching his feet, hands, watching his fingers flex, looking at his round head, his dark eyes. He as if grew right before my eyes, learning how to walk, holding my hand with his fingers as he followed me, and then again resting in my arms, and again walking about. My fantasies exhausted the last of my strengths that still remained in me, but I had to struggle, to resist depression as a result of not being able to do this.

This concluded the prison stage of my journey. Next was the labor camp. It was 13 months of interrogation at Lubyanka and then another 6 months at Lefortovo.

Daniel Andreev – The Prison Years

1948 – Continued

Daniel Andreev arrived at Vladimir Prison #2 on November 27, 1948. Although Daniel and Alla were only about 120 miles apart geographically, they would have no idea of the other's circumstance at all until 1953.

Vladimir Prison was considered high security. It was surrounded by a 10 foot brick wall and rows of barbed wire fence. Sentries walked along the wall during the day, and at night searchlights were on. An old hospital was located on one side of the prison, and on the other side was the cemetery with a surviving and functioning Orthodox Church. The prison had 4 major cellblocks and Daniel was assigned to #3.

The inmates were fed poorly, they were always hungry. Their bowl was filled from the common cooker or vat. They sat at a bare wooden table and concentrated on their personal predicament, silently they ate. For dinner it was greasy soup and either rice, lentils, cracked wheat or potatoes. Each inmate was allowed half-an-ounce of fat per day. To find a piece of meat in your soup was a treat. The ration of black bread was from 1 to 1-

1/2 pounds per day. There was a prison dispensary for the inmates with money, but they were very limited as to what they could buy or what was available. Twice per year the inmates could receive a package, should relatives know where they are.

Strolls were required – once a day for an hour. For 20 minutes they were required to march in rank and file. Inmates were not allowed on the roof, lest someone from the outside see them. The strolls were normally between the wall and fence where all could be kept in file and watched. During the winter the strolls were torturous, with the temperature 40 to 50 degrees below freezing point, and wearing clothing and boots that were not suited to resist such temperatures. A neck scarf or mittens were not assigned to the inmates. The cells were not heated well, and would drop as low as 20 degrees below freezing point.

Noise from the city Vladimir never reached the prison. The inmates only audible testimony of an outside world was the cemetery and the church next to it when funerals were conducted. They could hear the people gathered and then the bell from the church steeple. This was their only sound to testify to an outside world. The inmates were also buried at this cemetery.

Once every 10 days, the inmates had a bath and their sheets were changed. But even the bath in winter weather was often a torture.

Their beds were made of iron grating or lattice. The light in the cell was always on, and they could not turn it off. The stench of the latrine bowl never left the cell.

Twice a week doctors would visit the cellblocks. It seems everyone would sign up for a visit, but any promise of a visit to a medical clinic or hospital was dearth, but inmates went to distract themselves from their circumstances. It was also rare that an inmate had good health. They were plagued with tuberculosis, ulcers, gastritis, cataracts, catarrhs, hemorrhoids, neurological and psychiatric disorders – especially among the innocently convicted, and of course, innumerable heart disorders, as Daniel would also develop.

The newspapers delivered to the prison library were censured and at least 2 months behind. The local Vladimir paper and the Soviet *Pravda* were available. On occasion a personal request was granted.

One item to the benefit of the inmates of Vladimir prison was that their library held the largest collection of any single penal institution in the entire USSR prison system, with over 10,000 volumes. Daniel would have taken advantage of such information to assist him in later composing *Rose of the World*. Many of the books were considered antique, as well as including books otherwise prohibited for public distribution in the USSR.

One popular entertainment was chess. The inmates played it passionately and even organized tournaments.

The next distraction from prison regimen was writing. Inmates that could acquire a piece of paper and pencil wrote vehemently, page after page, and on whatever was on their mind: poetry, novels, history, and always taking advantage of the prison library. So did Daniel, once he adjusted to prison regimen and conditions became tolerable for him, compose his *Rose of the World*. Writing was not prohibited for the inmates at Vladimir, although prison officials would not allow criticism or slander to be composed. Guards likewise confiscated what they wanted at a whim. It was not until the death of Stalin in early 1953, that rules were relaxed and more freedom of expression in composition was allowed.

Daniel was housed in a dormitory room of 10 persons. Natural sunlight hardly penetrated the room through the lattice over the window at a high elevation, but the one light bulb that hung from the ceiling provided sufficient light for reading and writing. After the horrors of both Lubyanka and Lefortovo, Vladimir prison was adaptable, but never to be comfortable.

The descent into the punishment cell was a cruel experience: it was a prison within a prison. An inmate was fed once a day; the window was so high and dirty it was of no use; the light bulb hanging from the ceiling barely flickered; there was no where to sit; sleep was next to impossible. It was cold and no warm clothing was provided. But what tormented Daniel the worse when he was confined in it was that smoking was not permitted.

The ascent from the punishment cell was liberation and a return to the inmate's own cell. Daniel would later utilize the same experience in the descents and ascents to and from lower and higher worlds in the *Rose of the World*. Cellmates could empathize with others when they were assigned time in the punishment cell.

A fate worse than the punishment cell was the search of Daniel's cell by guards. All that he composed over the initial 2 years since arriving at Vladimir were confiscated. It was all his attempts at recreating what was destroyed by cremation at Lefortovo.

Daniel's closest friend became Vasili Vitalyevich Shulgin, a popular deputy of the State Duma during the latter part of Imperial Russia. Shulgin was an ideologist of the Mensheviks and indirectly involved with the activities of the White Army. He had 2 books to his name, *Days* and *1920*, both published in the Soviet Union, but as a result of their contents, he was arrested. Shulgin had emigrated from Russia after the Civil War and defeat of the White Army, and settled in Sremski Karlovci, Serbia, leading a quiet life as a nondescript person. One day he was asked to come to the local police station, and once he walked in he was arrested by Russian soldiers, December 24, 1944. His alleged crimes dated back to his role at the State Duma and involvement with the Mensheviks. He was first taken to Lubyanka, and then the 70-year old Shulgin was given a 25-year sentence. He arrived at Vladimir Prison on July 25, 1947. As Daniel recollected, Shulgin spent his days reading in the library.

1949

Daniel was unable to deal with the loss of all that he wrote in the past, and regularly suffered bouts of depression while in prison as a result. He attempted to resurrect as much as he could by memory. One associate in his cell recollected the following:

> Regardless of any superficial laughter, every day he covered the pages of his notebooks with his precise handwriting, using magical words that he difficultly developed. As many times as these pages were confiscated during regular frisks, the same number of times would Daniel Leonidovich again resurrect what he wrote by memory.

Once Daniel acquired a mental balance and was able to adapt to the regimen and accept his fate for the long-term, he returned to writing and poetry. However over the first year at Vladimir, hardly a dozen poems survived the guards. In 1956, Daniel wrote a letter to Alla with the following statement:

> I told you back in '47, and you did not believe me, that I would conclude *Wanderers* with some verses. This lingered in my subconscious, and sometimes even in my conscious, particularly because I felt it could not be published without you. The recent few years I had plenty of leisure and plenty of concentration, which this isolation has provided me, allowing me the ability to continue.

Although *Night Wanderers* was never recreated, a few fragments from Daniel's recollections were composed during these years. Otherwise, Daniel wrote like he never did in his life. All that he lived and experienced and encountered over the recent decades now initiated a cosmic cognizance, a new burst of purpose for his existence. Daniel's visions and mystic experiences of earlier years seemed to provide him a presentiment or premonition of impending supra-historical upheavals and sub-historical collapses. He felt himself close to receiving additional mysterious revelations, and conceiving mentally new concepts, seeking a new language. And what was primary and repeated was the close proximity of these other worlds.

Daniel's first visions and mystical encounters at Vladimir prison occurred in September after his move to his new cell, and he stated the following:

> I still had insufficient experience to compose *Rose of the World*, as much as I acquired on the route of comprehension so far. But the motion itself along this route brought me to the point that I seemed capable of consciously adopting the effects of certain Providential powers, and the hours of such spirit encounters became more of a perfected form of meta-historical comprehension.

This encounter evolved into one of the concepts that became the basis of *Leningradski Apocalypse*. Daniel would work on the poem intermittently until 1953, when he completes it.

For a thousand nights on his prison cell cot, over a period of 4 years, beginning that evening in September 1949, and until the final revelation in November 1953, Daniel departed on transphysical journeys in his nightly visions, as Daniel called this transcendent state. To him was disclosed and unveiled much that was unknown and from an unexpected, clandestine region. He relates this in 2 places in *Rose of the World*, both very similar:

> Finally, something similar, but already fully free from metaphysical terror, I experienced in September 1949, in Vladimir, besides, it was at night in a small prison cell as my sole comrade slept, and several times later in 1950-1953, also at nights, in a common prison cell. The experience collected on this route of comprehension was insufficient for *Rose of the World*, but the very movement along this route brought me to the point that finally I seemed capable to consciously absorb the effect of certain providential powers, and the hours of these spirit

encounters became more of a perfected form of meta-historical comprehension, than what I just described in writing. So the route of meta-historical illumination, contemplation and intelligence was supplemented with trans-physical journeys, encounters and conversations.

Particularly in prison, with its isolation from the outside world, with its unlimited spare time, with one thousand nights that I spent in vigilance, lying on a cot with other sleeping comrades, it was particularly in prison that the new stage of meta-historical and trans-physical comprehension began for me. The hours of meta-historical enlightenment were frequent. The long series of nights turned into a solid constant set of contemplation and meditation. The depths of memory was sending into my consciousness more and more distinct images, illuminating the events of my personal life and history and contemporary events with a new meaning. And finally, when awakening in the morning after a short but deep sleep, I knew that day that what I saw were not arbitrary dreamings, but something else entirely, they were trans-physical journeys.

Daniel likewise had a vision of the deceased poet Aleksandr Blok, who accompanied Daniel through the dark worlds just as did Virgil for Dante. Together they traversed the *Duegguer*, the world of deceptions and temptations of youth. Daniel wrote of the journeys of the 2 of them:

I saw him in the summer and autumn of the year 1949. The need to say something about this is not only my right, but also my obligation. I first met him in trans-physical journeys a long while back, many years, but lost any recollection of this. Then it was again in 1949, the circumstances of my prison confinement provided me the conditions to remember, and even remember the day, and the impressions he left upon me during these night journeys with him.

He showed me the *Agr*. No sun and no moon were there. The sky was black like a solid canopy. But certain objects and buildings that shined on their own were there, and they all had the same brilliance, from a distance it reminded me of our color scarlet.

In September 1949, Daniel was moved from the cell he shared with Shulgin to another. It occurred at night while Shulgin was asleep.

1950

In January he begins composing his poem, *Encounter with Blok*. It is a portrait of Aleksandr Blok as Daniel remembered him in earlier years. Only a fragment still remains at present. Even though Blok served as a guide into the nether regions, Daniel felt that he definitely needed a new language to express these concepts correctly for his readers: using earthly language to describe his journeys through other worlds.

Some of his earlier compositions utilized modifications of old Slavonic terms or those based on early Slavic mythology, but somehow they did not fit his purpose because the subject matter transcended Russian culture. But Daniel did speak of sirins and alkonosts of Russian folklore since he felt that global culture would eventually rotate around the Russian meta-culture.

When wife Alla was later helping Daniel with editing *Rose of the World*, she recollected her comments:

> I disagree with the use of *assumption*, because the word is known to tens of millions of people, and they do not need a dictionary to figure its meaning, just like any person knows what Christmas is, and also Ever-Virgin. You cannot have some archaism accidentally dropped in-passing and then have it disappear like some ghost.

Expression is one of the central means of these concepts that are disclosed in subsequent stages. Another word that is out of place in the text is *throne*.

Both assumption and throne are not used in the final edition of *Rose of the World*.

The most productive year in Daniel's life was 1950. Every day new verses were composed. Daniel started 3 of his major works this year: *Russian Gods*, *Iron Mystery*, and *Rose of the World*. He composed more this year than all of the previous years combined, and of them, about 120 stanzas or paragraphs have survived the frisks and confiscations and the censurers. Many of his poems dealt with his childhood, and these seemed to be the ones that were confiscated and destroyed, more than others. Daniel likewise did his best to recomposed poems that were reduced to ashes earlier.

Apart from poetry in its strict narrow sense, Daniel's periphery expanded to what he initially called – over-history, which he considered a departure or variation of history from strictly one angle of view, and soon this perspective became known as meta-history. From this kernel of universal perspective, where Daniel concluded poetry and religious feelings to be inseparable, he began to cultivate a new series of writings to extend to the end of his life. Now what Daniel called doctrine, concepts, ideology, ethos, began to acquire a visible materialization. Parallel with this, Daniel began to write based on his recollections of his forest hikes and his meta-physical journeys of Trubchevsk. While in his cell, these other worlds easily connected with the corporeal, becoming also unrealistic and existing only behind prison walls. This is to what his searches and visions and compositions led while in prison: a logic of history beyond history, and worlds beyond worlds, and his personal destiny.

Daniel also surmised that it was best for these revelations of other worlds, spirit-vision bursts to occur while he was in prison. He believed this unconditionally and the revelations started, initially as imprecise dreams, then they increased in clarity and sensations as though he migrated directly into the vision as part of the vision itself. Due to his poetic inspiration, Daniel felt he could adapt to possessing a spirit cognizance, and in his search for this entrance he mentally returned to the banks of the Nerussa River, where his initial immense confrontations with the cosmic reality and comprehension overwhelmed him. But the actual transfer of his *I* from the corporeal and into the astral body, as he read in Ramacharka, this he encountered later.

From February to September Daniel created his first poetic collection, called *Russian Octaves*. The notebook survived, and it contains 7 of his hand-written penciled poems: *Gods and Pines, Floodplain, Stroll, Barefooted, Forest Blood Red, Marsh,* and *Spring of Life*. All of them are based on his hikes in the Trubchevsk region. Daniel was hoping to created a trilogy of such volumes to unveil more of his meta-physical concepts. As time progressed each of the poems were supplemented. Some of *Russian Octaves* were transferred into Daniel's later book, *Vagrant,* and the balance increased in number of poems and stanzas to become his poetic ensemble, *Russian Gods*. This volume begins with a Moscow-based theme, with the author seeing 3 Moscows: the earthly, the historical and the heavenly. The earthly is mundane and comparable to residing in an abyss, while its historical twin is decorated with sacred jewels, and its representation in heaven is crowned as the heavenly Kremlin, the dream of the population.

The symbol of Moscow as a citadel appears in *Russian Gods*, representing the Stalinist, infernal Moscow, the support and emblem of God-defying authority. Around the city rotates a continual whirlwind that is saturated with demonic influences.

In *Iron Mystery*, Moscow as a citadel is the symbol of totalitarian Soviet dominion. In 1947, Stalin celebrated the 800-year anniversary of the founding of Moscow in 1147, the first reference in Russian history to the existence of the city, then a small town. To someone like Shulgin, who read Daniel's composition in his cell at Vladimir prison, the conclusion was solely political.

To announce that Moscow is a citadel represents worldwide revolution, equivalent to declaring war against all the bourgeois governments. Subsequently, there is no reason to expect any kind of stable peace in the near-future years.

Later Shulgin told Daniel his opinion that the country was again on the brink of war, and Daniel completely shared the same opinion, and felt that an altercation between the USSR and the west was inevitable. The devastation of the previous war would logically continue into the mystery play of global history with a new and awesome warfare on the gigantic scale of the atomic age. As a result, Daniel's primary topics of composition of his prison years after 1950 were directed toward the abolition of tyranny and war, which Daniel considered the most formidable of dangers for humanity. Daniel started on *Rose of the World* December 24, 1950.

Daniel's contemplations flowed one after another and arranged themselves into a poetic model of the universe, connected with the undermining intents of Daniel's purpose. Moscow was one of the centers of this universe. In *Russian Gods*, the Kremlin was called the cradle of the fatherland, with the child tied to the umbilical cord of the Russian Orthodox Church. The Moscow Library, Bolshoi Theater, Cathedral of Vasili the Blessed, and the Church of Christ the Savior, were sacred jewels embellished upon the child.

In the poems of 1950, Daniel traversed the cycle of his life a 2nd time: Moscow childhood, city wanderings as an adolescent, the Trubchevsk hikes, the mystic experiences, war, adjustment to civilian life. The concept of *Rose of the World* grew out of this cycle. Old poems were rewritten and supplemented. Of course, all that Daniel wrote was not fictional, but derived from his mystic experiences and studies in the same spheres. The *Symphony of City Days*, written at the end of 1950, was the most expressive, anyway in Russian poetry, of the depiction of Stalin's Moscow.

Regarding the start of *Rose of the World,* Daniel introduced the book with the following passage:

This book began when the danger of unprecedented calamity was already hanging over humanity; when the generation that barely began to depart from the agitation of the Second World War was shockingly convinced that over the horizon there was already curling, thickening, a strange deep darkness, the warning sign of a catastrophe that is even more terrible, a war that is even more devastating. I began this book in the extremely mute years of tyranny that prevailed over 200 million people. I began it in a prison that had the designation of political isolation. I wrote it clandestinely. The manuscripts I hid, and good efforts of people – and even those who were not human – hid it for me during times of search. And every day I expected that the manuscript would be confiscated and destroyed, just as my preceding work was destroyed, which deprived me of 10 years of my life and brought me to political isolation.

Prison regimen often caused depression and mental dissipation, but less here than in places designated for direct torture and execution, such as Lubyanka and Lefortovo. One person able to keep his psychological balance by the use of personal gymnastics and yoga was Shulgin, as he recorded:

Nerves in prison easily crumble. It is often the monotone prison procedure, the poor food: soup, rice or potatoes, the ritual of getting a bowl of it from the pot, the continual gloom of the cellblocks, especially the difficulty of autumn and winter when the windows are frosted over. Daytime came late and night came early. All of this drained and exhausted the soul of even the most resistant and agile inmate.

What especially was painful and devastating was the unknown: what was occurring to wife and friends at home, and also those who may have been likewise arrested for some alleged crime.

In 1949, Shulgin sent 2 letters to his wife, but they were both returned for the address not existing. Later when he saw the envelopes, one numeral was not correct in the address.

The inmates had the right to 2 letters per year to send and to receive. The size of the letters were regulated. For a long while Daniel only had one address which to use, and this was Alla's parents. His mother-in-law, Yulia Gavrilovna would respond. She refused to reveal Alla's location to Daniel, afraid if she had the right to do this. Yulia was also afraid that should Daniel now correspond with Alla, she would no longer do the same with her parents, especially with only 2 letters per year allowed. After the arrests started, they were hardly pleased with Daniel. From the day Daniel was arrested in 1947 and until rules were relaxed in 1952, there was no direct communication between Daniel and Alla or even knowledge of the other's location.

The Bruzhes' home was turned upside down with their daughter's conviction as an enemy of the people, as well as her 25-year sentence. Alla's father, Aleksandr Petrovich, was fired from his job as a result. Yulia continued to correspond with Daniel, and she was his only communication with the outside world, the sole relative who extended any effort at all on his behalf, who would take the risk. The balance of Dobrovs were either arrested and sentenced themselves, or distanced themselves from Daniel and his predicament. Yulia would sent money and parcels. Daniel responded in a letter, about summer of 1950:

> I turn to you with a request, although I am not aware of your financial circumstances. If you could possible send to me during the coming year about 25 to 30 rubles a month, this would allow me the possibility to supplement my daily needs. But if this be a burden to you, then just

forget about my request, as though I never brought this to your attention.

Another request is to forward to me my wife's address. When I turned to you in February 1950, you denied my request. Why do you doubt that you have the right to satisfy my request. But this is the matter. During the summer of 1949, I was able to get my wife's address from another agency, as they granted my request, but I was only able to use this address in a letter in January 1950. What happened was that the letter was returned to me. Somewhere the address was changed. There is absolutely no way for me to find her address from anyone, except from you. Try to imagine that it has been 4 years that I know nothing about my wife and am unable to utilize the one right I do have here in prison, to correspond with her.

But due to her fear of what might happen to her, Yulia refused to forward Alla's address to Daniel for some time into the future.

Still having serious medical conditions, his spinal disorder, Daniel wondered how long he would survive in prison. Toward the end of 1950, Daniel wrote the following in his poem *Springs of Life*:

> I will not hide my depression
> As death may come upon me at any moment.
> And I am not comforted by distant worlds.
> Weeping, I embrace the past close to my heart.
> I turn to my final friend,
> The fragrance of green grass,
> Install a plain and wooden eight-pointed cross.

Daniel later mentioned to Alla, that toward the end of 1950, his personal destiny was not at all clear to him. But he endeavored not to capitulate to some undesirable fate and so continued forward, especially with his motivation for writing.

1951

In January Daniel started on *Morning Oratory*. As he described it:

> It is different from works of drama, first of all, due to the absence of defined visual reality. Freedom is applied to the visual imagination of the reader or listener, and limited only by short remarks or sounds or repeating voices, or an exchange of words, and the content of their retorts.

Only some fragments of this poem survived his prison term. It begins with a choir of demiurges, the national leaders located at the piedmont of the global *Salvaterra*. The choir consists of the demiurges of the ancient Greek and Roman supra-nations, the Ancient East, the young demiurge of the countries of the west, and *Yarosvet*, the demiurge of Russia. This also provides the basis of the system of meta-cultures, supra-nations, and their demiurges that are arranged in *Rose of the World*.

Another started composition was *Fevronia*, consisting of 5 parts. 1: The Ancients, *Stikhials*, Princes; 2: *Suekhovei*, *Velga*; 3: The Moscow Hill; 4: Conception of the *Yuitzraor*; 5: Birth of the *Yuitzraor*. The oratory of *Fevronia* was never much completed, but became the basis for Daniel's later poem, *Fevronia and Vsevolod*. But none of any of these likewise survived his prison term. Daniel mentions the state he was in when he received these images and worlds, disclosed to him as a dream-vigilance. The fragments contain the date of April 1951. Then the work was interrupted, and he continued to supplement *Oratory* in September of the same year.

During the week prior to Easter of that year, which occurred April 20, Daniel returned to recreating his lengthy poem, *The Twelve Evangelists*, which he had written 20 years earlier and was cremated with his other compositions. But as with others that he attempted to recreate, his success was limited.

Daniel defined his poetic method as penetrating-through-reality or meta-reality. *Demrosver* became the demiurge of the Russian supra-nation, but later he decided in favor of *Yarosvet*. The female great suppressor (*Velikiya Gasitilnitza*) became *Velga*. The female sculptor of the nation's body (*Vayatelnitza ploti naroda*) became *Vayapola*. Daniel described his onomastics as follows:

> There are no more than about 10 appellations and terms that I fabricated myself, among them being *Navna*, *Yarosvet*, meta-culture, *Velga*, and the others. But about two hundred or so appellations I did not fabricate and did not acquire, but heard them in one or another state, and some of them many times. Their transcription using Cyrillic letters is only a close approximation. But some of them I was just not able to decipher precisely. Among them are terms that sound really bad, for example, *Erl*, *Propulk*. Yet they are still very expressive and proper.

In October, Daniel wrote to his mother-in-law:

> Over the previous year I have received from you, deeply respected Yulia Gavrilovna, 350 rubles. Words are hardly sufficient for even the smallest indication of my expression of my gratitude and they can hardly display to you the significance this amount of money has for my health and in general my life.

Daniel would spend the money on food and toothpaste, and especially for paper and cigarettes. Every inmate seemed to smoke in the prison, and Daniel was a chain smoker. Chewing tobacco would always go fast if any inmate was able to get any.

Yulia Gavrilovna gave Daniel their new address. The Bruzhes were forced, and to add to all their other misfortunes, to move from their large apartment to a single spacious room in a communal apartment. But Yulia mentioned nothing about Alla to Daniel, and even though he asked for her address Yulia ignored the request. The Bruzhes blamed Daniel for their daughter's sorrowful predicament. In his letters Daniel did not ever justify himself, but instead attempted to get some information on her whereabouts.

> If you are going to write back to me, do not deny to communicate to me this kind favor. Also I really need to know if you have a photograph of my wife, even a small one, and preferably one that would be recent.
>
> My thoughts of love for her compels me to continue to live, even though separation is completely powerless in dissolving our relationship.
>
> But if matters should turn around in a different direction at some time in the future, that she would decide to build a new personal life without me, I would accept her decision as my deserved punishment for not being able to provide for her welfare. And if this should give her even a flicker of light, even this much happiness, then I would likewise be also happy for her.

Daniel abruptly ended the letter at this point.

Three uncommon inmates who were incarcerated together in cell 45 of cellblock 3, were referred to as the academics. They were very different in appearance and temperament, but their profession seemed to draw them together as they were all writers. The 3 were Vasili Vasilyevich Parin, Lev Levovich Rakov, and Daniel Andreev.

Rakov was arrested once before in 1938, and was confined a year at Krestu Prison, Petersburg, in the psychiatric ward, for alleged terrorism-related activities. Much like Daniel, Rakov was conscripted into the military, and was a veteran of the war and a hero in breaking the blockade of Petersburg with 2 awards. His highest rank was major. In 1947, he was assigned as director of a local Petersburg library. From testimony of those who knew Rakov, he loved the students who studied at his library, and he had a reputation as a ladies' man and dressed and conducted himself very elegantly.

After the library he worked at a military museum in Petersburg, one that commemorated the suffering of the residents during the blockage and its liberation by Soviet troops. But according to the Soviet agencies, Rakov did not attribute sufficient credit to the role of the Communist Party and Stalin in the city's liberation. As with Daniel, the agencies accused Rakov of involvement with an anti-Soviet group. Because Rakov was also in charge of antique military weapons at the museum, he was accused of hoarding an arsenal to be used in an assassination attempt against Stalin. Two weeks before his arrest on April 20, 1950, he married. He was interrogated and confined for a while at Lefortovo. On October 31, 1950, Rakov was sentenced to 25 years prison and 5 years deprivation of civil rights. He arrived at Vladimir prison on August 20, 1951. Daniel was able to identify with Rakov and the 2 became close.

It was in this atmosphere of the academic cell that the wit-filled book, *Newest Plutarch* was written by the 3 authors. The book was subtitled as *Illustrated Biographical Dictionary of Imagined Famous Activists of all Countries and Eras from A to Z*, and Rakov was the initiator, primary author, chief editor and illustrator. Other creations of theirs were a cycle of tales called, *In a Drop of Water*; a couple of literary essays, one called, *Onegin's Fate*, based on Pushkin's novel length poem, and *Letter about Gogol*, in additional to much humor in order to pass the time away and distract themselves from the critical environment. Rakov considered himself a writer of prose and with no sense of poetic composition.

On April 3, 1953, Rakov was moved from his cell with Parin and Daniel to another cell, #35. There he continued to composed, supplementing *Newest Plutarch*.

After contributing to *Newest Plutarch*, Daniel wrote some humor on his own, something he says he was inclined to do since a child, but that he was always distracted by reality and mysticism and writing for a living, and never seemed to have the time to write humor, but now was able to with the spare time available. Only 2 stanzas survived Vladimir prison from his lengthy poem titled *Moscow Childhood*, and nothing of *Old House*.

1952

Essentially, *Rose of the World* as a book was something that Daniel thought of and attempted to write not just once, but his entire earlier life. In 1933, he wrote a book titled *Contours of Preliminary Doctrine*; at the end of 1950, it was *Tractate*, following it was *A Metaphysical Sketch*, which included a table with the changes of red and blue epochs. *Tractate* was written as an introduction and the first part of a meta-historical trilogy. Not only his concepts of multi-dimensional worlds and history driven by mystical powers, but the entire life of the author, was included in all the above. Daniel lived continually under the expectation of spirit breakthroughs and alien events, bright visions of a heavenly Russia, and a close proximity to the secrets of dark worlds. But he understood that these would be breaches and in some incomprehensible depth of his personal cognizance.

Doubt in the validity of the spirit-vision experience did occur with Daniel. Overcoming doubt demanded a certain conviction. In the traditional mystic teachings that were earlier proposed, he did not notice any unconditional truths, however he found many contradictions. Daniel concluded that this could only be resolved with personal experience, and not so much from education. As a utopia, Daniel's epos concentrated on the future, clearly divided into 3 primordial stages. Yesterday was the blood-filled, the day of battle, storm and judgment, a living hope, because it was the stage between the future general fraternity and the arrogant dominion that will be destroyed forever.

The day after tomorrow reminded him of the wilderness after the flood. The 3rd day will be the installation of the epoch of ROSE OF THE WORLD, the co-development of all the supra-nations of all the world. But the utopia of ROSE OF THE WORLD is religious, and so eschatological, and the entrance of the epoch of ROSE OF THE

WORLD will occur following designated stages. Daniel saw the arrival of the anti-christ and end of world history as we know it. The past is just as significant as the future, but not only because it arranges the karma of history, but because the historical past in a mystical sense in all its fullness enters the future.

The treatise from its start was composed slowly and so near September 1952, its arrangement began a poetic ensemble called *Russian Gods*. The chief demonic power of Russian history and characters of the book were personified as a monster called by the strange gnashing appellation of *yuitzraor*, the mystic personification of state authority, demonic due to its nature. The clandestine work of meta-history was dedicated to the comprehension of the mysterious life of the *yuitzraor*, that was unveiled in history.

In Daniel's cycle of poetry and prose dealing with his interpretation of history, he included Tsar Ivan IV the Terrible, the Imposters, and the Time of Troubles. The poem, *Ruin of the Terrible*, became a mystery play of Russian history, and upon which Daniel worked, little by little, during the winter of 1952 and completing it before spring. The undefeatable drive of tyranny predetermined the trans-physical destiny of Ivan the Terrible. The tsar, who is summoned to be an innovator of new comprehension, becomes a tyrant. To Daniel, this was one of the decisive meta-physical events of Russian history. Daniel describes the gloomy destiny of Ivan in *Rose of the World*:

> Certain qualities of his nature became his easily accessible and unconscious spiritual replacement, while unlimited authority unbridle his emotions, corrupted his will, agitated his mental balance, brought irreparable damage to his ethereal body, and transformed the bends of his individual route, or more correct, his fall, into a chain of catastrophes for the supra-nation and a catastrophe for his government.
>
> It is a lesson for the contemporary era, having appeared as an orderly attempt to convert absolute tyranny of the entire country into a work assignment,

although at the cost of the destruction of entire classes and that driving and terrifying humiliation of general creativity and their moral level, and which seems to accompany each tyrannical national system.

The events of the country's history, the result of the struggle between the demiurge of the supra-nation and the demon of autocracy, is mutually connected with the processes that occur in the demonic world.

The succeeding poem was *Symphony of the Russian [Time of] Troubles*, and was a continuation of the same meta-historical era. He started this in September 1952. Following this was composing the Introduction to *Russian Gods*.

In Daniel's verses the living and the dead are listed both, but not all is completely understandable. He discusses the post-mortem fate of the Dobrovs. His Aunt Sasha Dobrova will somehow hasten her own death, but she will save her mother from *Morod*, which is the 3rd stratum of purgatory, one of the higher category. It is the realm of absolute silence, where the residents are tormented by a melancholy state of great abandonment. Aunt Elizabeth's fate is still unknown to him. Dr Philipp Dobrov is designated a place that is "radiantly tranquil and creative throughout all the changes of eons."

The political prisoners suffered at the hands of the criminal prisoners. It was this way in all the penal institutions: exile, labor camps, prisons. As long as Daniel, considered a political prisoner, was in the same cell as other intellectuals, the relationship was fine. The difficulty occurred when a person convicted of some criminal offense was in the same cell with a person convicted of a political issue. Alla described this in the following manner:

> If we can imagine the type of people these criminals were who were sentenced to prison and not to a labor camp. When I was in the labor camp they always said that the murderer, bandit, embezzler or prostitute was a person,

but the political prisoner was not. So to mitigate this attitude, when these criminals who committed some horrible or serious crime were assigned to the same cell with Daniel, and Parin and Rakov, and they would greet the criminal in a courteous and friendly manner, and then start occupying themselves with their personal activities. Vasili Vasilyevich read them his lectures on physiology; Lev Levovich – lectures on Russian history, and especially his lectures on the development of the Russian military uniform, which was his favorite topic; Vladimir Aleksandrov – Russian art; while Daniel would compose some poetry relating to them personally and spend time teaching them grammar and writing.

This made it much easier for them to get along in a friendly manner with the criminals.

Another inmate with Daniel was Isaac Markovich Volfin, a teacher of the Swedish language. He was arrested in 1946 and accused of having ties with foreigners, and together with other teachers at a foreign language school in Soviet Russia, was convicted of espionage. He received a sentence of 25 years. Before the war, Volfin worked in Sweden, and then he returned to Soviet Russia at the start of World War 2 and was conscripted into the Soviet Navy in 1943. Daniel wrote to Alla about Volfin:

> This is a man of a different circle, with whom you and I will seldom have the opportunity to meet. He is a sailor, and sailed many seas and ports, and is also a great fan of swing dancing. He adores music and which is his life, but externally he is very rude, loves taking risks. His soul is heavily wounded, but he does have a very high regard of human life. He is just 44, and still has much young life ahead of him.

Another cellmate at some time was Zea Rakhim, or more properly, Zea Abdul Khakim Kirim Ogli, the most mysterious individual of all of Daniel's cellmates. He was an orientalist and arabist, and was arrested as an alleged Japanese spy in 1946, with no other evidence except for his scholarship in oriental studies. He appeared to be of Egyptian descent and was raised in an Islamic family. Together in the same cell, he and Daniel became friends, having his scholarship somewhat connected with Daniel's attraction to eastern religions. Zea was 30 at the time, he was scholarly and well-educated, from the history of the middle east and orient to contemporary physics, with an ability to listen and be attentive. Parin and Aleksandrov could not but be impressed by Zea.

There were also a few hard-line communists in the same prison against whom the party turned for some reason or another.

After his release from prison, Daniel related to Alla about an attorney who was also assigned to solitary confinement. Disregarding this, Daniel attempted to be friends with him, and he wrote to Alla:

> When he was released for a stroll, and all by himself, he took a few crumbs of bread with him to feed the doves. All the doves would land on his shoulders, and he would give to them the last crumbs of bread that he possessed.

In another letter to his wife Alla, Daniel states:

> During these years I personally met people with whom I developed a personal relationship of internal closeness, and such were those with whom I had a simple connection due to a fervent empathy, respect, and commonality of certain interests. Of course, initially there were just a few, or actually just one, but of the others, each was close to me from a different side of me.

In April, Daniel sent a letter to his in-laws, thanking his mother-in-law Yulia Gavrilovna for the 50 rubles she had been sending per month, and which made life considerably easier for him. He was also saving some of the money since now he was having tooth decay and was in serious need of dental work. Daniel promised his next letter for March or April 1953.

1953

Yulia Gavrilovna, Alla's mother, living within a circle of fear, always overexcited wondering if she would be the next victim of some nighttime arrest squad, was on the edge of a nervous collapse the entire time beginning with Alla's arrest. As many times as her son-in-law Daniel would request Alla's location and mailing address, Yulia would acutely respond in a subsequent letter:

> Let me repeat. I do not know and even if I did, I do not know if I have the right to tell you, and I have not any motivation to go to the authorities to find out. I have been very agitated and shocked over the recent events, and it seems it will always be this way and I will never recover. I am unable to transfer to you our experiences, and I have no words to describe it. They are so sharply penetrating, as the initial days.
>
> Please seriously consider what I am saying, very seriously, regarding my refusal to give to you our daughter's mailing address.

Recent newspapers were not circulated to inmates, and then from the beginning of March 1953, they ended entirely and for the next month and-a-half none were distributed. However, everyone did learn of Stalin's death quickly. One of Daniel's acquaintances related in later years how Daniel described hearing of the event:

> On the night of March 5-6, 1953, everyone was sleeping in the cellblock, but Vasili Vasilyevich could not fall asleep due to some persistent pain or illness; it seems

that the entire cellblock was sick in some manner, and where a healthy person can easily get infected or get sick anyway. And so Vasili Vasilyevich, in pain and unable to sleep, heard in the night silence a few fragments of words that echoed from a loud-speaker from a near-by street, "The leader of global proletariat... The sorrow of the nations of all the world," and more. He guessed what the matter was and in the morning quickly hurried to inform Daniel. But how? To just blare something like this would be disastrous to him, so Vasili Vasilyevich did the following: he walked up to Daniel, depicted a mustache with his hands and then pointed to the floor. Daniel sighed. Vasili Vasilyevich repeated the pantomime. Then, it seems, by 2 o'clock that afternoon, there was not one person in the Soviet Union who was not informed of it.

The dedicated communists and the political prisoners that were innocent of any crime, they politicized the event with loud wailing over the death of the "leader of nations". But they also knew that they would have to wait for more changes before gaining their freedom. The attitude of the state toward political prisoners did not quickly benefit them, but conditions were ameliorated.

What Daniel experienced at the time he transformed into a meta-historical picture in *Rose of the World*. Stalin's death was next in a series of fatal events of Russian history and meta-history. In Daniel's prison notebooks he has the following notation, "*Yarosvet* fought against *Yuitzraor* in 1855, 1881, 1904, 1923, 1933, 1949, and twice in 1953." Stalin's death in *Rose of the World* is depicted in a manner that as if Daniel is physically transferred from his prison cell to the specific place where the battle of the inhuman powers of evil was occurring. The spirit-vision, which Daniel viewed as absolute truth, acquired a poetic representation, and this was his stance of many years of Stalin being the personification of despotic tyranny.

In October 1953, Daniel in his prison notebooks recorded a few remarks pertaining to his meta-historical portrait of Stalin and what he saw in dreams regarding him.

Stalin: Face. Voice.
1. Torture.
2. Route to absolute tyranny.
3. Imagining he is Caesar; bleeding the nation, manic persecution, self-deification.

A shadow. Conceited. Tasteless.

The ingenuity of the state was shredded when he was still a child. The ingenuity of science and literature succeeded to advance until his birth. From that time forward it has become monotone verbosity and precomposed addresses. This is a crippled dark universal genius. But this can only succeed once. Now the *Yurparp*[48] knows how to protect its offspring.

Not at all did Stalin possess any mystical blindness. Materialism was just a mask. There was a moment when he even prayed in great fright: the coming perspective was unveiled to him, and its entirety, the fate of antichrist. But obstinacy and the insane unlimited thirst for authority overwhelmed him.

He hoped that science will succeed in providing him physical immortality, a dream he carried with him since childhood. He has fallen down as far as *Shim-Bieg*,[49] but his body is already emaciated and shredded. He migrated with the help of the demons of gloom. At one time he was very strong and awesome. Three of his *Sinklit* brethren[50] were imprisoned and to this time reside in the rear dungeon of *Druekkarg*.[51] Among them is Mikhail Yakubovich.[52]

---

[48] The great implementer of the demonic plan
[49] One of the 3 lowest of all the purgatories, reserved for those suffering many deaths.
[50] Human souls, these would be Yakubovich, Malenkov and Beria, mentioned further.
[51] Russia after Tsar Ivan IV.
[52] Mikhail Petrovich Yakubovich, 1891-1980, a social democrat who opposed Soviet

Stalin died as a result of a ruptured artery during the battle of *Zhrugr*[53] against the demiurge[54] and [*Zhrugr*] was defeated. Those who saw this concluded it was a stroke. During the time from his stroke to the deaths of Malenkov and Beria, Mikoyan (even though he was not directly involved) and Khrushchev worked hard for none of this to survive. Beria had no other exit because he was defeated.

Molotov was agitated. The crime of Beria was the death of millions of innocent persons. There were 3 reasons:

1 To confuse Stalin.
2 To keep the country in a state of terror and mutism.
3 An unquenchable thirst for blood.

He had a dark mission, but his comprehension was planar, flat like a table. At his interrogation he exposed them all, and this was his vengeance against them, and he was able to take vengeance. They sat opposite to one another, despising each other. Among them was not one person who was not aware of the crimes of the others. They were all entangled in the same web.

The details of the picture were not clear at first. From official newspaper announcements, that finally made their way into prisons, the death of the tyrant, the state demon, did not seem to Daniel as something usual, as a death of an old and ill person, but the result of the effects of meta-historical powers that materialized in the persons of their characters. Daniel further described the situation from his meta-physical perspective in *Rose of the World*.

---

authority, and likewise spent must time in prison.
[53] Russia
[54] The demiurges are all who create for the glory of God, from love of the world and its primordial Creator.

During the initial days of March 1953 there occurred a decisive duel between *Yarosvet* and *Zhrugr*. The channel of invocation uniting the entity of the *yuitzraor* with its human weapon, was severed at the blink of an eye. If it was possible to have done this earlier, so than much earlier would the life of the human weapon been severed. When this did occur, there were no human strengths available that were sufficient to restrain the burden lying upon this psyche and on this physical organism. This occurred about 2 o'clock in the night. After half-an-hour his cognizance vanished, but the agony persisted, as we know, for several days. The *yuparp* grasped the ruptured end of the channel of invocation and attempted to pour into the perishing person some strength and consciousness. This did not succeed, and in part because several men, standing along side his death bed, made sure that he would not return to life.

The motives that guided these people were diverse. Some feared that if he were to remain as head of the state, he would release a war, a war that they pictured as a great calamity for every one and a fatal danger for their Doctrine. But among those that were close to him stood one who for many years guided the rudder of the mechanism of safety.[55] He knew that the leader already marked him as the next serial sacrifice, next in line to be silently purged, knowing that the nation was complaining about him. It would have been proper to place before his eyes the full responsibility for the masses of millions of innocent persons he destroyed. The end of Stalin would provide for him another chance to replace him, take his position. The course of his activity during the life of the leader delineated 3 motives: to confuse Stalin, inflating and innovating physical dangers, as though they were threatening him on every

---

[55] This was Lavrenti Beria who was head of the NKVD, National Committee for Internal Affairs, which he later merged with the MGB, Ministry of Government Security or Safety.

side; to retain the country in the reins of fear and mutism and so be able to quench his personal thirst for blood. Such a person was the agent of a dark mission, including the increase of nations sufferings, but his comprehension was planar, flat and non-mystical, like a tabletop, while the size of his individuality and talent was worthless. He was the Maluita Skuratov of the 20th century.[56]

Finally the great minute arrived: Stalin released his spirit.

Gashsharv[57] quaked at this strike against him. *Druekkarg* echoed with wails of terror and anger. *Zhrugr* howled from rage and pain. Hordes of demons exited from their lower depths to the higher strata of the infra-cosmos, striving to slow the fall of the dead one into the depths of the magma below.

A sorrowful demonization was transmitted to *Enrof*.[58] The funeral of the leader, or better said, the transfer of his body to a mausoleum, was transformed into an idiotic erection of a monument. The manipulation of his name and actions was so great that hundreds of thousands of people regarded his death as a tragedy. Even in prison cells some wept over the fact of his demise. The crowds, who were never considered sufficiently worthy to see the leader while he was alive, now hungered to see his face at least in his coffin. Moscow displayed itself as a picture of an insane asylum, one as large as the capital city itself. Crowds flowed into the center of the city attempting to get close to the Palace of Unions, where the corpse of the tyrant was set for public viewing, and where anyone could join the mourning procession. The adjoining streets turned into Khodynka Field. People died in the process, crushed against the walls of houses and street lights, or were trampled underfoot, or falling

---

[56] Skuratov was the henchman of Tsar Ivan IV the Terrible.
[57] One of the basic strata of the demonic anti-cosmos among the worlds.
[58] The physical universe, according to *Rose of the World*.

from the roofs of many-storied houses, hoping to somehow bypass the medley of crowds below. It seems, that as though he, having nourished himself all his life with the odor of suffering and blood, even now in his coffin, was still drawing people into his infra-cosmic sorrow of sacrifice.

Stalin died and the wind began to blow in a different era. On June 26, Lavrenti Beria was arrested, and he was executed by shooting on December 23, by the order of Nikita Khrushchev.

The first amelioration for inmates occurred in August, when now they were allowed to write one letter per month. On September 1, the OSO was disbanded. The release started of inmates who were tried and sentenced innocently.

Daniel's night visions during the events of 1953 turned into a picture of the power struggles of the wrong side of the world and where the fates of the nation's history was decided. On October 22, Daniel wrote in *Rose of the World*:

> The *Raruggas*[59] are completely insane. They revolt among themselves. They surround their pagan temples, they do go allow the *igvies*[60] entrance. The statue is overturned. The *igvies* do not want war. The *Raruggas* are only capable of massive suicide in the event that a global victory is not attained.
>
> Khrushchev did not leave his residence for several days due to fear. But he needs to soon in order to attend the Presidium of the Central Committee. There a storm will occur. No one knows how it will end.

Daniel explains these events such that the demonic intellect rejected the idea of a Third World War, and the power struggle

---

[59] The second of the race of anti-humanity, presenting itself as those entities that traversed innumerable incarnations in the strata of demonic materiality

[60] The head or first of the race of anti-humanity. The highly developed intellectual demonic entities

ended with the victory of the moderates. He viewed Khrushchev's character as not cruel by nature, but he remained in essence a person who possessed many flaws, but that they could be traversed without difficulty, he was a person of the "invocation of bright principles" compared to his predecessors.

On October 29, the first of the changes inmates expected in the labor camps and prisons materialized when Vasili Vasilyevich Parin was released and could go home.

Rakov likewise attempted to somehow get his release, and on November 25, he wrote a request to the Presidium of the Central Committee of the Communist Party of the Soviet Union (CC of the CP of the USSR). He explained the absurdity of the accusations made against him and requested to meet with delegates or agents of the CP, since he was a member of the CP in good standing in earlier years, in order to explain to them the matter. In conclusion, Rakov begged them not to send him back to Lubyanka or to Lefortovo, for more tortures during interrogations. But he never received a reply.

In November, Aleksandr Bruzhes started an aggressive campaign for the release of his daughter Alla from the labor camp.

For Daniel the most important contribution to the penal system after Stalin's death was the opportunity to correspond with his wife. Somehow he was able to ascertain her location and the address of the labor camp and his first letter to here was on June 21, 1953, after not communicating with her directly since their mutual arrests some 6 years earlier, even though Daniel says it was 7.

> My precious, my favorite girl!
> It is difficult to show you how much it will mean to me when I receive your reply to this letter, lines written by your own hand, and I will read them as a definite reality, and not just in endless and innumerable dreams about you. I feel this pain for you, the worst of all tortures that I have even experienced in my life. But it is

hardly necessary to speak about this, as you know this yourself. This thought in my mind of the conditions in which you reside endlessly gnaws at my conscious and soul, and thinking of this causes its own category of torment every day. For 7 years I held the notion that my love to you was great and bright. But it is just a pale illusion in comparison to what it is now. I do not know if it was this way in the past. I cannot say if I could have saved you from the horrible attacks against you, all of this occurred so independent of my will. But in any case, we would have stayed together.

How intolerable are now the irritation I caused myself over trivial items, my inner emaciation, not understanding the great gift of those who were sent into my life. In general, I got what I deserved. I cannot seem to forgive myself, even if all of them were to forgive me. And even if the conversation dealt only with me, I would willingly find meaning in my life past and the present.

In order to keep the meaning of you retained in a certain positive reflection, in order to do this, it is obvious I need to rise to such heights from which I am still very distant. Every evening after 10 o'clock, I mentally converse with you or recollect our common affairs, or else I dream and try to transcend them. This is obviously a trait of my character.

As far as my health is concerned, in order to evaluate it properly, it is necessary to view it in terms of my previous conditions and then compare. Other than this I can state the following: Since leaving Moscow I no longer use a cane. I can walk for an hour, but then I need to rest. Otherwise, I wear light shoes or slippers as I used to wear when I loved to stroll in the villages in earlier days, but then I was able to go further. As far as my headaches are concerned, those that cause excessive pain last only a short while and now occur about once a year.

I seem to be cold all the time and have lost weight, but the condition of my heart is better. Radiculitis[61] now seldom affects me. I have worn myself out much due to tooth decay, little by little I have lost almost all my teeth. I suffer, as I have always, with insomnia, but staying awake at nights is sometimes inwardly productive.

My memory is now weak, but alongside this, and forgive me please, for having such self-confidence, I undoubtably have become smarter. I still am involved in many things. Obviously, in some other situation a person would devote strength to do his best, so I do the same under these conditions. I am sure you can imagine the best I can do here. If I was to compare the fruits of my activities here with those earlier, these would seem trivial, mundane and even infantile.

A long while back you expressed the desire for me to devote more attention to humor, a region of mine that I have half-discarded. But of course, not under any circumstances will it come to your mind that this is actually possible under the present conditions.

I have read much that is good and interesting, my periphery has somewhat expanded. Almost every day I rest as I play chess or simply have shallow conversation with others. This may seem strange to you, but little by little I am learning how to joke again, I say something stupid and sometimes even laugh. In general I strive to not lose my courage. I sense that I still possess an immense store of inner strength and energy. My wit and depth and even, although this may be paradoxical, a freshness in me has blossomed. And I am convinced that persistence, the endurance of my nature, have considerably increased, more than I expected, even under these conditions and because I have still not discarded hope.

May the Lord be with you. I hug you and kiss you innumerable times and pray for you constantly. What is primary, the most important, is not to lose faith or

---

[61] Daniel calls this spondyloarthrosis in other documents.

become morose. I feel that I could not express what was actually most important, but even then this is impossible to do in words.

Your Daniel.

P.S. That love is eternal is not just a statement.

Based on prison regulations, Daniel could write his next letter to his wife in February or March of the following year. But he did not receive a reply from Alla until 7 months past, in April.

The summer of 1953 was the accomplishment of a certain stage. Two of Daniel's poems were completed: *Leningradski Apocalypse* and *Rukh*. The poetic ensemble of *Russian Gods* was also arranged for the most part, but Daniel still wanted to add one more chapter. Daniel was having a difficult time writing his *Rose of the World*, starting on it and then stopping. He was still unsure if he would ever reach its conclusion. Daniel wondered if enough spirit agencies were revealed to him, and whether he had sufficiently participated in the necessary amount of cosmic cognizance to create such a composition. As he wrote in *Rose of the World*:

> The revelation of spirit agencies consists in of the ability to view these disclosures face to face and discuss them, and not forgetting any of it. Then the journeys, along with my body, which were other-worldly at this time. My *daimon* is here and they see him, although I was the only one initially. The first exposure was at the square in front of the Temple of Christ [the Savior].[62] The practical abilities of knowledge will occur on their own. They were not annihilated and cannot be annihilated, because they are unseen. The pain of my heart will stop with the revelation of the spirit agencies.

---

[62] This was in 1921.

But for a person to have such revelations or visions was not so unusual within the confines of prison walls. Shulgin filled about 100 notebooks with records of his dreams. Shulgin also possessed a mystical composure, but prison painfully altered his psychological stability, causing depression and a withdraw from reality. This increased his susceptibility to listening to voices occurring within himself. It is difficult to say whether this was good or bad.

In was during late autumn of 1953 that Daniel received the exceptional, the culmination of what he was expecting his entire life, with the previous revelations just being an introduction. Daniel recorded this in his diary on February 7, 1954, attempting to codify what occurred and evaluate its content:

> October and November of the previous year [1953] was an extra-ordinary, unprecedented era in my life. But what occurred at this time? Some revelation? A delusion? Insanity? The grandiosity of the revelation was the extent of a global panorama, incomparable, and transcended the capabilities of my faculties, and I think, even my subconscious. But this panorama included a perspective of ages recently passed, and disclosed to me that the role of the subsequent epoch was different than what I previously thought, it was absolutely incompatible with any of my earlier data and any potentials that I envisioned. From the view of a spectator, this might appear at its face value as *mania grandiosa* integrated with religious craziness, except that 2 facts still need to be considered in this evaluation: that I was unable to give total and full credence to the revelations imposed on me due to their colossal significance (even though those suffering with *mania grandiosa* seem to believe all without question); and likewise that the veracity of this information would be affirmed only in the situation if a complete series of prognoses of a general and personal character would be affirmed.

Several months, or at least even a year, had to pass before it was possible for me to ascertain this properly. Several bits and pieces, obviously, were already provided me, and they confirmed for me other predictions that were presented to me and had fulfilled. All of this accompanied a tremendous and incredible encounter – the tangible perception of the close proximity of great brethren from the *Sinklit* of Russia. I am not able to relate their names, but the close proximity of each of them colored in an unrepeatable manner the individual current of feelings: one summoned the strength of the heart's beating, a blessed veneration, fervent love, and his tears flooded the city. Another greeted my entire essence with an inexpressible, kind, warm love, as a precious friend who was able to see me as though penetrating into my soul and loving it and bringing into me his forgiveness and comfort. The appearance of a 3rd summoned my necessity to get on my knees in front of him due to my admiration for him as a great and powerful person standing immeasurably above me, and his close proximity was accompanied by an austere and triumphant sensation. Finally, the close proximity of a 4th was accompanied by the sensation of a joyous happiness enveloping me and tears of ecstasy poured from me. There is much that I can doubt, and much in my inner life that I would approach with skepticism, but not to these encounters.

This period was interrupted by my transfer to another cell. In December, I was consumed by work on this treatise. Part of the information transmitted to me during the month of November entered into it.

In another part of *Rose of the World*, Daniel speaks of those of the *Sinklit* of Russia who accompanied him his entire life and whose presence he always felt.

Did I see them as individuals during the times of these encounters? No. Did they speak with me? Yes. Did I hear their voice? Yes and no. I heard, but not a tangible sound of a voice. It was as if they spoke from somewhere deep in my heart.

So he defined these encounters as being of a spirit nature. The first of them that Daniel met was Seraphim of Saratov, whose icon always accompanied Daniel: during the war in his uniform pocket or on the wall in his prison cell. He appeared to Daniel once in 1933, in the Church of St Vlasia, and Daniel never forgot this vision. We can guess at the 3 others based on their repetitive and positive mention in *Rose of the World*: Feodor Dostoyevski, Mikhail Lermontov and Nikolai Gogol, and since they are mentioned below by their first names.

The revelations of late 1953 then stopped abruptly as he recorded them as inclusions into *Rose of the World*. Daniel was still expecting more and as confirmations of previous spirit visions and journeys. Daniel understood it better later and explained this in *Rose of the World*:

> No matter how unconvincingly this might be declared to the overwhelming majority, still I have no intentions of hiding this fact, that even though they were weak and fragmented, but for me they were conclusive testimonies of bursts from the depths of memory that were disclosed in my life from childhood, and which increased during adolescence and finally during the 47th year of my life[63] began to illuminate the days of my existence with a new light. This does not mean that as though there transpired a complete unfastening of the capacity of my memory's depths, to reach this is still far away in the future, but the significance of the images, from wherever they were given me, became for me so tangibly clear and the images of these occasions were so distinct, that their

---

[63] This would be 1953, the year of Daniel's final series of revelations.

quality and focus distinguished them from regular memory or recollection, and opposed to the tactics of the imagination, they were indisputable.

1954

Daniel recorded the following in his diary, dated February 7, 1954:

A reaction occurred with the beginning of the new year.

The increase of the difficulty of my situation is rooted in the following. The inner connection was severed, and obviously the severance was as much unexpected for that side as it was for me. In any event, I was not forewarned about this. Night time encounters stopped. What was promised to me, which I anguishedly awaited day to day, the revelation of an inner vision and audio, when I will no longer nebulously feel, but will see and hear the great brethren of the spirit agencies, when I will speak with them and when they will lead me into the journey through other strata of the planetary cosmos – this revelation had not yet materialized.

For the verification or refutation of the external foretold periods, just a small amount of time passed. I shout between the sky and ground, not knowing what is occurring with me: what is truth and what is false. I do not understand how I should live and what I should do, what is being prepared for me, how it is being prepared, and what in general is being prepared. If what was foretold to me in autumn is not confirmed, then a genuine chaos will affect my deliberations, meaning, I will not firmly know even the most fundamental matters I need for the creation of *Rose of the World*, its historical role, my mission, my future, my meaning in the realm of literary and religious activism. The disclosure of this great concept that I started will remain just opened, but totally insufficient for preaching, whether written or verbal. So in general, all will just collapse and fall to the wayside. Meanwhile I feel that to deny my mission is not something I can do or want to do. It is better for me to go insane. But to state that it is impossible for me to do this, as long as even one chance in a hundred remains, I will not, because this is definitely my missions and not an illusion. And this chance remains, assuredly, always, and even in the worst of situations. Long ago, yes, long ago, it was not this difficult. What is horrifying is not an external prison, but an internal, a psychological: for the agencies of spirit communication to stop functioning, the absence of this connection with the spirit world, a pathetic limitation of the circle of knowledge.

I have traversed some type of life's seclusion, after which peace and life then became a valuable possession, but only to those under the condition of spiritual vision. Really, in similar circumstances, people in ancient times entered a monastery. And even if I was to have my freedom, and if monasteries still existed, this would not be for me, because my mission is not in departure, but in preaching, in organization. Lord, how my soul fantasizes. The physical drive is the need to clasp my hands, get on my knees in a position of petition, to prostrate myself – but all of this is impossible in the restraints of a prison cell. And especially in solitary confinement! It seems impossible to meet even a shadow of comprehension! Hopeless materialist torpor of those surrounding me, and their self-reliance is worthless! It seems the inevitable is to absolutely be silent about all of this, all that is occurring with me.

Lord, shorten the interlude of this intolerable expectation! Great brethren of the *Sinklit*, provide me a sign! Do not abandon me! I am exhausted from doubt, the unknown, I wander about and thirst. Support me on this road, this terrifying branch of this road, and acerbated double due to my incarceration. Father

Seraphim, open my spiritual eyes. Great brethren: Mikhail, Nikolai and Feodor,[64] open my spiritual audio! Why have my eyes not opened in 3 months? Great brother Vladimir,[65] related brother of Aleksandr,[66] appear to my soul, give me a sign, some kind of a sign.

Daniel continue to record his analysis of the situation in his diary the following day, February 8.

This is the first time over the past 20 years that the necessity has appeared for me to enter notes similar to those of a diary. The reasons for the attempt is the intensification of the inner life into a unity with absolute solitude. Surrounding me are 3 persons [cellmates], but I cannot stop shallow conversation with them. Their profanity does not seem to stop for even one hour, no matter how hard I try. One of the most intense tortures of prison is the absence of solitude. To read after 5 o'clock in the afternoon is almost impossible due to the lack of sunlight. The illumination inside for any pursuits or just plain meditation, if even for a somewhat nebulous daydream, is impossible when you have 3 people chattering in your ears at their full voices, if not about the poor toilet paper, then about the prison women who distribute food, whom we see on occasion through the kitchen, or about packages not delivered, or about something worse, like illnesses that are half-way real and half-way imagined. Nothing remains to be done during these hours except to plug into this transfusion from the vain to the stupid, striving to at least route it if at all possible to some kind of verbal communication, something that intelligent people might do. The result is the same, all these efforts are worthless at face value,

---

[64] No doubt referring to Feodor Dostoyevski, Mikhail Lermontov and Nikolai Gogol.
[65] Probably Vladimir Solovyov.
[66] Could refer to his cousin Aleksandr Dobrov, or the brothers Vladimir and Aleksandr Lenin-Ulyanov.

and I almost never complain, having learned whining does nothing for me internally or externally, and so I do not become morose.

Right now my difficulties are doubled due to 2 circumstances. First, my creative period is ending, that which begin in 1949. I am exhausted from the concentration and effort on *Russian Gods*, but do not think I will complete it. It is possible that a pressure is coming from *Buistvich*, but this will summon the most horrifying pressure and alarm.

In one respect, the *Buistvich* was similar to the situation of the inmates surrounding Daniel in prison. This is the 4th stratum of the purgatories, where the decay of living inmates is occurring, as though they reside in a spiritual lethargy, and their torment consists of a repulsion toward themselves as a result of their situation, having accomplished nothing at all during their life. It is apparent that another bout of depression was now affecting Daniel, something he would deal with about once a year.

A letter arrived from Yulia Gavrilovna that same day, letting him know about the start of intervention on behalf of daughter Alla and the need from his side to also write petitions for a review of the matter. Yulia believed that his intervention would also be a benefit. Daniel's reaction was that of irritation, since nothing regarding any effort on behalf of his release was mentioned. It was apparent the animosity of the Bruzhes prevailed against him, still considering Daniel the source of all their daughter Alla's troubles.

Daniel recorded in his diary the following on February 9:

Yesterday a letter caused the situation to become complex, and expressed in very strong terms. That which she wants and demands proceeds at a tangent from my wants and intentions, and likewise is contrary to my personal attitudes that are essentially indispensable to me in the interests of *Rose of the World*. However I reflected on the contents of this letter, and it still had a bad effect on my soul. I have suffered, but not just I, but the lives of many people in a long series have been shattered.

Undoubtedly, she and he are the sole people that have this inner right, to the extent it is strong and unquestionable, and I cannot just walk right passed them. In the final end, much, if not all, depends on the future progress of matters over the course of the next month. Until March 10, I will not occupy myself with anything. Today my hopes have increased in the resolution of the problem on its own with the present progress of matters. If this occurs no later than April, this will signify a justification, and a confirmation of the accuracy of the basic affirmations that I have received. O, if just all of *Night Wanderers* could have survived.

As difficult as Daniel's statements are to understand, he is reacting to the extremely slow release of prisoners and review of the accusations and proceedings with depression affecting him as a result of the circumstances, and having no one to help him. All his family is gone, either in France or died or in prison themselves for the same matter, and this is agonizing for Daniel, and there is nothing he can do but wait with artificial deadlines that mean nothing anyway, and vent his frustration over the manner events have transpired and completely out of his control.

The subsequent entry is dated April 18, the Sunday before Easter Sunday:

Yesterday I ended up having to interrupt working on my treatise, I was just mentally dead. Of course, I did do a lot on it, but 99 chances of a 100 is that this one will also perish. I plan to memorize *Iron Mystery* and any others I can. My depression is overwhelming and my surroundings are worsening it. These people are so mechanical, so materialistic, satisfied with their torpid state. They are suffocating mundane and squalid minds to the point I feel I am being strangled, and as though living in a grave.

So far over the 5-1/2 years here, not once did I complain about this prolonged term in such a wailing solitude. And these people suffer as a result of their conceit. Every minute.

Sometimes at night, when I remember my past, I see how stupid I conducted myself in a thousand menial items, and particularly stupidity and the most ordinary of stupidity. But in the large picture, I just plain do not see it, but looking at life from the sidelines, all of it becomes so clear. Pertaining to the trivialities of life, I was unquestionably stupid, and even disregarding the entire grandiosity of *Russian Gods*, *Night Wanderers*, and others. Otherwise, the fact is this, that I am slowly reflecting. There needs to be some subtle intuition, like an X, or something widely universal, like a Z, to ascertain all of this and with meaning something.

Although Daniel was surrounded by inmates, it was a new group after he was moved from his intellectual associates, and as a result he felt himself isolated from all of them and residing in a world of his own, and one with which they could not identify or even knew existed. So Daniel was on the verge of a mental breakdown now, so many items all converging upon him at one time, and he was crying out internally with no one able to listen or even know what was occurring with him. Under such a mental state, the menial mistakes of his earlier life were resurrecting and being inflated and so haunting him. He realizes they were small and mundane, and so seeks help to place it all in its proper perspective, so not to further irritate him, allowing him to proceed to more important matters.

Daniel's hope on the progress of matters was justified in part. Gradually the prison regimen became better. A set time was defined for strolls about the prison yard, rather than just at some arbitrary hour at the whim of guards, and often in the middle of the night. The grating over the windows were removed, allowing more sunlight to enter the cells, and in some cells the inmates could actually look through the windows and see the outside world. In September, the striped prison uniform was exchanged for a dark-blue, and they were issued new pants and jackets.

Rakov wrote a new petition on May 2, now addressed to Kliment Voroshilov, the Chairman of the Supreme Soviet, and then he was unexpectedly released on May 15.

On May 19, legislation was announced for procedures to review the sentences of all those who were convicted for political crimes or contra-revolutionary activities. That May, the commission created for this purpose began its review. Persons who were obviously convicted based on fabricated evidence, or sentenced by the OSO, were immediately released from the labor camps. The justice was a triumph, but so far it only pertained to selected individuals, and partial, and slow. The system that was accustomed to convict and sentence took a back seat and, it seems, just waited. Those who were sentenced along with Daniel also started to cry for justice. Shelyakin, who was completing his term at the Mineralski labor camp, wrote in May to some prosecutor, informing him of the injustice, that just because one of the characters in Daniel's novel could be described as a terrorist, his only involvement was listening to this chapter as Daniel read it to him and others. The interrogators then counted him as an accomplice to a fictional character and sentenced him to 25 years. Shelyakin begged this prosecutor to review the facts of the case and such a severe term when no crime or even any association with any criminal activity was evident.

But the prosecutors assigned to review these many cases were in no hurry.

Daniel became friends with a new inmate assigned to his cell, Pyotr Vlasovich Nikolaichuk. He organized and participated in a prisoners' riot at the Norilski labor camp in Siberia, demanding better conditions under the new regime, and so was sentenced to 10 years in a high security prison. Nikolaichuk arrived at Vladimir at the beginning of 1954, and was assigned to the same cell with Daniel.

Sometime in April, Daniel received his first letter directly from Alla:

> Danik, my beloved! So many years I have awaited your letter, and my expectation was fulfilled, and I saw you exactly in the same manner as I prayed you would be. Be calm, I have traversed a difficult and complex route, and right now I am also the same as you would want to see me, dreaming about me, I know this. I do not want to remember right now the bad that occurred, what occurred over the road I have traversed. I have paid for it, am paying, and will pay.[67] Do not torment yourself by remembering the years lost due to this situation, ignore my role also. Our past life should not contain any dark blemish at all for our future. The two of us possess such profound faith and mental strength.

Daniel took advantage of the new freedom to write letters to Alla. He wrote sometime in July:

> My memories of our previous life together are cloudless, and I always feel you to be my support, my protection and my calm. I am afraid that we were only guilty of being in love with one another too much, that we were egoistic too much. It seems to me that right now I love you in an intelligent manner, better and even stronger.
>
> There is nothing more to say about the pain that I have fully endured, and some of which has also fallen upon you. You know this yourself, and even then, this cannot be expressed in words. But secure faith resided in you and this was the basis of what supported me. But there is one matter that does not provide me rest to this time, it is the thought of the reserve of your purely

---

[67] Alla feels she was responsible for a lot of Daniel's suffering due to her statements during interrogation.

physical strength, of your health. You have hardly at all written to me of this facet of your life and I need to say that this contributes little to help calm me. I ask of you, my green willow tree leaf, do not avoid this topic in the future.

Something did occur that was new in my life. May 15 became a holiday for me. I received from your mother a majestic and beautiful gift: a Hindi-Russian dictionary of 33,000 words. I jumped in celebration as though insane. I discarded all my other involvements and for 1-1/2 months I did not raise my head from this well of wisdom. You can understand that involvement in any language other that this one could not exude as much joy and appreciation, and could not drive me to a speed as fast as this. During this time I first concentrated on learning the transliteration of letters and words, and surprisingly I was able to easily express its terms and able to sufficiently adapt to it. Even then, some of the letters seem to skip over each other, and are not pronounced in the place where they should be, suddenly they lose a foot or tail, and the other letters like squiggles are intertwined with other letters, and then are suddenly abbreviated. Such a combination of parts of several letters is called typographic ligature, and there are hundreds of these ligatures in this language. But all of this possesses its unique attraction, the script is amazingly ornamental and to draw these letters is just a pleasure in itself.

Second, I copied over 2,000 words that I need to learn as the first series, and learn them by repetition. Third, I started to familiarize myself with short grammatical phrases that are attached to the dictionary as an appendix. However, because this section is brief, it has caused more questions for me than provided any answers. Meanwhile, the especially vague part is the system of pronunciation, meaning, where the accent goes on each word. I am afraid that some Hindu will hear me pronounce something and will laugh so hard he will get cramps.

But one way or another during this year, if there are no changes otherwise here, I will at least acquire fluency in a few thousand words and learn the written language properly, and this will be a foundation, or better said, a foothold to proceed to advancement in Hindi. All the fictional literature, and especially poetry, in this language is truly beyond visualization. And I hope that even a bad ending will result in time with me acquiring sufficient knowledge to apply this to translating their poetry.

As a person who enjoys sunshine, and which always provided him mental exuberance, the summer sun flooded the courtyard of their daily strolls, warming the cement floor. So did his letter end with the passage of his enthusiastic mood, but the depressive environment still had a negative effect on Daniel:

I am so immensely grateful for the regular worries of your mother. The environment has provided me warmth, some amount of heart and it helps me overcome this suffocating feeling. Such contributes to my mental energy, but it will again exhaust. As far as the physical is concerned, it is difficult for me to state anything positive.

A few times this year I was able to see the tops of the trees, even though for just a few seconds from a distance. This boredom is especially torturous for me during the summer season, only God knows what this will lead to, sometimes I cry into my pillow late into the night. I am only confessing my weakness to you.

With infantile excitement Daniel undertook learning Hindi by studying the dictionary, and he could only have done this in an environment of isolation, like in prison. It was Daniel's primal love of India that served as the impetus. His next letter to Alla was in autumn that year:

> My *pri'ya* (in Hindi this means – beloved), *r'ee* (dear), *lallee-ee* (girl, daughter)!
>
> It seems to me that learning Hindi is better, now that I am able to do it. You do see in newspapers, the speed and extent that our cultural association is developing with India. I am ready to climb on the wall to see Indian movies. There is a trend presently of the translation of hundreds of fictional compositions, and poetry among them. So will not learning this language, besides anything else, provide us some concrete and practical benefit? But the shortcoming is that if I learn this language sufficiently by the time we meet again, then what remains is to deeply improve on it and polish it, but this is very doubtful. But what is still not understandable is how I can apply such knowledge to some city center where no publishing facilities even exist. One way or another I strive to cross over this bridge when I come to it.
>
> By now I have learned about 2,000 words, although I fear this is not a very substantial amount, and I am now involved in reading and especially writing. Since all I have is just a dictionary, this is what I do: I close my list of Hindi words, and then I take my list of Russian words, and write the same word in Hindi next to it. Since I have no other means of learning this is my only choice. The orthography is monstrously strange, I have to admit. If somebody can send me a grammar book and a reader of elementary text, my education will proceed even better.

The rain during autumn that year however made matters worse. In Daniel's subsequent letter to Alla he meticulously and aggressively deals with health issues. Having been raised in the family of a doctor, his concern was apparent, and he was not shy to inform Alla of his illnesses, and especially those caused due to the pressure from interrogations and residence in prison. So Daniel wrote his subsequent letter in late 1954:

> I will leave off the formalities. I have pains in my head, anguish due to my teeth and wearing this prosthesis,[68] occasionally I have an very rapid heart rate, some problems with trying to focus with my sight, and now something new that is affecting me: hemorrhoids (but do not get bitter or annoyed at this, dear one, since Alexander of Macedonia likewise could not escape the same). There are 3 other maladies that are more or less serious that I deal with: radiculitis, gastritis, and manic-depressive psychosis. During the previous year the radiculitis decided to expand to new areas and it seems that for no reason at all, these sharp pains appeared in the calves of my legs and in my groin and other places. Quartz light and infrared light and some other treatments have tied the hooligan and forced him into his burrow, my lower back. In this regard, I have felt much better since July, and better now since 1946.[69] I am able to walk without getting tired about 6 to 8 miles, and of course, only bare-footed.
>
> I am grateful for the excellent packages and as a result I have already gained some weight, and undoubtedly, I weigh more now than I did 8 years ago. Among other things, all of this motivates my mental faculties.
>
> The second is gastritis. This souvenir of fate unexpectedly erupted within me this summer. They are exerting effort to heal me, but whether they will be successful to completely liquidate this malady, it is still too early to guess.
>
> And finally your old friend, my manic-depressive psychosis. I did suffer bouts of depression in 1950, but

---

[68] This is his back brace.
[69] Meaning, just before he was arrested in 1947.

they were not heavy, and all passed without me taking any special measures. But this year it was very bad. Right now I am forced into a condition that is ideal for me to struggle and overcome depression. Other than this, I struggle with my neurotic and psychological oppression using tested methods, those that have helped me in all such similar situations: physical exercise and especially walking barefooted. You know my primal instinctive repulsion toward shoes, which I have had since childhood, and such habits that I developed while still a child. And now as an adult, it was with a good reason that I have so far walked thousands, if not tens of thousands, of kilometers, step by step bare footed through the Bryansk forests, Crimea, Ukraine, and other marvelous places.

I can fully and tangibly sense how the surface of the ground exudes some kind of emanation that penetrates through the bare soles and into my torso, and instilling into it, and especially into my nervous system, a beneficial and healing effect. I am not aware of any work in progress right now with specialists dealing with the emanations of nature, and the use of such emanations in medicinal treatments. But myself, due to my personal experience, I know its effective power as though no better exists. Meanwhile, for me it is undoubtable, and no matter how strange this may seem, that to walk barefoot upon the cold ground has an especially intensive effect, but of course, only if a person is adapted to it. However now I experience this beneficially healthy effect from this emanation [of nature] more now than I did earlier.

When in my cell and for a long while now, I have not worn shoes the year round. I enjoy the invigorating coolness of the cement floor. For some reason, not wearing shoes has also caused my grippe to go away, and this affected me earlier about 3 or 4 times every winter. Now I take my strolls barefooted and each time feel such a flood of vigilance, energy, and exuberance, as if I have now become a different person. After my stroll, I am able to further study my Hindi with double exertion for 4 to 5 hours straight.

I have firmly decided that once I gain my freedom I will subject myself to the torture of wearing shoes only in the most extreme of circumstances, and no matter how much others will misunderstand or ridicule me when they first see me.

Daniel eventually had to fight for the right to walk barefoot. Ending up in the prison hospital due to depression, and receiving a prohibition to stroll barefooted, he wrote a petition to the prison warden. His nervous condition is obvious in his petition:

My petition to you possesses an unusual character. So in order for it to be correctly understood, I am forced to explain the entire matter in detail.

My life was oriented such that during childhood, and as an adult, I became accustomed to walking barefoot most of the time. I always suffered dryness in the skin of my soles. I always hated shoes and rarely did I wear any, except during the winter frost or for especially official engagements.

I walk the year round in my cell in prison barefooted, and outside during summer during my strolls.

At the present time I am in the prison hospital in an isolation cell, where I was placed as a result of ... due to a relapse of my neuro-psychological disorder. It is characterized by a feeling of depression, a repulsion toward association with others, fear of loud noise, and so on.

Long before I was incarcerated, I was convinced that walking barefoot, and especially in cold weather, had a beneficial affect on me, not only in the sense of cooling my entire body as an organism, but in the sense of improving the general state of my mental faculties. Now after my strolls, I return to my cell as literally another person, having experienced a flood of vigilance and energy, and subsequently I am able to routinely attend to tasks for several hours.

However right now this rule is now imposed to force me to stroll wearing shoes because it is no longer summertime. But I am no longer a child! At my age and maturity, I should be able to decide on my own what is harmful to me and what is beneficial to me. At first glance this question may seem trivial to you, but for me it has great meaning, as it applies to my physical and psychological and neurological conditions.

I turn to you with a convincing request to release me from wearing shoes, and to allow me to decide whether I should use them, and whenever I should feel the need.

Walking barefoot was obviously just a panacea for Daniel and because, understandably, he was barefoot when he received all the original revelations that would be included in *Rose of the World*. Daniel even contemplated how he would walk about Moscow streets barefooted, and somehow not annoy any other pedestrians. But Moscow is not Madras, where almost everybody walks about barefooted. But Daniel in this one respect seems to live in the past, in his previous incarnation in India, where he no doubt did walk barefooted all his life. So it was easy for him to apply at least this area to the present.

Hope for a review of the criminal matter and Daniel's eventually release seemed to be in sight, and in a letter with Alla they defined their future in more distinct terms. Yet, it was not separate from the past and the present. Alla wrote to Daniel:

I fear very much the feeling of guilt that you retain in regard to all those who suffered as a result this matter. I already wrote to you, my dear, that there were no adolescents or mentally retarded among us. All that occurred, occurred logically and could not have been otherwise. What meaning is there by being offended by history and seek the guilty party in some catastrophe that would have occurred anyway. I fear your feelings of guilt toward your friends because they can interfere with your health and tranquility, and interfere with an ability to ascertain the future properly, and perhaps even the life that is beyond this life.

But Daniel did not want to just brush aside any of his previous associates, be did not want to deny his guilt or responsibility toward those who innocently became part of the alleged conspiracy. As Daniel wrote to Alla:

My attitude toward my previous friends remains as it was in the past, and how could they have changed anything anyways? They are not at all the ones to have been blamed. It is another matter that I do not forgive myself for certain matters, just as would any other person who would be standing in my place and with just a milligram of conscious. I have meditated and re-meditated on this a thousand times. And although many parts are still unclear to me, and some of which can only be explained with face to face meetings, but the very fact of my guilt in regard to several of them is clear like day. And if in the future I will have some success in meeting with them (and if they do not just have the intent to tell me to go to hell because of this matter, and then acquire a great satisfaction should this actually be possible in happening), this will be of some help. I might even be able to help Shura [Dobrova] and Aleksandr [Kovalenski]. I cannot imagine their attitude toward me right now, even if they are alive, or would even want my help in the size of a mustard seed.

What can be resolved or even imagined ahead of time? Our individual capabilities have been much severed from reality and will be much declined. I fear, for example, that during this initial period, it is not us who will be able to help those older, but the opposite.[70] And no matter how possessed I may be as a result of such thinking, just any plain and stable thought will verify its correctness. It is another matter as to when we will be supported, but then, how long and how will we be supported?

But I do still retain some pride, Alla, and I imagine myself as a 50-year old chick, whose painstaking parents are shoving worms into my beaks every minute. Is there any enthusiasm to be gained with such an allegory, tell me please?

Also thank [your parents] for their marvelous packages and money.

Alla's parents continued to intervene. Mother Yulia continued to write letters to both Alla and Daniel, nervously explaining her efforts in providing new information to the judicial institutions and state agencies that were involved in the alleged conspiracy, but her letters pertained only to Alla. Daniel wrote to Alla's parents in response:

I wrote my first petition and mailed it. I plan for a second one after the [Christmas] holiday and will send it to [Kliment] Boroshilov, the Chairman of the Supreme Soviet, as one person advised. But I still think that the matter will be investigated even without these petitions, the question is a matter of time. What is important is the result of all the petitions and review of the matter. Will it implement a quick release? And this is what I think. Or to shortening the sentence under the conditions of residence as confinement is at present, or to shorten the sentence and also ameliorate the poor conditions at the labor camp. I have to admit that these latter options seem to me the least attractive. Until that time, I cannot

---

[70] Referring to Alla's elderly parents helping the 2 of them, who are younger.

return in any way to a normal life and I have no ability of going anywhere at all until the matter is settled.

Daniel was more afraid of being transferred to a labor camp as the result of a rejection of his claim. It was easy for the agency to change the terms of his sentence. He felt he would not be able to complete *Rose of the World* at a labor camp, and so had to remain at Vladimir prison, plus with all of his maladies, life would be completely intolerable at a labor camp. It was impossible for Daniel to explain this to his in-laws, who were only worried about Alla's release. In the same letter to Alla's parents, Daniel requested some items to be sent to him:

> The matter is that certain items have not been able to endure the test of time so far in my incarceration. Particularly my shirts are no longer repairable. Other than this, in case I should be transferred elsewhere, even in the event of movement out of this place somewhere else even local, I will now be in an desperate situation as though locked in a box. For this reason I ask you, if you can, to send me the following items:
> 1. A few of some kind of plain or sateen shirts, for example, pull-overs, and the color does not matter, as long as they are not expensive.
> 2. A large strong bag with pockets sewn into them, similar to a knapsack, but without any metal parts.
> 3. A pair of small purses, for crackers, sugar cubes, and stuff like that.
> 4. A brush, something plain, and one that is firm.
>
> For the time being, I do not need anything more. Excess items just tend to make life more complex for me.

On November 10, 1954, Daniel wrote a petition to Comrade Malenkov, the Premier of the USSR. As Daniel informed Alla of the letter:

I expounded all that was significant in detail and it was rather verbose, much more than the first petition. More than all I worry about its precision and its absolute accuracy. But I am content with it. Now I will very calmly await a decision, knowing that the agency, upon which all depends, has this request regarding our matter and all has been explained in a proper order and manner.

But the honesty of Daniel would hardly be considered as beneficial to his cause of release. Such detailed explanations would only cause his release and rehabilitation to become more complex, because it was exactly for such open information admitted by suspects that they were sentenced. Later Daniel recorded in his diary:

My malicious attitude toward the Soviet system has as its basis the denial of not only the economic side of this system, as much as the political and cultural. In part, I do not see genuine democratic freedoms in our country and, alas, my personal destiny has confirmed this. So now, as it was earlier, my attitude toward Soviet authority depends on that level of freedom of writing, the press, assembly, religious activity, to the extent that Soviet authority factually permits it, and not just in announcements, but in its materialization. A person will not be convinced of the existence in our country of original, guaranteed, democratic freedoms, and I right now cannot rise to a position of full and unconditional acceptance of the Soviet stratum. It is indispensable for me to point at this circumstance directly, so there would not appear some erroneous understanding of my political convictions in these agencies that will investigate my matter.

At the beginning of December, Daniel was overcoming his depression and was able to write his next letter to Alla.

You are agitated over my health for completely no reason at all. Some of these unimportant maladies that affected me from May to October have conclusively ended. My brain is still sluggish and often seems vacant, but I am incomparably more tranquil. I have not attained to my previous capability of normal work, but my strength is returning to me.

Although he says this to comfort Alla, he spent that entire year of 1953 in nervous tension, writing difficulty, and felt his efforts to be fruitless. His petition to Malenkov did not help any.

In December, Daniel's health failed acutely and he was diagnosed with anthrax. On December 30, 1954, Daniel was moved from cell 49 to the hospital wing, cell 52.

1955

So did Daniel greet 1955, and he wrote to Alla, but avoiding mention of his latest medical diagnosis, so not to scare her:

My beautiful little flower, my spring patch of green grass, my happy summer breeze! The snow that quietly descends on the white Christmas ground! Incidental circumstances, although in essence do not have much significance, have restrained this letter. But only with the New Year, and even with Christmas Eve, I am only able now with this opportunity to congratulate you.

I do not plan to deal with superficial items in this letter. However, I am still somewhat affected by grippe with the winter, and I write this letter while lying down and with considerable effort.

We have not spoken to each other in many years. Letters are almost nothing, these are scattered fragments deprived of any ties. It is natural that much in my condition and views may seem strange to you, and you are inclined to supplement the empty spots with your personal contemplations about your Daniel, the one to whom you were last close 8 years ago. Then a series of mistakes occurred.

My invaluable friend. I could never express in words the anguish I endure to be close to you. And no matter if any doubt exists in any of this, you and I will search and discover an arrangement for our life together, one that is compatible to both of us. This is humorous to me. But you know that I belong to that category of humans where there lives a certain something in the depths of my character, and which resides from cradle to grave, something higher that defines for them the value of life's revelations, a categorical director of life's imperative goals and obligations.

This is the reason many of these applicable facts summon from my side another reaction, different than yours, but not owing to accidental mistakes, illusions, whims; but only because I am I. Consider also that my life has been halved. You for example write, "If we should exit this situation with a hard and austere adjustment to life, we will still live." Yes, but not at all do all arrangements of life possess an unconditional worth and meaning,. Yet they pertained to me when I was 20 years old, and will at 50 years old, and will if fate should allow me to live to 70 years. So these [arrangements] do pertain to me, since I have the possibility to directly or indirectly work for a good benefit, and I consider this to be my obligation and activity, and meaning and justification of my life. If a prolonged period should arrive, when all becomes dampened and suppressed due to my simple struggle for existence, I cannot look at this in any other manner except for years lost. Lost, true, and for the sake of extending myself toward other matters, although they may have absolutely no autonomous worth to me personally. But right now I take into account every year and even month: do not forget that I am almost 10 years your senior.

This one thing is sufficient for me, that I prefer to remain here where I am now, and if this should depend on me, and for several more years. Here I am not able to speak even on item not true, or even make a motion. Here I cannot disdain myself. I can, however in part, do in general what it is I live for. I will expend all I have in my struggle towards growth, although I will acquire such great joy, as life with you. Understand me! Do not condemn me! You are my gold. My heart is filled with such feelings, and my mind with such thoughts, and the kind that I could only transmit to you through an extra-sensory route.

Meditating on some of the items mentioned in previous letters have, pathetically, created a certain image of my bewilderment of life. Not really a bewilderment, but a defined angle of view, and which has been over defined. I do not know if I was able to sufficiently convey this understanding to you. In any event, the ideal genuine person remains for me as alien as a person from Mars. But progress of time does not stand still. I believe that I will live to the days when there will no longer be any need to struggle for growth. I would want our destinies particularly to unite us during these days. I would want to exit here and under the wide sky and go where my heart, my beliefs and my talent, will lead me.

At the beginning of February, Daniel recovered from the effects of anthrax, and he gradually returned to his normal routine, but still in the hospital ward. The indispensability of his completion of that project, one in which he had no doubt, and to which he felt he was predestined, supported him.

Daniel later wrote again to Alla:

Winter was very mild for us this year. Even the thaw has come early. But thaw in the middle of the winter season will benefit the destitute. Now by the way, this is already past, and winter has grasped the region with greater strength. This was to be expected. Have you read Ehrenburg?[71] He deserves much credit and praise for his work. Being in his situation we can find a retrospection of life's realties. He is faithful to himself and courageously carries the cross of the repercussions of his novel. The immense majority do not even suspect the existence of such phenomenon.

But I have some bad luck. If not one thing, it is another. Right now I lie flat due to lumbago. I write in a most uncomfortable position, and wearing a karakul.

Do not anguish over me. All will conclude fine. I am assured of it. But for something to end well does not mean that there will not be any more upsets. If the planetary cosmos did not present itself as a system of variously significant, multi-dimension worlds, from the global *Salvaterra* to the lucifuric anti-cosmos, and if the route of the monads did not penetrate them as high as can be, to the levels of the demiurges of the galaxy and even higher, to the very sun of the world – then there would be room for despair.

Over the several recent years I have encountered something immense in this direction. And what remains for me as a special joy is just this, that I have found for some of them a manner of expressing them. It is strange, not similar to anything at all, but it seems, it is well directed without missing the goal. When this unproductive year ends, which actually started the previous autumn, I will return to working on my final project.

---

[71] Ilya Ehrenburg wrote a book named, *The Thaw*, about conditions in the USSR under Nikita Khrushchev, just published.

Annoying thoughts about the future did not help Daniel with any hopes about leaving prison. Alla's parents, hearing of amnesties, of the liberation of prisoners, continued to write petitions to whomever they could possibly. Alla's father Aleksandr Bruzhes was now in a better mood. But Daniel was not enthused about the so-called thaw. After his letter to Malenkov, he turned to Khrushchev in February. Alla responded to Daniel's efforts:

> It seems the matter is being reviewed, obviously, in its entirety, that is, it concerns you as much as it concerns me. If you have the freedom to write an unlimited number of official letters, then consider the following: the chief military prosecutor, Major [Mikhail] Tarasov, has a big reason to write to the CC, there they know about our matter: Secretary of the CC of the CP of the USSR [Mikhail] Suslov, and also [Ivan] Dedov in the administrative department of the CC. Today I wrote small petitions to the first 2, and in a few days I will write to the 3rd. I little understand why you would write particularly to Khrushchev, but this is not a bad idea either.
>
> Does Aleksandr Petrovich have any basis for his optimist conclusions? Are they based on observations or just on his imaginations? Or has he actually received some information?
>
> There are no replies to any of my petitions that I sent to the capital city. I have not received anything at all, and I do not even have information about the status of any of my petitions, and so far 4 months have already passed.

From his cell in the prison hospital, Daniel returned to his previous cell on March 12. Anthrax somehow also affected Daniel's psyche or mystic nature, and he no longer received revelatory visions of other worlds or traversed journeys into the spirit cosmos as he did in the past. This connection with the spirit realms seemed to now end.

While Daniel was in the hospital Zea Rakhim moved into the same cell, with whom Daniel sat earlier in various cells. This did make Daniel feel somewhat better.

At the beginning of April, Daniel wrote to Alla:

> Now I again started, obviously, a new stretch. My health is excellent. Second, the period of my unproductiveness has finally ended, which lasted over a year. This stimulates me also to proceed on this pencil-written manuscript that I hold in my hands, and which I had not seen for several years and ¾ forgot about. And 3rd, a person who was earlier close to me, whom I mentioned to you before, and whose association was very important and valuable to me, is now with me. This is for me a great blessing.
>
> Except for a short while when I was lying flat due to my heart problem or due to lumbago, I walked barefooted the entire winter. I walk of course, and only during a strong freeze do I wear any slippers to cover my bare feet, and this is about half of the time when I stroll. The effect of this, and especially walking directly upon the fresh fallen snow, is that it has a strikingly beneficial affect on my health. It even benefits my heart problem.
>
> I still do not have sufficient time for all that I do: my literary endeavors, Hindi study, some time to stroll, a short rest playing chess, and the day is gone. I lie for 2 or 3 hours unable to sleep, but even then, this time is very productive.

The Hindi-Russian dictionary resurrected the Indian part of his soul. What also inspired Daniel was that more and more Soviet newspapers were carrying articles on India. He wrote to Alla's parents to send him a few books: a Hindi grammar and a couple of books on the history and philosophy of India. Having recovered from his anthrax, he again dedicated his study to learning the language.

Shortly after he did receive from his in-laws a book titled *Introduction to Hindu Philosophy*, and he wrote to Alla, sharing his enthusiasm over it:

> The book is written in a clear precise language, objective and very detailed. So far I have studied the introduction, streamed through the enjoyable system of carvaka,[72] a style of materialism that seems to be similar in part with Epicureanism, but more coarse, studied the amazing philosophy of Jainism, and especially its attitude toward ethics. Among other items, Jainism possesses the following meaning:
>
>> "Prosperity is an external shelter of life, and to violate the prosperity of another means to create damage to life. Without prosperity in one or another form, human life is impossible, so then a person's deprivation of prosperity factually materializes as the deprivation of his essential conditions upon which depend his life and spiritual development."
>
> Now I am migrating to the philosophy of Buddhism. All of this I have studied earlier, between 1930 and 1935. But at the time I was utilizing it for the most part on my work dealing with the history of religion, but I am delving into depth with it as compared to what I did earlier, I find conflicts with my earlier studies. But ahead of me is still 6 orthodox philosophic systems of Hinduism: yoga, Vedanta, and others. You cannot believe what a pleasure this it.

Daniel's in-laws sent him additional books on India and especially now with the thaw in international relations between

---

[72] Also known as Lokayata.

the USSR and India more was available: *History of India* by Arunodai Sinkx and Victor Banardji; *Opening of India* by Jawaharlal Nehru; Tagor's Indian folk stories; *Diary of a Journey into India and Burma* by Ivan Minaev; some reproductions of photographs by Soviet artists who visited India. Daniel was enthused like a child upon receiving all these books.

Daniel highly valued Nehru's book and stated the following in his next letter to Alla:

> He is one-sided, rational, condescends to scientific facts, and he does not incline toward emphasizing his personal ideology. But on every page a tremendous culture is felt, the width and maturity of the scale of his personality. What is primary is that he is a beautiful person, a humanist in the genuine sense of the word, and his merits on behalf of India are colossal. He is a brilliant person.
>
> India is intimately so close to me, like no other country, except obviously Russia.

The unexpected return of some of his old notebooks that were previously confiscated during searches for contraband gave Daniel some hope and motivated some optimism in him. He told Alla his feeling that the subsequent year of 1956 would bring a tremendous burst of productivity in his literary efforts now with more freedom in writing. That perhaps *Night Wanderers'* manuscript did survive, and that it was not actually cremated, also stimulated hope in Daniel. He even began to meditate on creating a new revision, considering introducing 2 more characters and several chapters. But this was just a fantasy because the manuscript was definitely destroyed.

In his letter in October to Alla, Daniel sent the beginning of his new poem *Navna*. This is the name of the conciliar soul of the Russian supra-nation. According to the concepts of ROSE OF THE WORLD, every supra-nation possesses its bright guiding demiurge – with Russia this is *Yarosvet* – and its bright conciliar soul. It is one of the manifestations of the eternal Womanhood in its historical process. The name *Navna* was just arbitrary, but its existence is a reality. *Navna* as Daniel explained it:

> It is what unites Russians into one nation; what summons and draws the separate Russian souls higher and higher; what motivates Russian art with an unique fragrance; what hovers over the most immaculate and supreme figures of Russian tales, literature and music; what causes a nostalgia of refinement to be born in Russian souls; what causes Russia to possess a predestined obligation.

Navna is the soul of the Russian people languishing under the authority of despotism, and soon to be liberated when ROSE OF THE WORLD triumphs. But meanwhile it is the prisoner of the *Zhrugrs* in *Druekkarg*, the residence of the Russian anti-humanity. Its liberation is the goal of Russian meta-history. Daniel as the author of *Navna*, dreams of this occasion, but nowhere in the poem does Daniel mention any visions, but his subject is the progress of Russian history in a poetic form culminating in its destiny.

Daniel wrote to Alla:

> Let me describe it this way. What I present is not realism, but reality. This is not a play on words. True I do make mistakes on occasion, in my lines and more. I could also be mistaken here, but I do not insist on the possession of the gift of predictions. I am only convinced that I am not mistaken pertaining to the spirit side of certain revelations and processes and their direction. Every person has a specialty, a something in which they specialize. Mine is meta-history.
>
> All of this can be arranged in a manner that is totally sorrowful for you, but this will not in the least shake my attitude to such things, because they are based not on what is good or bad for you or me, but on a higher

objective reality. This is why I state that such an ideology is a reality.

Now able to write one letter a month, Daniel austerely wrote to Alla at the beginning of each month for all of 1955, except for May and July when he wrote to her parents regarding books on India and thanking them for their regular stipend.

Alla received Daniel's poetry from prison, read them, but could not decipher a lot of it. She was used to the poetry he wrote in earlier years and was still unaware of the extent of his visions and revelations pertaining to other worlds and other levels of the universe, or spirits and demons, and the other spirit entities of the other side, the realm of spirit. Alla was still not totally familiar with Daniel's meta-historical concepts and his mystic cosmos and this puzzled her. These bewildering names, terms, and even the subject matter was infused with new meanings that were beyond her ability to grasp.

Reading the introduction and start of *Navna*, she hurried to comment:

> Pronouncing the words and the originality of the context is just a marvel. It is plainly majestic beauty and totally an item of your essence. But why and where did you get these names, which you could not have known, and I do not understand. And these names and likewise the lines, such as:
>> The *stikhials* sing lullabies to the cosmos of the tangible stratum.
>
> And the entire composition, as I can fathom it, is a genuine mixture of immense and incomprehensible fiction combined with things of questionable existence.

Daniel responded.

> What can I say in regard to your thoughts about simplicity? The question is complex and impossible to explain in the manner you asked it. I will limit myself to

the following. You are right and you are wrong about my views. The matter I can explain this way: It does not enter the head of someone to demand of mathematics that he should manage the theory of relativity or vectorial analysis in a manner understandable to someone in just the 5th grade. Art likewise has its vectorial analysis. What is primary is that the task, at face value, is unprecedented, and so it is necessary to present it at least in general characteristics, in order to ascertain it in stages of simplification. Certain of my phrases can unpleasantly resonate, and you will notice in them signs of a strange self-assurance, an arrogance that is out of place.

Unfortunately this bewilderment is inevitable, and I cannot find means to convince you through such letters, that this is not entirely self-assurance, but something that is qualitatively and principally something else. Never before 1947, did I have such a modest opinion of myself as an individual as I do now.

Just wait awhile to judge *Navna*. Know that from one side this is just a start, but from another it stands alone, complete in itself, now I need to complete the body. If it is possible for you to leave your special opinion for the future as to what pertains to R. Steiner, but the case is that this does not pertain to Sheiner at all, but only to certain concepts that lie beneath or behind all the texts and constantly are surfacing in various series of strata and figures. These are not accidental lapses, but dashes in the orthography. There now exists a certain new genre as a reality, called poetic ensemble. Some type of theme, very wide due to its volume and complexity, can find an adequate expression, not in a poem, circular or drama, but in a genre that is complex and integrated. All of its parts are tied one to another with the unity of this theme, the various aspects and sub-themes in them are developed, and at the same time each of them appears as a composition which is autonomous to a certain stage.

I affirm all of this, but still you do not want to hear it. It is not in vain that I lie down flat, I estimate about 1,500 nights and without sleep.[73] Few situations like this occur.

As far as such terms are concerned, let me repeat in summary, that if you were familiar in the entire composition, then you would be assured, that the text would be impossible without them.

The terms *Shadanakar*, *Nertis*, and many others are derived from the same source as those names that scare you – *Liyurna* and *Nivenna*. Over the course of a series of years I have adapted them into their defined purposes, which in time I will strive to explain to you in personal conversation, of God should give us to opportunity to meet. The number – 242 – is the sum[74] of all the strata of the various materialities, with the different number of spacial and time coordinates or dimensions. All of them together comprize *Shadanakar*, that is, the system of various materialities of planet Earth. Such systems are called *bramfaturas*. There is a vast amount of them, since the *bramfatura* possesses a large quantity of stars and planets. Galaxies have their meta-*bramfatura*, with many hundreds and even thousands of various materiality planes. For example, the one-dimensional bottom of *Shadanaker* presents itself as if a line, with one end resting on the star Antares (Alpha Scropii), and the one-dimensional worlds of all the *bramfaturas* of our galaxies twist themselves around it like a helix.

Nonetheless, such meager fragments of such enormous concepts can hardly provide you something.

I have acquired an immense enrichment this year. I hope this period of merit will stretch further, and that my maladies will not interfere. I will keep a hat on them.

---

[73] His 5 years so far at Vladimir Prison.
[74] Daniel's initial sum is 242, but within the text of *Rose of the World* there are another 6, bringing the total to 248.

Daniel attempted to convince Alla that the composition contained a hidden mystic knowledge. The subsequent chapters of *Russian Gods*, which Daniel forwarded to Alla, also required some explanation.

The first meeting of Daniel with someone outside the prison occurred in June, now that they were allowed by the revised rules. This was his first personal contact in over 8 years with someone outside the penal system. The first of his family to visit him was Yulia Gavrilovna, his mother-in-law, and this was in August. Her purpose was to speed the intervention and review of the proceedings by the proper agencies for Alla primarily, and Daniel secondarily, and she was worried that Daniel was not composing his petitions properly or not sending them to the proper persons. They met for 30 minutes.

Upon returning home, Yulia wrote to Alla, telling her that Daniel lost weight and looked pale. Yulia also asked Alla to tell Daniel not to write any more petitions, feeling that he was doing more damage than good. At the same time, Vladimir Aleksandrov, Daniel's cellmate recently freed, somehow came in contact with the Bruzhes, but he relayed to them misinformation on Daniel's penal situation.

Alla, after her recent letter from her mother and the letter from Daniel on his responses to his newest genre of poetry and their mystic inclination and subject, immediately wrote to Daniel. Alla was very abrupt about his "exclusion from social life and loss of perception of reality."

Daniel responded:

> Truly your notion of my exclusion only pertains to certain practical details, but does not pertain to my situation in general or its entirety. I read newspapers, magazines, new books, on occasion see new people, I rewrite my compositions, and yet I still have a head on my shoulders. I do not know upon what the opinions of this other man are founded, since they do not coincide with your earlier opinions, and incorrectly resort to a

very primitive explanation: that I have somewhere lost perception of reality. And then you combine this with the manner that I wrote the petitions. But they are not poems or prose and have no undertones of Dostoyevski. I have to admit it is obvious that I do not do well in writing official documents. But since my style of writing has a lyrical element, it naturally is included in such writing, and as a result, it indirectly excludes the special juridical and legal presentation that may be expected. Nonetheless, I can calm you by letting you know that I am not intending to further write just anything to just anybody.

Daniel likewise informed Alla that he sent 80 rubles out of the money that Bruzhes had been forwarding to him to his cousin Aleksandra Kovalenski. She had an undiagnosable illness that exhausted all her strength, and yet she was also arrested in the same matter and sent to a labor camp.

Alla responded that she last saw Aleksandra Kovalenski in 1951, somehow they crossed paths in the penal system being transferred from one place to another. What Alla told Daniel was not very comforting:

> She appeared sickly and disheveled, and her psychological condition was bad. This was not a human, but a tragic ruin: physically and mentally. Someone wrote to me recently about her appearance: she was bent forward, her skin was a dark shade, a very strange figure with bulging eyes. She just as well be Mephistopheles.

Daniel in response adamantly expressed to Alla of how painful it is for him to accept the berated condition and suffering of those incidentally involved in this matter. He cannot reach any further stage of personal guilt toward them. His own deprivation of freedom is one manner of atonement for what was caused to others, even though he was not the cause, but the agencies who developed the alleged conspiracy are the ones to blame. But somehow, he knew he will always be the target of all those that the alleged conspiracy included. Such guilt overwhelmed Daniel to such an extent that in one letter he blurted out:

> All the more and more I want to voluntarily terminate this account with life once and for all. But do not let this phrase scare you. This means of exit is prohibited and excluded. And I cannot have you deal with the anguish.

Daniel considered a prison with its unassailable walls as depriving a person of his inner freedom less than a labor camp, and not without good reason. Work would have been impossible for Daniel in his physical condition, and only distract him from traversing the spirit worlds and reduce his time to write. Daniel was also assured of his imminent release. Daniel was especially concerned about his ill health, and foresaw being homeless and penniless. He wrote to Alla:

> It is starting to seem that the opportunity for you and I to meet is getting closer than I earlier supposed. But this also designates certain complexities and difficulties, in the face of which I remain in complete perplexity. So how am I to conduct myself and what am I to do when released? You, unconditionally, do not even suspect any of these complexities. We need to suppose that the pension for invalids of the Fatherland War will be restored.

Pain in Daniel's heart made itself known. It started to be difficult to climb the prison stairs. On occasion Daniel had to take nitroglycerine, and several times in the prison hospital he was injected with camphor. In a letter that October, Daniel told Alla:

> In general, as long as I remain in one spot and without any special movements, all proceeds well. I work with all my strength and I have done much in the past 3 years.

My mental state is sufficiently stable and could be better if I could be assured that I will remain here until spring. I experience a deep repulsion to any transfer, and first of all because I imagine I will deal with it very poorly. Right now I am not even able to pick up or carry my personal suitcase, although it is not so heavy. But since the condition of my heart is getting better, although gradually, but truly, I hope that by spring I should be able to handle any transfer.

Yulia again visited him in October. Daniel told her that there was no manner that he could ever possible repay her for the persistent worry she has suffered and to return her daughter back to her. The 70-year old woman, pale, exhausted from the trip to Vladimir, always feeling in danger, motivated by a personal understanding that was blatantly false, her nerves disintegrating, wailing at any moment. Yet Daniel understood her condition. He also knew that it was Vladimir Aleksandrov who was disseminating fraudulent information about Daniel in prison. He wrote back to Alla about the situation with Aleksandrov:

> On his own, he is a good person and always treated me wonderfully, just as I did him, but he is person who is complex, ill, contradictory, and possesses immense conceit. Plus he is unreliable, suspicious, and plainly has a poor attitude.
>
> I do not know the reason for his antipathy toward me, but I feel bad that such echoes of conflict have reached you, and especially in such a distorted view. But to change this will have no lasting effect, or even any indirect benefit. But other than Aleksandrov, similar opinions were voiced by Parin about Rakhim, and later I found out that he was not the only one.
>
> Even though it is still the beginning of December, I say Happy New Year to my wife, since my next letter is destined for my mother-in-law. My joy, I am absolutely

assured that we will see each other the coming year. And you know that I am not such a reckless optimist. This may just happen, that you will visit me here.

Alla, at the labor camp, was not restricted any longer to the number of letters she could send, and for every one letter she received from Daniel, she replied with several. In November, she sent him photographs of herself, which was a major event in Daniel's life, to see her again, even if just a photograph and to know she was well. After an 8-year separation, a photograph brought him close to her again, regardless of comments he made earlier. The labor camp was now allowing photographs, as long as they wore civilian clothes and the camp was not noticeable in the background. All had to appear proper for public display.

Photography was not permitted in prisons and so Daniel had to provide a verbal auto portrait, so he replied to Alla:

> So that you will not scream when you see me in a few months, seeing what used to be an extravagant figure. True, you will see it in a somewhat softer form. But imagine an older and slenderer person who once wore a blue suit, which now covers his gaunt and pale and wrinkled body. His eternally cold head is crown with a dark-blue beret. His emaciated cheeks and swollen eyebrows provide evidence that their possessor will soon reach half a century in age. His gaze is gloomy, forehead is penetrating. However his militaristic nose testifies to only the flesh being weak, while the spirit is vigilant. His feet are still bare, and the local residents stare at him nonchalantly, as though his feet are his inspiration, like a personification of a challenge to the laws of nature, uniformly walking through the snow at regular intervals.

At the end of the year 1955, Nikolai Sadovnik, a cellmate of Daniel, was moved from Vladimir Prison to Dubrovlag, or Dubrovski Labor Camp 3, in Mordovia and close to the labor camp where Alla was located. Daniel described Sadovnik in one of his personal journals:

> It is impossible not to deeply respect a person of such heroic temperament, absolute integrity and, in addition, one possessing an amazing kind soul, and more than just one would notice this on the outside, touching on the inside. He is likewise courageous, with a high level of moral strength, and appearing to people as a primitive or conservative type of a gentleman. Upon his shoulders he carries genuine accomplishments, and in the highest meaning of this word. It will not be surprising if by the sunset of your years you never meet a man of such a far reaching limit of integrity.

Sadovnik took with him some notebooks of Daniel's verses. He took the time while at Vladimir to copy all of Daniel's extant compositions carefully and precisely, in small block letters that looked almost typewritten. The notebooks that Sadovnik was able to smuggle in his suitcase were the initial 7 chapters of *Russian Gods* – *Through Nature, Barefooted, Worlds of Enlightenment, Ruin of the Terrible One, Rukh, Holy Jewels,* and *The Blue Light*. Daniel requested Sadovnik to deliver the notebooks to Alla, who was at Mordovia Labor Camp 1 at the time.

1956

At the beginning of January, somehow Sadovnik was able to get to Alla and deliver the notebooks. She immediately responded in her next letter to Daniel, "No other word, except joy."

Toward the end of winter, Daniel sent Alla a 2nd auto portrait, but started it with a general issue. Then he continued with his specific purpose. After the freedom of years of wandering through Russia's virgin forests, and other vacations in nature preserves, now it was eight and-a-half years in the penal system and this took a worse toll on Daniel's psychological balance. Again depression set in during the winter. He complained to Alla:

> My popular overcoat was repaired last year: it was shortened, a new strap was sewn on, and now it looks more like a jacket than an overcoat. It is lighter and more durable now. From the lower section that was cut, a hat was made from it, or better described, a strange looking helmet with flaps over my ears. I have never worn anything so warm and comfortable over head.
>
> A state of ingratitude right now stains almost everything that surrounds me, and this I tolerate difficultly and because I cannot get back into the middle of nature. This little devil of depression is gnawing at me again and such a devolution is not a natural occurrence for me. But this song you have heard me sing before. But I do not expect myself to accomplish a termination as did Glinski;[75] this is something I do not think about. This is not actually a thought, but nothing more than an arbitrary feeling that arises on occasion.
>
> And in general my conditions, even desires, have evolved as being dualistic and contradictory. Eight and-a-half years of the one and same scenario pressing upon

---

[75] A character of *Night Wanderers* who commits suicide.

me causes me to have nausea or cerebral migraines more often. What makes it worse is that this causes other bad affects on my mental and physical health. Even the attraction for my beloved India is affected negatively. A photograph of the Taj Mahal in a newspaper led me to the state of remembering the feelings of Adrian,[76] when he ran from the street car and almost fell underneath a speeding truck, in order to meet a friend who was just walking about. But the alarm was no more than the same noise from some subtle buzzing of fleas. Unfortunately, feelings of this sort become a daily occurrence.

The lumbago, about which Daniel wrote to Alla at the beginning of December 1955, now was worse, and he wrote to her about it again:

This entire past month [January] I was only able to go for a stroll twice, and both times I was sorry that I went. Most of the time I just lay flat, and not because of this prosthesis that I need to wear, but now I have to. To sit in a chair for 3 or hours during the day is the ceiling of my present capabilities. I need to swallow nitroglycerine almost daily, and right now I am again on a course of glucose injections, but so far I have not noticed any result. My head, of course, is clear and I can read and have my time occupied, but after a ¼-hour of walking about the cell, again I have the same pains, the ones that started a year back, the obvious heart attack. So what saves me are hot-water bottles on my chest and back and the nitroglycerine. Now judge for yourself if I am capable in this condition of being transferred somewhere else or to survive a journey to somewhere there in Novo-Sibirski province.[77] It is very doubtful that I will even survive

---

[76] A main character of *Night Wanderers*.
[77] In south-central Siberia, bordering Kazakhstan, also the location of Soviet prisons and labor camps.

being dragged just to Moscow. It is better for me to last here another 2 to 3 months and at least make it somewhere, than to be torn from this place right now and not to make it anywhere.

Maybe the reason for the prosecutor to be prolonging any decisions, and as strange as this may seem, is for some good side of him to surface. Other than this, the very fact of postponement appears to be a better indication of the proceedings than a bad sign, and because negative decisions are usually decided quickly. In general and based on my surmise, I have an optimistic mood about you and so depend on the opinion of these persons who have the responsibility of resolving these things, and much better than I can. To be transferred to Podsosenski does not seem to me an empty venture, since it is only 70 miles away.[78] What also looms personally in front of me is another option: a convalescent home somewhere closer, at least for a while until you are stabilized in a new residence, and then I can drag my frail torso of a human body over there.

In January, Daniel received a decision regarding his petition.

> The Central Commission Statute of the Criminal Code 19-58-8, as supplemented by 7-58-8, punishment according to paragraph 17-58-8, 58-10 part 2, and 58-11, will remain as before: a term of 25 years prison confinement.

Daniel wrote to Alla that he was more than just agitated, but there was nothing he could do.

At the beginning of February, Alla's father, Aleksandr Petrovich, went to visit his daughter. He needed help to write new petitions, now hearing what occurred to Daniel. Alla then

---

[78] A street in central Moscow, where some hospitals and convalescent homes are located, and very close to the Bruzhes' residence.

wrote to Daniel, that the new petition was being sent to Nikolai Bulganin, who was now premier of the USSR, and that she would somehow get a copy of the letter to Daniel to help him in his next petition for another reconsideration of the matter. She sends a copy to Daniel and he responds in a subsequent letter his intent to send another, and now to Bulganin, but it will take him about 2 weeks to create it.

On February 18, Daniel again was admitted to the prison hospital and together with his cellmate and self-designated caretaker Zea Rakhim. Daniel wrote in his diary:

> My friend cares for me like a nursemaid. But he is himself very ill, suffering. It is his heart, rheumatism, and in general he has lost weight and become gaunt, but his attitude and worry are so touching. I move very little, I stroll seldom, and to my great regret. I take every medicine available here for me to take. My head, however, is still clear, and I do not abandon my studies, although I am at a point that they move slowly. What is primary is that I cannot sit long at my table. It is taking me 3 days just to write this letter.

In March, Alla wrote to Daniel about the death of his cousin, Aleksandra (Shura) Dobrova, Aleksandr Kovalenski's wife, who died February 9 from some internal illness in the labor camp hospital. Officials allowed her husband to attend and he spent 2 weeks with her until she died. Alla wrote about her personal grief to Daniel:

> What happened to me is that after I heard of the fact of Shura's death, I was 4 days grieving, and especially not knowing the accompanying circumstances. This was not easy. But having known about her condition I was inwardly ready and was almost waiting for news of this type. I did not receive any letters from him [Aleksandr],

and doubted anyway if I would receive any. However, thank you especially for your intervention.[79]

At this time I wanted to mention to you of the suffering that the past caused, and to assure you that not Kovalenski and neither your cousin retain any malice toward you.

Daniel sent his newest petition to Nikolai Bulganin at the beginning of April, demanding a new inquest into the matter. One item to the benefit of Daniel was the denunciation of Stalin and the personality cult that surrounded him by Nikita Khrushchev at the February session of the CC of the CP. A new wave of expectations flooded the labor camps and prisons and they materialized with the release of thousands of inmates. The first to be released were the seriously ill or the hopelessly ill, as well as the elderly.

The new review of Daniel's matter for the meantime was not moving forward, but some were being released. Those released at this time from the alleged conspiracy were Aleksandr Dobrovolski, Aleksandr Dobrov and his wife Irina, Aleksandr Ivanovski, Victor Kemnitz, Irina Armand, and Tatyana Volkova.

On April 2, Daniel's mother-in-law, Yulia Gavrilovna, came to Vladimir to pay him a visit. This time she brought regards from his friends, and it was gratifying to Daniel that their attitude remained as it was previous. This encouraged him, but just encouragement was not enough. Daniel felt he had recovered completely from the anthrax, as over the 6 months after leaving the hospital he had no recurrence. But then he started to lose his strength, although he did have respite regularly. Daniel confessed to Alla.

> During my bad days, or actually bad weeks, I am forced to lie flat, almost not moving. During good days, I can move a little, but to climb the staircase is now very difficult for me. It is almost impossible for me to gain

---

[79] Referring to the 80 rubles Daniel sent earlier.

enough strength rise or exert any physical effort, and the small upheaval causes an interruption in my movement, pain, and forces me to lie again down on my cot with heating pads on my front and back, while swallowing nitroglycerine tablets in the meantime.

I really need some tranquility, but letters and newspapers and political shifts and power struggles in the higher levels of state government, seem to upset my social balance. The prison radio deprives me of any silence and concentration. It is turned on at 6 in the morning and blares all the time until 12 midnight. This has become torturous. I stuff my ears with cotton and sometimes pieces of bread.

My child, I am not getting ready to die, although I strive to be ready should this occur. It is possible in conditions of ideal serenity, but not in the city, that I might succeed to squeeze still a few more years. I would greet a convalescent home with an exceptional smile.

Walking barefoot still helps me. If I had to wear shoes, it would kill me. Being barefooted is what keep me existing. For many this would seem psychotic and empty. But I know what I know.

Alla and her parents continued a persistent intervention and lived for this purpose. Premonitions and dreams started occurring to Alla and she wrote to Daniel about it:

First I congratulate you on your name-day.[80]

I again saw a church in a dream, but this did not seem good. I have seen so many of them over the recent years and of various designs. On the eve of my transfer to Lefortovo, I heard in a dream, "My soul magnifies the Lord,"[81] and I saw lit candles. This time, and truly due to

---

[80] Russian Orthodox Christians do not celebrate a person's birthday, but celebrate the day they were taken to church and prayed for with their name. For Daniel, this would have been March 11.

[81] Luke 1:46, a popular tune in the Russian Orthodox Church.

horrible nervous weakness, I saw something totally fantastic. In the middle of Moscow the London Tower was raised, and it was called the Westminster Abbey. I walk around the immense building searching for the Chapel of Henry the someone. I found the chapel and which appeared as a nice small structure with a high bright green roof. On the balustrade of the staircase there were drawn some type of pictures. I pushed the snow off of it using my hand and was surprised with the hardness of the paint. How depictive it was.

Father Aleksandr Bruzhes went to visit the military prosecutor Terekhov with the purpose of speeding the review of the matter of Daniel's alleged conspiracy. Aleksandr wrote to Alla regarding the situation:

My little girl. Here are some details from yesterday's visit with Mr Terekhov. The matter, truly, under his investigation, he called "monstrously stretched." He explained in detail all the ups and downs and the reason for the prolonged extension, and he let me know how intensively confusing the matter, as well as how wide the conspiracy, with as many Soviet personnel involved, and all the anti-Soviet statements made, and which were all solidly factual. But later he admitted that some of the evidence was based on indirect information from witnesses not completely reliable or was circumstantial.

The second reason for the difficulty consists in that the original material, Daniel's novel, is no longer available, regardless of the prolonged and intensive searches for it, and so obviously it was definitely destroyed by order of Abakumov. All that remains are some fragments of the novel that were obtained elsewhere, and this is all available at present as far as an accusation of the author's character is concerned.

In summary, as I understood his approach to the matter, all the testimony and evidence available for his consideration only apply to the charge of anti-Soviet agitation, and which has a sentence of 10 years.

Then he said that time is on side as far as our daughter was concerned. The testimony in the past that was earlier labeled as anti-Soviet will no longer apply as such in just a few more months.

Receiving Alla's letter of the status of the proceedings based on her father's visit, Daniel responded, and repeats his poor health much as in a previous letter:

> I need to say that right now I am exhausting my final strengths remaining to conclude this itinerary of my plans, because under any new conditions I will not have opportunity to delve deep into them very long, and perhaps maybe never. Unfortunately, the work is getting more complex, besides, due to my insufficiency of purely physical strength, I am unable to sit very long at a table, and other than this, I have been overwhelmed by a horrifying spiritual numbness, apathy, over the past 2 months. The matter is due to my heart, I am forced to change my daily pace and stop any further nighttime meditations and vigils, which I was somewhat utilizing as my spiritual nourishment. Every evening I am somnolent, and as a result of which I sleep 8 to 9 hours straight, and this is very good, and every plainly indispensable at the present time. But what this then causes is that the balance of the time I am numb, scatter-brain and sluggish, as though mentally retarded.
>
> Even the smallest upset causes momentary anxiety and causes weakness in my heart or else pressure in my chest, and this leads to heating pads and nitroglycerine and other means of easing the pain. I have become repulsive to myself, and the thought of what it will be like for you to live side by side with such a person deprived of vivacious strengths torments me. But I want to exit this place with fully developed faculties, so at

least in this respect you can be untroubled. I insanely and intolerably want to spent time, even for a short while, back in nature.

The wheels of the Soviet bureaucratic machine rotated but out of balance, and it was a feast or famine with the penal system. Now the gates of the labor camps rotated like a revolving door. By April of that year, at Labor Camp 1, where Alla was confined, about 80% of the inmates were released, leaving only about 70 persons, and most of them political criminals, like Alla. Fights and arguments started among those remaining who felt deprived of freedom. It seemed that as long as many were incarcerated they were all incarcerated, but now with the population down, those remaining felt cheated. After work they would wander out of the camp and into the forest to gather berries, walk to the river. As a result Alla and the balance of inmates were moved to a collective farm to work in the field, Farm Camp 17. Life for them hung between captivity and freedom, an undefined tomorrow and overexcitement of expected soon release.

Daniel continued to work on *Iron Mystery* during early 1956, and finally finished it. He wrote to Alla on May 2:

> Today I finished what has been occupying my time since I started this in 1950. I would like to celebrate with the boogie-woogie or some jazz, but looks like just in my heart.

Started at the same time as *Rose of the World*, *Iron Mystery* depicted the decisive events of 20th century Russian history, described in dramatic form. The rebirth of the mystery plays – a special sacred genre – was one of the tasks of Daniel's poetic reformation. The mystery plays, he felt, would inevitably blossom in the future and become one of the cultural portions of ROSE OF THE WORLD.

The historical activity unfolding in 12 acts of *Iron Mystery* became not so much a reconsideration of the past and present, as much as being prophetic regarding the events to occur at the end of the world. Historical personages, whose energy was nourished by the powers of darkness are presented in the mystery play as grotesque, a symbolic figure personifying the secret truth of the event. While the heroes of the powers of light are virtuous, ministers, while their symbolic hero is the poet or announcer, who depicts the highest integrity.

During Easter week, which began May 1, Daniel attempted to quit smoking and for a while was able to reduce his tobacco intake, down to 5 or 6 cigarettes a day instead of his previously 20 to 25.

They celebrated Easter on May 6, regardless of the austere prison regimen. In their cell they could hear the church bells. Daniel recorded in his diary:

> As usual I did not close the window shutters and so I heard the bells of Uspenski Sobor. And then in the adjoining cells I hear them shouting, "Christ has risen." The inmates there were women, most of them elderly, and so they sang, "Christ has risen," This meant that they did not sleep the first half of the night.[82] That afternoon I looked through the window and saw these Ukrainian women in nice dresses walking. So I shouted to them, "Christ has risen." So then they responded, "Truly he has risen." They waved their hands at me. Then I looked closer and I saw Shulgin walking and with him was the Georgian Beriashvil. I then again said, "Christ has risen." And Shulgin took off his hat and waved to me and said, "Truly he has risen."

Daniel lived in uncertainty. The releases so far did not impact the high security prisons, such as Vladimir.

May 4, Daniel was moved from his cell in the prison hospital to Cellblock 4, but then he returned straight back to the hospital.

---

[82] Orthodox Easter services are normally held about 2 AM, Easter Sunday.

Zea Rakhim was released from Vladimir shortly after. Daniel lost the one remaining person at Vladimir who was sincerely concerned for his welfare and who worried over him and who treated him decently. Daniel wrote to Alla about him and his condition:

> The thought that we are now permanently separated, and will not see each other again, is intolerable. What also torments me is what I feared and thought, that I have no strength left to revive *Night Wanderers* and compose it again. But perhaps God will grant it to happen somehow. In any case I seem to retain a somewhat inherent feeling of an unfulfilled debt. I say – somewhat, because in order to satisfy the debt in its fullness, I still need considerable time, at least a year or year and-a-half, and under the best of circumstances.

Nothing occurred with the agencies reviewing the matter in either June or July, and now it was already August. Daniel continued to worry about being discarded as a invalid and homeless by the state if he should ever be released. One extreme choice was to go to Paris and live with brother Vadim, even if this was possible, as Daniel noted in a letter to Alla, and for her to consider it as a last resort, or even if feasible.

Overwhelmingly distraught over lack of news, Daniel attempted to resort to writing, but ended up reading more instead. To take his mind off matters, he read Jacob Boehme, and then read Vladimir Ermilov's biography of Feodor Dostoyevski that was just published. The biography annoyed Daniel because of its blatant anti-religious approach to Dostoyevski, and he wrote to Alla:

> I fear that Feodor Dostoyevski is rolling in his grave without stopping like a watermill wheel. But in general, my inner life over the recent months, after I finish my last composition, has been struck by emptiness, insensitivity and lethargy. Without the ability to write,

my life becomes meaningless. If the matter should be prolonged anymore, and I am forced to remain here for several more months, I will try to return to *Rose of the World*, and so far I have finished about half of it. But I am afraid that no matter how hard I may try to concentrate on it, the radio will interfere. In any case, should I start on more poetry, the radio will cause too much interference for me to accomplish much.

I also included mention of this in my petitions to the Minister of Internal Affairs, as well as to Bulganin, and I still await an answer. But meanwhile, I suffer daily headaches and regular irritation of my nerves.

Daniel worked on revisions to his *Russian Gods*, adding a couple more chapters until he was satisfied with it. The chapter titled *Meta-Historical Sketch* was later inserted into *Rose of the World*.

Alla Andreeva – The Labor Camps Years[83]

1949 – Continued

Alla was a short time at Labor Camp 13; then 3 years at Labor Camp 6; 6 years at Labor Camp 1, and 3 months at Farm Labor Camp 17. The following is her record:

> We were piled together in a large group and forced into Stolypin railroad cars. There I saw Anichka Kemnitz, and she just looked at me with a small smile on her face, the same she had all the times we were together previously, indicating no malice toward me. I also saw walking by me the wife of one of Daniel's friends, Alenushka Lisitzina,[84] she was the prototype of one of Daniel's heroines in his poem *Forest Blood*. We were together during part of the journey, until she continued to Magadan labor camp.[85] I was taken to Potzma,[86] penal

---

[83] These are selections of Alla Andreeva's book *Sailing to the Heavenly Russia* (Плаванье к Небесной России), translated by the author.

[84] Elena, the first wife of Evgeni Beloyusov, who later passed away, and then he married Alla after the death of Daniel.

camp station 13, a small one, for transfer, where I spent a little time.

I arrived there, but of course, not as a normal person. I express this in part because I could not understand why I would be allowed to leave the barracks and go into the street on my own. I sat on my bunk and waited for the sentry to allow me to leave. It took me some time to understand that here people as myself walk about freely.

I do not know how men begin their journey to prison, but the women immediately start to sing and very soon start to dance, even if this sounds strange. Literally from the first days of labor camp, we sang, read verses, and it was amazing as to why all of this seemed so necessary. We reminisced to the amount we could. I, of course, quoted Daniel's poems, but not just me. Someone remembered Pushkin, and even more amazing was Gumilev's *Kapitanov*. For me this remained a riddle, as to particularly why they seemed to us so necessary, more than bread. Line by line we helped each other remember poetry.

Why were such fluttering sails needed for us? Lord! How *Kapitanov* saved us! How this occurred, I never did understand, and no matter to whom I explained this, no one understood.

It was during New Years of 1949 that I arrived at penal camp railway station 13. I left the barrack, wandered somewhere into the center of the labor camp, where some trees were and a bench. I sat on this bench until midnight and wailed despairingly. And these were my final tears in the labor camp until my very release. I do not know what I cried out that night, I do not know what occurred and how, but I rose without any more tears and, let me repeat, I did not cry even once again, and under any circumstances, to the end of my term.

---

[85] In the far north-east of Siberia, along the Sea of Okhotsk, previously known as Kalyma. The inmates at the labor camps were used for mining.
[86] In Moldovia republic, near the city Zubova Polyana.

When I reflect on my life over the past half-century, as I am doing right now, then you understand, how much of all of it was irrational, and how little it was that I personally did for myself, and how much a Someone invisible, bright, living and knowing, did for me. And He did this in the way he could, working with an artist or composer or poet. In no personal abilities of any type can I explain how I was when I stood, how I lifted my head and then walked about the labor camp, attempting to be happy, striving not to cause any harm, and only do what I had strength to do. No longer was the matter in my hands. This was He, who was with me, my Angel guardian, this was now all of His responsibility.

Life in any labor camp is all the same: insensitive and senseless. You rise, are searched, you work, are searched, and then retire. The main events are letters and packages. Letters arrive from only the closest of relatives. I received them from mama. I had the right to write 2 letters a year. Every labor camp was self-reliant and independent.

All of these years are remembered as links of individual events, individuals, and sometimes an adventure, in a chain. So I will relate a few of them. There were 2 labor camps in the region, #1 and #6, and I was familiar with both of them (camp 13 was just a transfer point).

Each labor camp is like a miniature Soviet Union, as all the officials are Russian and how they deal with the inmates, and in every aspect.

The paling surrounding the labor camp is very high, about 9 feet, made from the trunks of thin trees and forced one against the other with no gap in between. Away from this paling toward the inside of the camp is a fence made of 3 strands of barbed wire with an electrical current running through them. On the outside of the paling there is another fence of 3 strands of barbed wire with an electrical current. Alongside each electrified barbed wire fence there is also a trench dug that is also guarded by a sentry.

So 6 strands of electrified barbed wire and a fence enclosed us in a rectangular shape. At the corners of the rectangle or square that composed the camp, there were wooden towers with a ladder leading to the top of each. There sat sentries armed with automatic rifles. This type of sentry was call a popka[87] or a vertukh.[88] The automatic rifles were directed at those inside the camp. During my term, each of the labor camps held approximately 2,000 inmates. So constantly there were automatic rifles in these crow's nests directed at 2,000 unarmed women. There was also another fence in the center of the camp that separated the residence quarters with barracks from the factory or working area. At both of these labor camps they were sewing factories.

There we worked using sewing machines that were indescribably old and obsolete. The girls sewed pea jackets and insulated jackets. The working shift was for 12 hours; it was divided equally from 8 in the morning to 8 at night, and then 8 at night to 8 in the morning. During the middle of the working shift we had dinner. I only worked in the factory area for a short time, toward the end of my term. They assigned me to the easiest work: it was called – trimming. My job was to cut all the loose threads at the ends of all the pea jackets after sewing was complete. The norm was 70 jackets a day. I did not make my quota at all ever, although others would help. Even the easiest work was beyond my strength to accomplish. The basic or majority population of the women held in the camp, and who worked primarily at the sewing factory, were Ukrainian, Latvian, Lithuanian, and Estonian. As the stream of Russians into this camp were few, not many were assigned to

---

[87] From the popping sound of a repeating rifle.
[88] From the Russian word referring to the rotation of the gun cylinder.

work, and the prisons officials preferred foreign women in the factories anyway. On occasion a completely exotic person would show. For example, there was one Brazilian woman, but I do not remember why she ended up here. There was some Koreans. One incident involved 2 sisters and 2 brothers, all of them children about 15 years old, and who were captured somewhere or other along the Korean-Soviet border. They were arrested, sentenced as spies, and all 4 of them were sent to different penal institutions, and one of the girls was in our camp. The Korean Li Yunok became friends with the Latvian woman and they spoke with one another in Russian, each knowing a few words, and both were learning in the process.

The girls sewed quite well. After several years some female director of the commission dealing with the prison factory arrived, enthused over the 200% and more of the quota that we have been manufacturing. Her intent was to adapt our methods elsewhere. She almost fell over when she saw these antediluvian sewing machines, and which for a long while never had replacement parts. The girls in the factory would repair the machines themselves, and even make replacement parts with other machines in the factory, which all were able to do.

There was also seasonal work. This was usually forestry and the short-timers were sent there. A short-timer had a sentence of 10 years. Those with a 25 year terms will not allowed to go into the forest, since the officials considered this dangerous. In general they told us, "You are not persons. Others who are bandits, murderers, prostitutes and embezzlers, are persons, but you are not. And you will never see any other life than this one."

So did we exist, and in response, we raised our heads, sang and danced, and each of us, I guess, had our own reason of doing so. Tears of course were many. Despair also. As far as I am concerned, this is what occurred with me: I just decided to stop thinking about the length of my term. I could not stop thinking about Daniel, my parents, brother, and this of course was an open wound that resided in me always. But I did not think about my term. In some way I was able to convince myself that I will never have anything more in my life, ever, except this paling surrounding me. And then I realized that I am able to adapt and live under these circumstances: nothing to expect, nothing to want, to understand that this is my horizon, a fence enclosing me on 4 sides, and that I must live here.

I repeat, I cannot definitely explain what was occurring in the camps. What I view before me is a simple chain of events, impressions, striking scenes, encounters, experiences. So I guess I will start with what it was I did there.

I was only at labor camp 13 for a short while. Then I was ordered to be transferred to the large #6 labor camp, and because they needed an artist there. During the wait I was affected by an inflammation of one leg, turning into a scarlet color, and it swelled to 4 times its normal thickness. My temperature also reached 104. Officials at camp 13 were also interested in an artist and attempted to have me remain there, saying they could handle my condition. But the general disagreed and ordered the guards at to place me on a gurney and they transferred me to #6 labor camp, and I resided there for about 3 years.

While I was in camp suffering from this inflammation in my leg, I was allowed to write a postcard to my parents with a request for them to send me medicine. So this was the first news that they received about me since my arrest, a postcard with the words, "Send penicillin." Nonetheless, they were glad to receive it, recognizing my handwriting, now knowing that I need penicillin, meaning that I was alive. They send me penicillin, and I soon recovered.

Of course, my vocation saved me. I worked at what was called the K-V-Che: Cultural-Educational Department, except that the place had no culture and was the furthest thing from being educational. I was for ever writing some trash: endless slogans, exhortations, and I do not remember even one line of anything that I composed there.

Because I was an enemy of the people, I was prohibited using the red color. So throughout the entire camp there were hanging brown banners with white letters. I am not aware of how I suddenly developed this talent to compose such rubbish with extraordinary speed, it seems to have surfaced on its own. Then we issued these mundane wall posters dedicated to motivating all the inmates to exceed the quota and to continue to exceed the quota. Off season there was always other nonsense to display.

As an inmate, I was obligated to do whatever they ordered. One humorous incident was when an official asked me to do his son's homework and create a multiplication table in large letters. But I was to do this and not his son. So that evening the official comes to me and orders me to have this finished by morning so his son can take it to school. I sat and begin to draw the table. The next day the official took the table and did not even look at it and his son took it to school, and then the teacher noticed the table was wrong and a scandal occurred. Half-asleep in the middle of the night I wrote: 5x5=25, 5x6=26, 5x7=27. I was accused of doing this because I was an inmate, but I then explained that I was plain exhausted and could not concentrate.

How can I define a labor camp in simple terms? It is a mixture of never ending regimentation and servitude. We in Mordovia were no worse than all the others. There did exist labor camps in Magadan and Kolyma that were more frightening, but the conditions everywhere and always remained the same: complete lack of rights; complete submission to whatever someone wants you to do, and complete impossibility to change anything in regard to your fate. Soviet camps were designed for people to reside there to the end of their life.

The wardens who ended up here were of various types. Of course, some were repulsive, bad ones were found everywhere. Then there were those who just did their job as wardens, and these were good ones. Interesting was how regimentation was implemented at the labor camps, and some wardens treated us like soldiers under their command. I remember one warden asking me, "So what were you as a civilian?"

There were also suicides among the sentries. One of them could not tolerate the situation and shot himself. They told us that they buried him like a dog: dug a hole, threw him in, and filled it. Suicide was considered criminal. It was possible that he left some kind of explanation for his suicide. Perhaps the Lord will forgive such a suicide, because this person just could not do what he was ordered to do. In general such tragedies in the labor camp affected both the inmates as well as the regular employees.

We resided in complete servile dependence, and often plainly on the kindness of the warden. They moved people from one camp to another at a whim, and there was nothing you could do about it. We had no rights. Wherever you were sent, there you went. In this light I want to tell you about one characteristic event:

In our camp they collected a rather large crowd of invalid and old and ill women who could no longer work in the factory. I guess there were about 300 of them. In Mordovia there existed a special camp for such inmates and where they were taken every so often. At the same time, through transfers young and healthy women, would be collected and an exchange made. And so 300 would leave, and 300 would enter.

One summer the heat was intensive, it was blazing hot, and our ill and elderly women were collected, counted, searched, shackled together, and they were sitting on the ground in the residential area awaiting their exchange. But the next batch was late, something was holding them up. The sun was pounding on them. Of course, some of the women fainted while others had heart pains. But there was no way for us to help them, we could not move them into the barracks, or even give them water, because they were already counted and shackled together. I had more freedom than those who worked in the factory, and the entire time was near these women. But not just I. At some moment in time, I could no longer restrain myself and ran into the warden's office with a shout. He just sat and waited for the next batch of people.

I said to him, 'This is impermissible! What are you doing? People are dropping out there! They are losing consciousness. What a terrible situation!"

I will never forget his reply, "Andreeva. Up to this point you still do not understand what in general a penal camp is, that it is a penal camp. What is so terrible? Why did you run to me, if a terrible situation is all it is?"

Eventually the next batch arrived. They entered the gates and drug out all those waiting for them. At the gates a mother and daughter met each other. The daughter was entering while the mother was drug out. All of a sudden the warden displayed a rare humane gesture: he allowed the mother to remain for a few days to spend time together with the daughter. But then they were separated.

In general, particularly in the labor camps I noticed what is called humanistic ecumenicalism. We had Orthodox, Catholics and Protestants. Orthodox Easter and Catholic Easter occur on the same day only once every 4 years. Christmas is never simultaneous. Nonetheless the holy day was still a work day even if it fell on a Sunday. So we managed to compromise. On Orthodox Christmas, the Catholics would take their shift in the factory, while the Orthodox would remain in the barracks and performs their rites, and it would work the other way on Catholic and Protestant Christmas, and the same for Easter. There was no debate on dogmas, but only so all of them could somehow celebrate their respected holy day.

In 1951, I was transferred to labor camp #1. And this was definitely #1, since I was told that it was founded in 1929, when the kulaks were removed from the farms during collectivization, and these were all honest peasants. They were brought here during the winter, thrown into the snow, and told, "Build." We lived in the same barracks they built.

I noticed over the course of all my years in labor camps, that there were people in each of the camps, like myself, who were affected by this prejudice, and we together decided to fight against it. Maybe this will seem strange, but one of the means of our struggle was amateurism, or better described, creativity. It did particularly help to quench this mutual hate. All of a sudden at the local Mordovia camps, people surfaced who wanted to participate in these amateur productions, and they participated after their working hours, after a 12-hour shift: they would practice singing and dancing. The camp officials did not stop us, they thought it was a great idea for the women to devise some amateur productions.

Soon after I arrived at Camp 1, I became friends with a Ukrainian woman from Lvov named Lisa, and she was an intelligent and kind person. She was able to succeed in getting an accordion from some aunt, and she became our accompaniment. This was the best means of working with people: choir singing and group dancing. But the hard part was convincing the Ukrainians to dance with the Latvians and Lithuanians and Estonians in their national dances. It was also difficult to get the Baltic peoples to sing Ukrainian songs with the Ukrainians. For the Russians it was easy to do both. We were also able to get a Ukrainian girl who was a member of the sect Jehovah's Witnesses to participate, since stage performances were incompatible with her sectarian convictions.

One woman named Dita Elsner, a German ballerina, we assigned to dance. There was another beautiful ballerina from Minsk. So almost all the Ukrainian women ended up singing, and Lisa accompanied them with her accordion.

Initially I made all the costumes, and out of rags, discolored material set to be discarded, and I managed to make everybody something. Then the others got involved with costumes.

Interesting that one of the inmates was Galina Mayakovskaya, an actress at the Radlova theater and the wife of film director Vladimir Iyogelsen. She was very professional and ended up taking charge as director of the stage performance at the labor camp.

When I started my sentence, I wore the clothes that I brought with me. But in 1950, when I was at Labor Camp 6, they were taken from us and we were issued prison dresses and white head shawls. The dresses were black, blue and dark brown, whatever you were issued, and on the backs they used bleach to insert a number. My number was 402-A. The same number was inserted on our winter coats and our skirts, and with black paint on our head shawls. I will never forget that horrible day. It seems they deprived us of all that we had left to us, our name, and we were no longer a human, but just a number.

But because Russians are Russian, not one of the prison officials the entire time that I was in the labor camps ever called any of us by that number, but only by our name.

We looked ugly and grotesque in our prison garb, but at least we were able to do some white needlework on the collars. The officials did not like it but eventually gave in. Sometimes there was enough scraps and discarded pieces from sewing that we could actually make a dress for ourselves, or at least a new blouse and skirt, and when we were finally released we would wear them. If there was any white pieces remaining, we also used them for curtains in our barracks.

Even though we were not allowed to possess needles, scissors or knives, we all had them. Women would steal and hide them, and the officials would have to requisition more, and there was nothing they could do.

When Easter came along we women had to improvise the best we could without priests. Each person that remembered parts of prayers would write them down until we had a sufficient amount. Then on Easter Sunday we gathered in groups and each person who could read well would read the prayers that we composed. Although what we did was not dogmatically right, but we did the best we could, and the prison officials did not interfere.

I also drew postcards for all the women there, and they would send them to friends and relatives. In return they would share with me the packages they received.

Come New Years and Christmas, we tried our best to celebrate. We were not allowed an evergreen tree on Christmas, but the officials did allow us one for New Years. We would fabricate toys and decorations in our spare time for the trees, and those inmates with children at home would send them as gifts.

We did have the right to send 2 letters a year, and I would write them to my parents. At Camp 6, the censurer was malicious and he would only allow us 2 lines in a letter. So my letters initially consisted only of the following:

> My dear ones! All is well with me. I am healthy.
> Please send (and I would list what I needed).

Of course, all the time I would ask my mother whether Daniel was alive, and he at the same time would ask my mother if she would send him my address. But mother feared getting husband and wife connected, meaning her daughter with husband, and she felt this might be illegal. So she refused to give me Daniel's address.

Then Yulia Gavrilovna wrote to daughter Alla on March 5:

> Daniel is alive and well. I send him money, just as I do to you, and the same amount. As far as his address is concerned, I will not give it to you, not only because you will stop writing to us, but I do not know if I am permitted to do this.

Alla replied hoping to comfort her parents, but still about communication with husband Daniel:

> My beloved, my trusted.
>   How can I find the words in order to comfort you a little? I tell you the truth that I am not deceiving you: I am well, content, happy; I have the ability to always find meaning and happiness in life, in all things, and even in what I have had to live through, even though this has been difficult.
>   My fate has closed all the light in your window, but even then, you are unable to correctly evaluate this fate. Take care of yourselves, my beloved, you must have some kind of support, you need to protect and preserve yourselves. We will see each other, we will be together. Daniel and I will somehow repay you, even if just a little,

for the horrible incidences you have endured as a result of us, and that you are still enduring, and for all your effort on our behalf. My suffering beloved. I write to you very poorly, I am insufficient of words, consider this.

If you only knew how grateful I am for your financial assistance. I just did not have the courage to ask you about this, but it torments me day and night, just how he is residing. You have absolutely no idea how important this is for me.

Why would you think that once I got his address I would stop writing to you? I was always on poor terms with you, but not this much! Daniel best of all will understand that as long as this is the situation with writing letters here at present, I will write to you, but that all I write to you is also interesting and important for him, because this is my life, and this is why you need to take my letters to you, and after reading them, send them to him. I will ask him to also write only to you, since our addresses may change, while all your letters I always receive on time, but for God's sake do not forget to include a return address. My dear ones, I understand your fear and your caution, but is it just getting out of hand, right now, the manner you are handling my request? You were not at all ever involved in this matter of ours, so to help two loving persons that want to know just a little about each other over the course of so many years, there is no law that would prohibit this, as far as I know.

My sunshine, beloved, favorites, I am always with you, and I am much better off than I was earlier. My life, although mama does not believe it, is nonetheless calm.

I read, work, sew. I are working on a decorative bird on gray linen. I still play the piano a little, accompany another, figure some new tunes. The theatrical plays were curbed for a while, because we no longer have a director, but I have not stopped my public recitations. Many pretty flowers grow in the area and I will occasionally spent some time with them, and this is also joyful for me. My favorites. It is possible to live in Moscow, be dressed and happy, but at the same time sense less the depth and meaning of life than at any time here. Danya knows this, because he is also traversing the very same road, and please believe what I have to say.

[end of letter]

Mother did visit Daniel. She noticed that seldom did the inmates there shave, and Daniel mentioned how mother arrived and saw him in with what she considered a most unpresentable face, since he had not shaved in a while.

Mother refused to even communicate to me whether Daniel was alive. So in the summer of 1950, or maybe it was 1951, I received a letter from mother where she included the following phrase, "Your Danya is alive." My God! I ran through the labor camp happy as can be and shouting out, "He is alive, alive, alive!" No one asked me who it was that was alive, they knew very clearly. This was the first news I received about Daniel since he was arrested some 4 years earlier.

The first letter I received from Daniel was on June 21, 1953, over 6 years since we were arrested. I likewise responded.[89] From that time forward we regularly corresponded. Later, after Stalin's death when regulations were relaxed, we were able to send lengthier letters. Over the years I was in labor camp, I sent Daniel 126 letters, and he sent me 26.

Such an amelioration of penal institution regimen started in June 1953, and the reason was only obvious, that a little earlier, in March, that monster – Stalin – died. The reaction to his death was interesting. Some, such as the Russian prostitutes here, sincerely cried, and likewise some of the hard-line communists were sorrowful, and I could not figure why. For some unknown

---

[89] A translation of these letters are located in the chapter above.

reason, we were searched in our barracks, not in the roadway as usual. I was forced into the back and at the end so no one would notice the triumphant joy on my face at his demise.

What I did cry about, and this was at the monster's funeral, was how he turned Russia into an inferno. And then howling all over the camp through the radio and loudspeakers, all about the monster, and it seemed it would never end. I cried and started to pray, but of course, not for his soul There is no reason to pray for such souls, the progeny of satan. I prayed to God so that nothing of the sort would ever occur in Russia. I wept and prayed, "Lord, Lord! Save Russia from a repeat of this terror."

After Stalin's death, events began to unfold one after another. Right now it is difficult to bring all of them to memory in decent order, one seems to merge into the next, and they occurred so quickly one after the other as though linked together. This effectively started in 1954.

The most unexpected things occurred first – amnesty. For all those who were labeled as war criminals, and plainly soldiers who fought for their homeland, were the first the receive amnesty. Subsequent to them was amnesty of the petty criminals, but this did not pertain to us. What pertained to most of those in our labor camp was the amnesty for the youngsters. The next edict legislated was the released of all those who were arrested under the age of 16. Although there were not many of them, but they were plainly set free, and I guess enough of them to make a special legislation. So these youngsters who arrived at the labor camps at the ages of 14 or 15, now left, and a portion of them left as mothers with children, wherever or by whomever they were conceived, and having raised their children in the labor camp. And so these mothers who lost their 14-year old daughters to the penal system, received them back home as adults and some with grandchildren. The number of such tragedies I cannot guess, but it broke their lives and their parents lives, and now they had to adapt back into the system with their parents, if they were still available.

In one respect I was glad that Daniel and I did not have children, or I would be raising them here in a labor camp. It was so sad for me to see these young mothers raising their children in such a horrible environment, and who knows who the father was, and which nobody in private life could imagine.

The year 1954 continued into 1955 and then it was 1956, and releases were slow but consistent, and the Labor Camp 1 population decreased. The first of the political prisoners to be released were those short-timers with a term of 10 years, regardless of how long they were confined so far. But my sentence was 25 years. When I arrived here the population was about 2,000, but only 11 of us female inmates remained by spring of 1956, with 2 sentries and a guard dog.

So then I was moved with the balance of Camp 1 to Camp 17, which was a collective farm. It was about 8 miles away due south and took 2 hours by truck, such are the roads in Mordovia. Those at the farm were mostly petty criminals, and it was considered very low security. The inmates there were not about to escape anyway, because they would have no identification papers and so no one would risk taking them in.

The warden at Farm 17 now had a difficult time, since he was used to having thousands of inmates to supervise on the farm, and now he was down to a handful, us and a few other brigades. We were assigned our dormitory, so not to associate with the original residents. Also when working, they had us distant from the others also. Our small group formed our own farm brigade and I was designated brigade leader. They gave us hoes and our job was to weed out the wild grass that was almost a yard high, and because beets had been planted and they needed room to grow. The camp supervisor was always there watching us. We were near the Vad River, but we were not allowed to go near it. The weeds reached above our waists in some areas and we could see the sprouts of beats above the ground as we cleared the plot. The supervisors claimed that we only fulfilled 24% of our quota, which was absolutely unacceptable, but this is all we were able to do that week and there was nothing they could do to us otherwise, except complain. Our work to the end of our term continued much the same, I guess I was there about 3 or 4 months. Of course, we were also asking the supervisor when our term would end and when could we be released as with all the others.

Unlike the labor camps, here we had the freedom to leave the farm for short periods. By this time the sentries did not worry about anybody escaping, and especially, as I mentioned, without documents.

The Mordovian forest was thick and wild: the trees were immense, the grass was higher than myself. Here at Farm Camp 17, we were permitted to wander about the forest, and we knew we would be foolish to run off while the Commission was working on our matter. I ran insanely through nature and the other female inmates would just stare at me.

Each day someone was released. One evening, I guess it was August 11, the camp supervisor walked into our dormitory and said, "Andreeva, gather your things, tomorrow you will be released." I slept like a rock that night, and in the morning gathered my belongings and then I did something strange. I just left them on my cot and walked out of the farm camp by myself. I walked alone through the Mordovia forest in the direction of Labor Camp 1, about 8 miles away. When I got there I bid farewell to the 3 or 4 elderly women who were still living there, but they were employees and not inmates. And also an engineer still there.

After visiting for a short while, I walked right back to Farm Camp 17, getting back before evening, and I stayed there another night, and my official release date was August 13, 1956.

Alla was given her identification papers and taken to the railway station at Zubova Polyana, and placed in the next train. She first went to Potzma, which was already packed with released inmates, and was on the next train to Moscow. On August 15, Alla arrived in Moscow at her parent's home, to an unguarded life, the first since her arrest 9-1/2 years earlier. Alla's parents were at their summer house at the time in Zvenigorod, so she left Moscow and took a bus there, spent some time with them, and returned to Moscow. Alla then busied herself running errands and catching up with matters, and getting registered again as a resident, and making an appointment to visit the prosecutor assigned to Daniel's matter.

She wrote to Daniel the next day:

> My dear! You of course are perplexed as to why I have not yet traveled to visit you. I also thought that as soon as I placed my suitcase in Moscow, I would fly straight to Vladimir. I have become accustomed now to living without identification papers for many years. Of course, I have certain matters to take care of first.

On Thursday, August 23, Alla met with the prosecutor, and the next day she took a train to Vladimir.

Alla described meeting her family in her memoirs and one bad affect of the matter on Alla's father:

> So I went to see my parents in Zvenigorod and spent a few days there. My beloved Zvenigorod, the city of my summer vacations during my childhood, was of course,

not the same now as it was then, but was still somewhat the same.

One day, after strolling about the outskirts of the city, because much of it was like the Mordovia forests, and I could not get enough of running about the open land, I returned home, went into the room and there sat a person who was completely unfamiliar to me. He jumped up, grabbed me by the hands and started to drag me about the room. I then grabbed him by the neck, thinking, "Lord! Who is this? Who can this be?" And I immediately recognized him, as he could only be my brother Yuri. Nine and plus years I left him as a skinny tall boy that just finished high school. Now he was a wide-shouldered and solid adult man, and appearing nothing like that teenager as I last saw him.

One unfortunate incident affected my father badly, but I do not remember exactly what year this occurred. He worked at the Obuv Institute of Professional Diseases, and while there he built a laboratory for the study of eye reflexes. This was his pet project. An interesting man with the Russian name of Kulibin worked for him and built a lot of the apparatus. This laboratory was my father's life, and then they took it away from him.

One day he comes to work and there is a sign on the door announcing his retirement, he, a solid scientific researcher, having the title of Professor *honoris causa*. The reason was plainly clear: his daughter was in prison; his mother was abroad. My grandmother, my father's mother, left Russia at the time of the revolution and went to live in Prague. After, father went to work at the Institute of Scientific Information, since he was fluent in varying degrees in 7 languages. He now felt he found his calling here at this new employment, but he never got over the trauma of his sudden expulsion from the Obuv Institute.

THE FINAL YEARS OF DANIEL ANDREEV

1956 – CONTINUED

At the Vladimir prison Alla finally saw Daniel again after 9-1/2 years, but under the surveillance of an armed guard. She later recorded the event:

> They brought me into a tiny room. In it was a regular table, 2 empty chairs, while a female guard sat on a 3rd chair holding an automatic rifle. They brought Daniel in. He looked just the same as he did before, except that he was now very thin and gray-haired. We were so overjoyed that we did not notice how exhausted the other was. But I was not thinking about any of his illnesses at that minute. Daniel grabbed my hands.
> The guard likewise appeared happy at our encounter.
> Daniel then, under the table, gave me a hand-written notebook with his verses. I took the notebook and hide it in my dress. Daniel then asked me to buy him a volume of Esenin's poetry.

Alla returned to Moscow by train. After a few days, Daniel wrote to her:

> My dear sunshine. I think that both of us displayed ourselves to each other in the best possible manner, than what we actually are in reality. This is the result of a nervous exuberance. Now I am terrified about the hurricane you are now in. Instead of absolute necessary rest, you for 2 weeks have been bouncing back and forth between Moscow, Zvenigorod and Vladimir and back and about Moscow.
>
> My little leaf. Perhaps at my age and situation this is hardly the place to confess such items, but I cannot keep silent about this with you. The matter is that above all variations of feeling and attitude that I have toward you, after our meeting, I am again in love with you, as a little boy. No joke, this is a fact. I want to be with you and nothing more.
>
> But meanwhile we need to in any case bear patience. This of course would be easier if I could, as earlier, be more involved in my projects. But there is no reason to think about this until the time until the loudspeakers silence for at least 2 to 3 hours in a day. But in the meantime it is even impossible to just rest a little bit and deliberate on it.

The radio did not allow Daniel time to concentrate, so he turned back to associating with the non-smoking and cold-blooded Shulgin, playing chess with him from morning to midnight. Daniel again started chain-smoking.

After his meeting with Alla, Daniel wrote a new petition, now to Kliment Voroshilov, the Chairman of the Presidium of the Supreme Soviet. But when Daniel was just about to mail it, he received a directive issued by the Commission of the Presidium of the Supreme Soviet of the USSR, dated August 23, stating:

> We have concluded that there is no basis for your conviction and sentencing according to Articles 19-58-8, and 58-11 of the Criminal Code, and your sentence of punishment has been reduced to a term of 10 years prison confinement according to Article 58-10, Anti-Soviet agitation and propaganda, which is still applicable.

So Daniel's judicial review was finally completed and the more serious of the crimes were mitigated, however he still had another 8 months at Vladimir prison.

Except for those who died in prison or labor camps, the balance of those involved in Daniel's matter were already released and acquired rehabilitation.[90] Alla wrote of this to Daniel:

> The machine is beginning to rotate again from the start. The matter is that many of our associates, who were caught in the web with us in this alleged conspiracy, have submitted petitions for full rehabilitation. They of course are fully justifiable to get it. I an intervening to get it also.

In the process of acquiring her rehabilitation, Alla accidentally met Victor Vasilenko in the waiting room of the prosecutor's office, and also Aleksei Shelyakin's wife, who just returned from Syktyvkar, the capital city of the Komi Republic, near Inta, where both of the men were in labor camp. They were likewise applying for rehabilitation. Vasilenko wanted to return to the universtity, while Shelyakin back to work as an architect. Alla of course wanted back into the **Moscow Region Union of Artists** and to return to work. The review progressed slowly for everybody, with many people in line, all those millions released from prisons and labor camps.

---

[90] After release as a political criminal, rights were limited, and the former convict had to go through a process known as rehabilitation to have full-rights returned as a Soviet citizen. This way they could again get a residence, work, and pension.

Alla likewise hoped that Daniel would be released from prison earlier due to his serious health problems, but they refused her petition and upheld the final decision for Daniel to complete a full 10 years before his release. She likewise petitioned to get them to drop all charges, that there was never any anti-Soviet agitation displayed or intended and that none of it was ever propaganda. Alla's argument was that Daniel's novel *Night Wanderers* was a total work of fiction and fantasy. This attempt was likewise categorically rejected.

After her visit, Alla communicated to Daniel the results of the meetings, and Daniel then wrote a letter to the Chief Military Prosecutor. He informed them of his disagreement with the decision of the Commisson to retain the 10-year sentence, based on the premise that he was not guilty of any violation of Article 58-10, or any other of the charges. Daniel detailed his argument with the following points:

1. The unfinished novel *Night Wanderers*, that appears to be the basis of my accusation, is not anti-Soviet. It was directed at separate ugly scenarios of reality that have recently received the deserved condemnation under the designation of [Stalin's] cult of personality and the excessive authority of the agencies of the Ministry of Internal Affairs. I wrote a fictional composition, reflecting the complex and completely contradictory proceedings of the old Moscow intelligensia of the period surrounding the year 1937. The various personages of the novel appear as representative of the various sides of the psychology of the intelligent person of that era. Not just one of the personages was displayed with certain characteristics, although often I utilized distinct traits of persons who surrounded me, and often just conjured characters in their entirety. One of the characters that personified the negative element was Serpukhov, and I placed into his mouth statements from a terrorist point of view, and as fiction, these

are not my genuine convictions, since I subsequently refute them in my novel through a character of positive elements, the hero Glinski.

The novel was never completed and I never viewed it as propaganda or with purposes of agitation, summoning others to some kind of malicious activities. My goal was to write the truth about the life of a very narrow circle of people, all who were very diverse, seeking each his individual paths under the conditions of a difficult and far from stable environment.

2. I do not consider myself guilty of anti-Soviet agitation, because never and not one of the number of my associate even attempted anything of a terrorist nature, and not even anything that resembled any activity that would be considered malicious to the Soviet government. Nothing in my novel can be concluded as being conducive to anti-Soviet agitation.

3. The investigation that was conducted in agreement with the instruction of the criminal Abakumov and under his direct control was subjective and from the very beginning had the fabrication of a conspiracy as his goal. In addition to this the investigative agencies presented a list of some 40 persons they felt involved, and who were just people who plainly entered our apartment, not counting all of our friends and relatives and my wife. They told me that I had to confess in order for the proceedings to proceed, so the agencies could immediately arrest all of these persons, and so much of what they did was obvious blackmail in its ugliest form to acquire more names.

I was not a person completely well from the side of my nervous system, because the nighttime hours-long interrogations and the entire atmosphere of force and provocation, all of which dominated the MGB in the years 1947-1948, very quickly brought me to a state of being incapable of fully controlling myself under what was done there to me under the appellation of investigative proceedings.

These are the reasons why I subscribed to falsified confessions that completely distorted all of my statements and my views and in general my entire individual self.

It was because of such zeal that caused them to destroy my manuscript, and all that now remains is a few isolated quotations recorded in other places. I feel the novel was cremated against my categorical protest because back in 1947-48, they felt later this manuscript would not serve as a reliable means of accusation, but on the contrary, that it would in time serve as a means to remove all accusations from me.

I petition you for a new review of the matter and full rehabilitation.

Daniel wrote to Alla regarding his latest petition, but admitted that it would have little affect on the matter, since the agencies were too authoritative and powerful for him to defeat, and they cared next to nothing about him anyway, having many others in line also with the same intents.

Soviet legislation of September 14, 1956, allowed the release of prisoners before the conclusion of their terms. On September 21, Shulgin, Bereshvili and 7 others at Vladimir, were released. Before Shulgin was released, as part of the mitigation of his sentence, he had to sign a document that he would not advertise or repeat to anybody the conditions of prison confinement, and he did, since he was already 78 years of age, and had been sitting at Vladimir now 12 years. He just wanted out.

September 19, Daniel was released from his cell in the prison hospital and was assigned to cell 46 in cellblock 3. Knowing he had time to still serve, he immediately returned to writing, and to *Rose of the World* for the most part.

Further work on *Rose of the World* developed characteristics of an interesting and unique philosophic, religious, mythological, and political treatise, and that he – Daniel – was its announcer for its dissemination among humanity and especially Russia. In one of his poems, Daniel stated regarding himself, *I am an announcer of that future day.*[91] In one of the earliest versions of the text, *Rose of the World* was divided into 4 major sections where his concepts are expounded:

The first section was from the worlds of enlightenment to the worlds of the trans-myths. The 2nd was the demonic worlds. The 3rd was from the *stikhials* to the worlds of the *daimons* and the supreme worlds of *Shadanakar*. The 4th section was a supplement that consisted of chapters titled: *Structure of the Human, Cosmic, Changes of Eons, Demonic Plan, Space and Time, Karma, Meta-Biography, Meta-History of the Contemporary Era,* and *Personal.* All of the text composed at this time at Vladimir prison eventually made its way into the finished volume, except the final chapter, as Daniel decided it was best to separate his personal self from his concepts.

Daniel, as a result of his spirit journeys, defined a structure of the universe that he describes as strata or worlds and, apart from a few, all have a distinct appellation with a defined purpose.

Daniel still could not adjust to working with the blare of the radio, and with a caustic humor complained to Alla:

> As far as *Rose* is concerned, even flowers love quiet and are unable to endure loudspeakers. And if they are exposed to an incessant stream of loud sounds, the vibrations cause them to decay, and they loose that aroma that we rightly expect from them. This is a fact that you can read about in textbooks on plant growth.
>
> It seems that all is going very well, and if they stretch it to February, I will be glad for the reasons that I already mentioned to you, the most important being

---

[91] This poem is located at the beginning of this volume.

time to decide our future. By the way, so you do not forget, when you receive my telegram at the time I leave here, travel here as soon as you can, and bring a suitcase with you, since I have no way of taking all the books I have accumulated over the years and also all my notebooks.

On November 17, the Military Board of the Supreme Court of the USSR took note of Daniel's matter and directed it to another agency for supplementary examination. He was the final person of the entire proceeding who still remained unreleased. It was not until December 2, that the documents reached Vladimir prison, and then Daniel's feeling that the circle of hardships was coming to an end was justified. He wrote to Alla:

I just read the decision of the Supreme Court. Practically, or better said, psychologically, I am prepared for a possible trip to Moscow, although I very much hope that this can be circumvented and he will travel to visit me here. Or maybe they do not want to see me here behind these walls and so know where and how I have been residing 9 years since I saw these people last. But maybe I want to go to Serbski.[92] But no matter what you do, nothing will help except fatalism. I will tolerate this final train ride as their final imposition of suffering upon me.

On December 12, Daniel sent a new petition, this one addressed to the Chief of the Investigative Department of the KGB. His purpose was to protest the supplementary examination to which he was ordered to attend. In this latest petition, Daniel brings to their attention his earlier letter to Premier Malenkov.

I a previous petition, written over 2 years ago, I brought your attention to the fact that it is impossible for me to

---

[92] A state-operated mental institution and convalescent hospital.

accept the existing Soviet establishment, until such time that you materialize in a factual manner the freedoms of speech, press and religious instruction. Since that time, important movements have occurred in our country, such as the XX Congress,[93] however no changes have occurred in regard to freedom of the press – and no matter what is stated in the Constitution – from the era of [Stalin's] cult of personality and the present era. It is all the same. So what is the matter?

At no time did I cause anti-Soviet agitation or distribute propaganda to incite this, and I never voiced my convictions in a public square, or in any social assembly.

So tell me. Of what does my crime consist? What is the basis to retain me in prison for 10 years? I have well documented my complete innocence in all the petitions submitted so far.

Daniel left Vladimir on December 16, to an inside jail cell at the KGB, and then he was transferred to the B.P. Serbski Central Institute of Penal Psychiatry. All of his possessions and all his notebooks remained behind in Vladimir. Alla went to claim them, and when she arrived she met with the deputy prison warden, Captain David Ivanovich Krot. Alla recorded her conversation with him:

"You know that your husband left."

"I know, but he is physically unable to lift anything, and so he had to leave all his things behind."

The captain called an attendant, that is, the prison purser (a woman).

"Well, did Andreev leave anything behind?"

"A entire bag of stuff."

"Bring it."

---

[93] This was Khrushchev's speech denouncing the cult of personality that surrounded Stalin.

She brought the bag. Now my prison custom kicked in and I figured he would do a search. So I started to take the stuff out of the bag.

Krot interrupted, "Not necessary. Leave it all there."

Then I said, "As you want, Mr Warden."

He then send the purser away, stared at me very carefully and said, "Take it and go away!"

I understood what he meant, and I grabbed the bag, mumbled some words of gratitude and ran out of the room.

Returning from Vladimir, while in the bus, I stuck my hand into the bag, and felt all of these notebooks, books, rags, linen, letters, and postcards. I withdrew just something from the bag, and it was a notebook, one of the sections of *Rose of the World*, written with a pencil.

1957

Daniel began the year 1957 in a hospital room in Department 4 at the Serbski Institute for Penal Psychiatry. The institute was located on Kropotkinski Lane, just around the corner from his old residence on Mali Levshinski. The area for political prisoners was separate from the criminal. Daniel arrived here at the intervention of Alla, because of his maniac-depression disorder from the war years and the bad effect that the prison years had on him, with his related illnesses while at Vladimir prison. Alla hoped for a quick discharge of all accusations made against him should the diagnosis be to his benefit.

While at Serbski Daniel befriended a young artist named Rodion Gudzenko. He was likewise arrested for anti-Soviet propaganda and as a result of his interest in French art. In 1947, he had plans to leave Soviet Russia to France, and was apprehended just before his ship left Leningrad. He was arrested for attempting to illegally flee the country. They became close over the 3 months Daniel resided there.

The director of Department 4 was a well-known psychiatrist named Daniel Romanovich Luntz, by profession he was titled a doctor of prison sciences. After several evaluations, nothing was concluded as far as Daniel's judicial matter was concerned, although he was diagnosed as having maniac-depression as a result of his World War 2 duty. In the middle of March, Daniel was released and he was transferred to Lubyanka.

Daniel returned to the same type of prison cell he had from the interrogation period at Lubyanka for another month. Alla described Daniel's final release from the penal system after 10 years and 2 days:

> By this time April was nearing its end, but I would still regularly visit the prison director attempting to see Daniel, but was not successful. So then about April 19 or 20, the director calls me personally. The first thing that came to my mind was that Daniel was terminally ill. He told me that all was fine and he would get back to me in a couple of days.
>
> Then April 22, rolls around, the time that Daniel should be released, and the director calls me and tells me, "Relax. All is well. Tomorrow he will be released. Come here tomorrow, and when you arrive, we will have him ready for you to take home."
>
> The next day, April 23, I arrived. I took with me a copy of Yevgeni Tarle's book on Napoleon and his Russian campaign of 1812. I was flipping through the pages but could not get myself to read any of it. Daniel entered the waiting room, where I awaited him. I rose and we took each other by the hand. We left and went to my parent's residence, and because there was just nowhere else in the world that he could go. It was a sunny day, just as it was on the day that Daniel was arrested.

As he expected, Daniel moved in with his in-laws on Podsosenski Lane, only taking one corner of the apartment. On May 10,

Daniel was issued new identification documents. Now he was free to travel. They likewise submitted documents for Daniel's rehabilitation, but with Soviet bureaucracy, this would take time and more petitions.

As soon as Daniel regained strength he went to visit Aleksandr Kovalenski. He received rehabilitation in November 1956, and in January 1957, was readmitted to the Union of Writers. But he was still ill and the death of his wife in a labor camp affected his nerves seriously.

After a few days, Irina Yusova came to Podsosenski to visit Daniel. Such visits with previously close friends brought some happiness and consolation to Daniel. His first wife Aleksandra Gublyor also unexpectedly came to visit him. She wrote a few letters on his behalf to the Union of Writers to have him accepted. Also Tatyana Morozova visited.

Daniel and Alla lived frugally. For all practical purposes, they had nothing. No residence, no possessions, no work, no money. They were living on the financial subsidies of her parents for the most part. Some of Daniel's old friends from school days, after they heard of his release and fiscal situation, sent some money. People would come by and slip an envelop under the door and leave. Daniel could not collect his veteran's pension until receiving his rehabilitation, or any other royalties from his father's works, until he could prove his validity as heir in a Soviet court. Somehow, Daniel and Alla managed.

Now Daniel and Alla had to find a place to live. Without documents indicating rehabilitation and a residency registration, they were forced to live 70 miles outside of Moscow, so they sought residence elsewhere. They decided on a friend's aunt, Alla Davidovna Smirdova. So they traveled to Vishenki, a village south of the Oka River and near Kopanovo, east of Ryazan. They were well received and spent the night there. Then they attempted to register for residence, but their application was refused, as they were still too close to Moscow.

The next stop was Torzhok, in the opposite direction, northwest of Moscow. Victor Andreevich and wife Anna Kemnitz lived there, and he was working at an airplane manufacturing place. They both moved here after their subsequent releases from labor camps. Daniel and Alla were able to register to live in a small 2-room apartment. Torzhok was likewise the home of many other released inmates.

They resided there for 3 weeks and Daniel was able to recuperate and regain some of his strength. Daniel rode the local bus and electric streetcar. Evenings were spent reading poetry to guests funneling through their apartment.

Daniel did not forget about previous acquaintances and he wrote to Galina, Rodion Gudzenko's wife, wondering what became of him after Daniel's release from Serbski. He also wrote to Peter Kurochkin, who was still assigned to Vladimir Prison.

Then Daniel's health failed at the end of May, and Vasili Parin, a former cellmate from Vladimir Prison, intervened on his behalf and had him assigned to the Moscow Vishnevski Institute for treatment. Friends rotated in and out of his hospital room on a regular basis. Tatyana Morozova, Sergei Ivashev-Musatov (who was Alla's first husband), Galina Rusakova, and Zoya Kisilova visited. Zea Rakhim traveled all the way from Georgia to see Daniel.

But Daniel was hardly able to write while at the institute, as he recorded in a diary:

> I am seldom lonesome. I am lonesome only when I am surrounded by circumstances or tedious work that interferes with what I consider to a certain extent to be my debt, my cause, my justification for existence.
>
> Right now it is particularly this way: the ward is noisy, nothing is comprehensible, and it is impossible to get involved in anything. The lack of patience I have developed due to waiting for my release papers so I can leave and go to Kopanovo grows with each day and hour. I am convinced that this circumstance and therapy will pass quickly. What is important is nature, freedom and calm. And for Alla to be along side me.

Daniel was released from the Vishnevski Institute June 22, in the morning. The diagnosis was not comforting: the results were myocardial infarction (heart attacks), angina pectoris, and arterial sclerosis of the aorta. He learned little that was new about his medical conditions. As far as Daniel was concerned, he only had one medical treatment to rely on: nature, and Daniel was eager to run from Moscow. That day at Bruzhes' apartment, he penned a letter, replying to Lev Rakov:

> In a few days, Alla and I are leaving, finally, to the countryside, along the Oka in Ryazan province, not far from Eseninski place,[94] for 2 months. Literally we will be gone exactly that many days and hours. I can no longer tolerate being away from nature, and my wife and I have not had any opportunity to have some private time together due to the turmoil of the first month and as a result of my time in therapy. She is exhausted to her limits. The concluding period before my release from prison was the most difficult of all for her.

Daniel and Alla did have the opportunity to visit the Kremlin before leaving for the countryside, a place he did not visit since a teenager.

The day before Daniel's release from the Vishnevski Institute, June 21, a review of his matter was concluded by the Plenum of the Supreme Court of the USSR and the accusations were ameliorated. The news came later, just as they were leaving. Now he was able to register to live in Moscow, but he could not do this until autumn, and the reason was that he still needed his documents to indicate rehabilitation. Another reason was a Moscow city-wide festival that was planned, so until then he still had to reside outside the 70 mile boundary.

---

[94] The birthplace of poet Sergei Esenin, Konstantinovo, Ryazan province, south of Kopanovo, where Daniel and Alla were earlier.

On July 1, Daniel and Alla took a motorship at the Moscow River and traveled to Kopanovo on the Oka River. The trip took 2 days, and they rented a room in the hut of a widow with the family name of Anankina. They called her Aunt Liza, as did everybody else. Shortly after arriving, Daniel wrote to Lev Rakov on his impressions of the area and their plans:

> Right now I am writing to you, sitting in a village hut that is only a 2-minute walk from the Oka River, which is so majestic here and its seems to be as wide as the Neva River at the Palace Bridge. There is absolutely no conveniences of any type here, the level of life is no different than during the childhood of Esenin.[95] No electricity, but to a certain degree this is counterbalanced by quiet, tranquility and the beauty of nature. We have a kerosene lamp and a wood stove. We wash our clothes and dishes at the river.
>
> Nevertheless, we have only been here 2 days and with my limited movement I was only able to see the closest of surroundings. But because I yearned so much for nature, that right now just the sight of any tree brings me great joy, and even more is their immense sizes and the extent of the forests around me.
>
> We have made arrangements to stay here all of July and August, resting and working. Alla Aleksandrovna goes out to do sketches, ignoring her grippe and the complete hooligan weather. I am getting ready to continue a work I started earlier and, among other things, I am thinking about a preparing a small booklet of verses about nature. Essentially it is already composed, but I still need to refine it and make some revisions, and I hope by autumn to submit it to a publisher. I cannot be assured of its publication, of course, to try this anyway will not affect me any. The

---

[95] Sergei Esenin, born 1895; died 1925.

title of the book is *Barefooted*. But in general, I have a stack of new verses that I would like to share.

A week later Daniel wrote to Tatyana Morozova:

The nearest post office and telegraph is 3 miles away, and the road is through an empty field. No pharmacy, or the closest is about 8 miles away, and the fastest way to get to each is still to walk. I also need to add that the weather is repulsive.

Yesterday was the first good day so far, and today it is overcast again with a cold wind from the north. I do not even want to talk about bathing. Both of us are getting ill. Alla's polyneuritis[96] started up, and her back and feet hurt. To make matters worse, there is not even a sapling next to the house to lie under, we need to go to the forest. True that the further we go it is very beautiful and colorful, rich with mushrooms and flowers, but this is at a distance, but nearby the place is filled with insects, and to the point you cannot even sit on the ground. Most of the time we just sit in the house. Alla has hardly gone to do any sketches, and I do little work, maybe 2 hours a day, and *Rose of the World* is moving forward.

It was here on vacation that Daniel developed the concept of Eternal Womanhood, prior to this time the concept was only called – She, impersonal, bright and good, and he had a revelation during the night that provided him the appellation of *Zventa-Sventana*.

Within a week the weather improved and the June sun changed their attitude.

---

[96] Also known as Peripheral neuropathy

While at Kopanovo, news came to Daniel and Alla that Vadim, Daniel's brother, was returning to Russia for a visit. The brothers had been separated now 40 years, and Vadim was working in New York since 1949. They were on a ship traveling from London to Leningrad and had just arrived, and with him was his wife and children.

Daniel was beyond just excited and insisted that his brother travel to Kopanovo and stay with them. But all of a sudden rain started and Daniel caught a cold, but Alla suspected it was pneumonia, as his temperature increased to 104, and there were no doctors or medical facilities in the area. But Vadim was not allowed to travel to Kopanovo without special permission, since he was from abroad, and so Vadim could not even leave Moscow. Since no ship or train would give him a ticket as a result, not having the proper documents, Vadim hired a private taxi to take the risk and drive him to Kopanovo.

Never had Vadim been in this region of Russia and it left an exciting impression on him, especially being near the birthplace of Sergei Esenin. But he had to leave the taxi at the city Shilovo, and take the final 25 miles by boat on the Oka River. The local boat owner did not care about documents, but only to get paid for the trip. Later Vadim recorded the event in his memoirs:

> Never in my life have I been in these regions, but I was able to identify with them. Every turn in the river unveiled to me something that was familiar and related. The white willows with their immense clumsy branches hanging over the river; the gray-blue bottomland between the flooded meadows; in the distance were the skeletons of abandoned churches; ravens nested on the hay-covered roofs of ancient villages. All of this was mine, native to me, all of this entered into me as Russian books and verses, all of this was somehow becoming part of my blood.

> I arrived late evening into Kopanovo, into a gray thick gloom, and I could hardly see the street. A woman's voice penetrated the darkness.

Alla met him at the dock and immediately recognized him, different from the others who left the boat and somewhat resembling Daniel. Vadim described the encounter between the brothers after 40 years:

> We went into the hut. The similarity between the 2 of us brothers was amazingly immense and obvious in just the first minutes we were together. The same graying hair, the same forehead, the thin face, the characteristic Andreev nose, and the dimples on each side of our mouths. We kissed and hugged and then talked on shallow matters for a few minutes.
>
> That night, Daniel's temperature dropped, and all of us had a long conversation, and it was interesting that we talked to each other in partial phrases, that one starts saying something and the other finishes, as if we had lived together all our life.
>
> Then Daniel read to me some of his verses and I was impressed at how professional and talented a poet that this boy became, and I remember how I would play with him and drag up and down the building fire escape ladder outside. His fluency and mastery in Russian was obvious, and the manner that he recited the words with such self-confidence and relaxation.

Vadim and Daniel spent 4 days together at Kopanovo. Vadim took the same route back to Moscow, and no one even knew he was gone.

After 2 months vacationing at Kopanovo, Daniel and Alla took a motorship back to Moscow, arriving there August 12. Vadim and his family met them at the dock and they spent some time together there also.

While at Kopanovo, documents arrived from the Military Supreme Court regarding Daniel's rehabilitation. Dated July 11, it was signed by Deputy Justice P. Likhachev, and stated:

> The decision of a special meeting of the KGB of the USSR of October 30, 1948, and the decision of the Military Supreme Court of November 17, 1956, regarding the matter of D.L. Andreev, that it will be removed and the matter terminated.

Now came the necessity of finding a residence, having received the proper documents to acquire a Moscow residency permit. For all practical purposes, Daniel and Alla were destitute and homeless. Daniel was still suffering from the illness in Kopanovo, and complained in his memoirs:

> What a nasty situation. Heart attacks with heavy vomiting, fainting, and unexpectedly, as in the subway. What is the worst is my severe limitation in movement.

Alla parents attempted to be as hospitable as possible, and Daniel wanted to take advantage of it while it was available. Daniel wrote to his cousin describing the situation:

> Aleksandr Petrovich works at home for the most part, in the same room. Alla has her graphics spread all over the other room and on which she needs to work. For me to do my writing I need quiet and calm, but now everybody's nerves have reached their limit. Yulia Gavrilovna had a heart attack. After this prolonged vacation I brought – not physically but located in my cranium – material that I need to immediately transfer to paper.

Daniel's mother-in-law, Yulia, with her self-sacrificing worry for her daughter Alla, one day screamed, "Deliver us, God, from such geniuses!"

It was a week after the couple's return from Kopanovo that Vadim and family left Moscow to return to New York. Daniel and Alla then went to visit their old friends, Gleb and Lubov Smirnov, at their summer house in Perlovka (today known as Mytishchi), just north of Moscow. They made their home there and Alla would go into Moscow each day and intervene on his behalf for his pension to be reinstated, and for back pension to be provided him, to arrange for future help due to his disabilities, and for a place to permanently live. Alla did not have regular work and the travel and commotion wore her.

The one job she did find was at a publishing firm for medical books, but the income was hardly enough for basic needs. Her first try at a pension for Daniel succeeded, but the amount was very meager for their existence. The future was not promising.

Daniel worked on a collection of poems about nature, which he titled *Barefooted*, and he termed it, "the last straw to grasp onto for survival." It included 52 poems of various facets of nature and the most of it based on his experiences in Trubchevsk. The balance of Daniel's time was dedicated to *Rose of the World*, still unfinished and on which he worked almost each day.

Daniel wrote to Tatyana Morozova and was very blunt about their situation:

> Dear Tatyasha. I did not write recently and the main reason is that I am overloaded with work and every day after I finish it I am not worth much to do anything else. Now in a few days we need to travel to visit Kornei Chukovski, and he lives in Peredelkino. I cannot seem to gather enough strength, and which I indispensably need for such a trip. I was only there once since returning to Moscow and I barely made it here to Perlovka. All our effort is concentrated on finding a room and getting my pension and the people with whom we need to deal are motionless. Living here in Perlovka, it is impossible to get them to move. Looks like we can stay here until October 10 – but only God knows for sure – but to stay

any longer is impossible. Alla has found some work, but it brings in little money, and her amount of business and visits has been excessive. She heroically attempts to do this all at the same time: put her painting in exhibits, traveling to Moscow, painting (otherwise they will expel her from the Union of Artists), caring for me, and handling domestic chores.

Recently Irina Yusova has been an immense help, but she needs to return to Moscow in a few days.

The mood here is already depressing.

Irina Yusova, in her self-sacrificing attitude toward Daniel, took a leave a absence from her employment and found a room in Perlovka in a communal house near the Smirnov summer home. She would take care of Daniel while Alla was in Moscow all day.

At the end of September, Daniel and Alla gathered what little they had and their strength and traveled to Peredelkino, southwest of Moscow, to stay with Kornei Chukovski for a while. He was a poet and prose writer, literary critic as well as a language teacher in a local school, and so he and Daniel had much in common. But this only lasted a short while, a couple of weeks, especially with Alla spending so much time in Moscow anyway between work and business errands on behalf of Daniel. So in mid-October, Daniel and Alla left the hospitable home of Kornei Chukovski and returned to her parents in Moscow. No sooner did they return that Alla became ill with bronchitis, and she was bed-ridden for a week, they blamed it on the sudden cold of autumn weather.

Alla's efforts in finding a residence finally proved successful and they moved into a apartment in Building 14/1, at the corner of Ashcheulov Lane and Sretenka Street, in the center of Moscow's business district. The apartment was compact: one room with a kitchen and bathroom, including gas, electricity and a telephone. As his habit was, Daniel would leave the apartment at nights and walk the streets barefooted in the snow. Such strolls, he was convinced, instilled new strength in him. But his health did not improve, and for the most part, he would write lying on his back, and even with the typewriter on his stomach.

The entirety of November and December were occupied with various business meetings on behalf of Daniel. To restore his pension as an invalid of WW2, he had to fill out all the inquiries and provide documents to the VTEK (Medical-Labor Expert Commission). On November 22, Daniel was again acknowledged as an invalid of the 2nd Category (meaning that it was not combat service), and he was assigned a monthly pension of 347 rubles. Bu this was totally inadequate, since the apartment they were renting took 900 rubles. Next step was writing a petition to the KGB for the amount Daniel felt was owed him when they confiscated his entire library of 2,000 volumes when he was arrested. Daniel tried to prove to them that many of these books were rare and valuable and needed, and he also attached a list of them to his petition.

Unexpectedly and thanks to Kornei Chukovski, Daniel was assigned work: the translation of a book of short stories by the Japanese author Fumiko Hayashi. He was not thrilled about it, since he spoke no Japanese. So Zea Rakhim, who was familiar with Japanese, became involved. Zea's responsibility was to produce an interlinear literal word-for-word translation from Japanese into Russian, and then Daniel was to arrange and refine it into a readable translation. He had to supply 20 typed pages of text before July 1, 1958, which gave him 7 months. Daniel felt the book would be of little significance, but it was work, yet he still felt that his first priority was *Rose of the World*.

Daniel had also hoped that Kornei could help him with the publication of his book of poetry *Barefooted*. But this was also a dead end as Daniel could not meet the demands of the publishing houses for the content and manuscript submission they required.

Even then, guests and friends circulated through the apartment on Ashcheulov, and almost daily: Sergei Ivashev-Musatov, Tatyana Morozova, Zoya Kisilova, Ekaterina Bokova, and Anna Smirnova, and then later the following year, a person to become an important part of the Andreev couple's life: Boris Chukov.

While in prison, Daniel became lonesome for the movies, as he wrote to Galina Gudzenko:

> I cannot tell you how much of an exciting passion I have toward this form of art, and how in specific periods of my life, under certain conditions, there grew a particular demands for movies. How I dreamed of seeing even a few categories of any good films. And so, imagine, over the past 6 months, since now the opportunity has surfaced for me to satisfy this demand, we have only succeeded in being at the movies twice: for *Don Quixote* and *Swan Lake*. We just did not have the time or strength over the balance of time: either time during the day or strength during the night. But we did manage to go to the Bolshoi Theater to watch *Romeo and Juliet* starring Galina Yulanova. Our admiration has no limit. She is not just a ballerina, but something much more. The decorations and settings were beyond any kind of complement.

Daniel received bitter news the beginning of December: his cousin Alexander Philippovich Dobrov died on November 30. His death was attributed to a combination of tuberculosis and cirrhosis of the liver, and he suffered immensely the final few months of his life. Daniel also wrote to Vadim in New York to let him know. Now for all practical purposes, Daniel had no relatives on the Dobrov-Veligorski side remaining in Russia, and just the very few in Leningrad on the Andreev side.

In December, Alla went to a medical clinic due to the growth of a tumor. It was the same one that was surgically removed years earlier when she was at Labor Camp 3, and they diagnosed it as fibroma, but now it was again growing. The next month January, she had it surgically removed. In addition to this, Alla was also diagnosed with anemia and Basedow's disease, also known as Graves' disease.

1958

Daniel hoped to continued working on the Japanese short stories at the Maleevka Writers Union outside of Moscow. Even though he was not a member of the Writers Union, he hoped to get a permit to use the facilities based on the fact that he was the son of Leonid Andreev, who was a member when he was alive. It surprised many of the members that he sat in prison as a political inmate for 10 years, and they accused him of writing monarchist compositions, but Daniel's rebuttal was that it was the Russia of the era before socialism.

Daniel and Alla were permitted to use the facilities and they took advantage of it. It became his little corner of paradise, where everything was dedicated to literature. They were assigned a small room as their temporary residence. Alla was glad for him and one less worry for her. Daniel wrote to Tatyana Morozova about working at Maleevka:

> We rise at 9 AM. Then wash up, have breakfast, and a routine here at the institute. Alla and I go for a walk and she does some sketches and I just enjoy the environment. She will go to some picturesque spot and set up her easel and drawing board, while I take off my shoes and go my way and wander about the forest. These places are marvelous, with sanitariums on 3 sides, surrounded by a stream that flows down a deep slope. It is so beautiful and quiet here, and especially because the slope is overgrown with trees. But with my heart I prefer places that are flat. I stroll about 40 minutes and then return to start on my work. Lunch is about 3 PM, then again I work until dinner, but before dinner I go for another stroll. After dinner, for the most part, we watch a movie, and they do have interesting and cultural films here.
>
> There is just not enough time to read. Over the 11 days so far I have only succeeded in reading Knaz

Serebranni,[97] which just accidentally fell into the library here.

They feed us quite well here. We try to eat everything that is on our plate, but even then this is sometimes not enough.

The people here are polite, always smiling and excusing themselves, but little is interesting. We have only met a few of the residents, and there are still a few dozen we do not know.

Even though I was initially accused of writing monarchial literature, the era has substantially changed, and now they are publishing Feodor Dostoyevski and Leonid Andreev. Their conversations also mention other authors, although in a low tone of voice, such as Boris Pilnyak, Nikolai Klyuev, and Osip Mandelstam, writers that were on the forbidden books' lists at one time.

Even though Daniel was rehabilitated and free to travel and to reside in Moscow, yet he still retained a paranoia and feared a subsequent arrest as a result of his writings. The first on his mind was all the letters that he had received. Daniel was convinced that should he be arrested again, all the people from whom he received letters would likewise be suspects and subsequently be arrested likewise and the cycle would repeat. So Daniel had Alla cremate all the letters he received so far. Inside of Daniel something was still bothering him, he felt he was still suspected of something as a result of his writings that he was attempting to publish.

Alla recorded the following in response to Daniel's suspicions:

Later we discovered that Daniel was right. For a short time while we were living in Ashcheulov Lane, and Daniel was able to still walk, this girl Allochka started to visit us, a nice girl who said she did not live very far from

---

[97] A novel by Alexsei K. Tolstoy.

there. At night she would accompany Daniel on his walks, and in the darkness he could walk barefooted. Allochka, we found out, then went to the secret police with questions about us. She did not tell us anything, but then quietly exited from our lives and stopped associating with us. I met her several years later and she confessed that she did this and said no more.

Daniel was very insistent that I tell no one at all that he was still writing, and especially about *Rose of the World.*

Boris Chukov later said that Daniel did destroy all of his writings that might appear to be seditious or anti-Soviet.

Daniel decided he had to somehow protect himself. After his return from Maleevka, he wrote a letter to the Central Committee of the Communist Party of the USSR, and included in the package a copy of his poems: *Rukh, Ruin of the Terrible, Nemerechka, Navna, Holy Jewels, Green Bottomland, Barefooted, Ancient Memory, Lyrica,* and *Worlds of Enlightenment.* A few selections of *Rose of the World* were also included. Daniel then sent the following letter:

> I turn to the CC of the USSR with a much unusual matter, that it must be accompanied by my manuscripts, of which I ask the CC to familiarize themselves, and this letter that explains the reason for such a petition:
>
> Almost my entire conscious life has been tied with the literary field. I was an artist, a graphics artist, and later wrote and published 2 scientific books of popular interest on geography, and at the present time I am editing a collection of short stories translated from the Japanese. But always parallel with this work, I was occupied with fictional literature. During this time I wrote to the extent I could and what I could, and not necessarily conforming to market demands, and for a long while I did not even think about having any of my

compositions published, since I did not consider them to be at the same level of present fictional literature.

In 1947, I was arrested and all my manuscripts were cremated. After 10 years of prison confinement I was released and rehabilitated.

Among my destroyed manuscripts there were several notebooks with lyrical verses and poems and a large novel on which I worked many years. To restore all this stuff, of course, is impossible. My memory does not retain such a voluminous amount of material over this long of a time. While in prison I was able to restore a certain portion based on my memory and reproduced it. But likewise these were confiscated and destroyed, or plainly discarded. I again attempted to restore them and in addition I wrote much new stuff. Under the conditions of prison confinement, as implemented by Beria and his confederates, these were again confiscated and destroyed.

The reason for my petition is for the Central Committee to become familiar with my works, and while I resided in psychologically difficult state. I did not write anything clandestinely. But at this point I am lost: do I have the right to read my stuff, and to a limited circle of listeners, and decide on their dissemination, whether or not they be submitted for publication?

So do I explain my petition to the CC, for you to become familiar with my basic compositions.

Daniel sent the letter February 12, and on February 26 he was summoned to the CC. Their decision was to allow Daniel to be free with his compositions, and based on the selections of *Rose of the World* that he submitted, he could continue and complete it.

The beginning of March, Daniel took his collection of poems titled *Barefooted* and submitted it for publication in the magazine *Vremya* (*Time*).

Another burden upon Daniel was his wife's illness. After their return to Moscow from Maleevka, they were informed that Alla's tumor that was surgically removed was actually malignant. Now Alla started radiation treatments on what still remained in her body, and for the next 2 weeks she traveled to the other end of Moscow for treatments. When she returned from the 2nd treatment, Alla collapsed in her cot, totally exhausted of any strength and was unable to more.

At the same time matters were not going well with their apartment, as the rent was beyond any pension Daniel was getting, and now with Alla's radiation treatments, she was unable to work. Daniel sent a letter complaining about the matter to the Supreme Court of the USSR, asking for an increase in pension, and at least enough to cover the rent on their apartment. But later they would loose this apartment and have to look for another.

But Daniel continued working on his primary project – *Rose of the World* – each day, while the translations of the Japanese short stories took a back seat. Still by May 1, he finished 4 of the short stories and hoped this would be enough to satisfy the editors and, if possible, terminate the contract and be paid for the amount done. Daniel's health was barely strong enough and he was hardly interested in the translation anyway.

With spring Daniel's angina pectoris and arterial sclerosis exacerbated, and on March 16, he just collapsed. Now there were 2 ill persons in one room. Daniel was forbidden by the doctors to move, and was advised that he only occupy himself with projects no more than 1 hour a day. Alla lay motionless due to the internal burns from the radiation and she did not walk for several days. Of course, it was Yulia Gavrilovna again to the rescue, who nursed the both of them.

Due to the efforts of Chukovski, and again through the Union of Writers, he was able to get a one-time personal payment to Daniel based on the income from all of his father's writings over the past 40 years, even though Daniel's rights were already terminated. This would be an honorary grant, and especially since 1956, more of Leonid Andreev's poems, plays and dramas were being published, now after many years of their prohibition. During spring of 1958, Daniel and Alla received the final and total sum of 40,000 rubles, enough to pay all of their past debts, some to use as a contribution to others, while the balance was enough for Daniel to live comfortably through the end of his life. At the same time, the Soviet Military Court increased Daniel's pension to 900 rubles a month, and this also helped.

The first contributions that Daniel made were: 300 rubles to Valeri Slueshkin's mother so she could travel to visit her son at the Serbski Institute, and 200 rubles to Galina Gudzenko.

The middle of April, Daniel again was admitted to the Vishnevski Institute, where he was the previous year. Daniel spent somewhat over a month here and almost confined to his bed. Once Alla's health improved, she did not stop with her petitions to the Soviet agencies about a new residence.

While lying in the hospital, Daniel received an answer to his collection of poems, *Barefooted*, that he submitted to the magazine *Znamya*. The poet Konstantine Levin was very blunt in his response as to why the magazine rejected Daniel poetry:

> The verses of Daniel Andreev cause a strange impression. From the one side, there is no doubt that in front of you is a genuine talented poet, and you will be surprised that you have never seen his name in print. However it is impossible to print verses without the visa of our era, it is impossible to include in our publications any contemporary verses not somehow impregnated with the Soviet spirit.

The response was hardly decipherable to Daniel, but he understood their objection, it was part of nature that was outside the secular atmosphere of Soviet press. Levin especially made note of the difficulty of fathoming Daniel's obsession with walking barefoot, and that this made no sense at all.

So Daniel sent a letter attempting to explain his style of poetry and included a copy of *Rukh* and *Navna*. The subsequent letter of rejection came from Dmitriev, the editor, and contained no complements to begin with and was very straightforward:

> Our magazine needs poetry possessing the precise pulse of the era: poetic and political realism.

The month or so that Daniel spent confined to his cot in the hospital improved his health a little. He complained to Tarasov in a letter and hoped to visit them in Izmailovo:

> If I arise, it is just for a short while, and not in order to walk, but just to sit up awhile. But what is worse is the extent of the limitation I have to work, it is almost impossible, and what is ludicrous is that I cannot hardly talk with people. The doctors demand that I talk the least I possibly can. Any conversation that excites or stimulates me or aggravates me causes pain in my aorta, and this easily leads to a heart attack, and then I need to be injected with coramine,[98] and then I am confined to my bed for the course of several days.
>
> But nonetheless, the month I spent in the hospital did provide me with some improvement. I think they will release me in about another week.

After Daniel's release from the Vishnevski Institute, the 2 of them went to the movies and saw Dostoyevski's *The Idiot*. Daniel enjoyed it very much and recorded his opinion of it:

> I was ecstatic over the primary hero. Mishkin is totally undefeatable, and even more than Dostoyevski himself. This is a masterpiece. I have never seen such a good movie in a theater.

---

[98] Also known as nikethamide.

About this time, Daniel and Alla decided to formally marry. They purchased the most inexpensive and thinnest rings available and selected June 4 as their wedding date. They invited Boris Chukov to be best man and Vera, the daughter of Tatyana Morozova, to be bridesmaid. Boris later recorded the event in his memoirs:

> On the morning of the wedding at their Ashcheulov apartment I gave A.A. a large bundle of tulips that my mother raised. A.A. wore a white wedding dress. Then D.L. and A.A. left for the Church of the Rizopolozhenia on Donskoi Street. In the automobile, D.L. told me that the evening before he confessed and took communion, and on the way home his heart attacks started again and would not stop, but now they had subsided.
>
> Chukov noticed that on the drive to the church, Daniel asked the driver to take streets that would avoid the buildings of the KGB. The ceremony was performed by Fr Nikolai Golubtzov. Afterward the 4 of them returned to the apartment on Ashcheulov for a small celebration dinner.

Regardless of Daniel's negative portrayal of the Russian Orthodox Church that he writes in *Rose of the World*, he always treated the religious institution respectfully during his life and considered himself a devout Russian Orthodox. The marriage rite for the Andreevs was a special sacrament, something they experienced together and pertaining to the future. Alla wrote of the special nature of the wedding in her memoirs:

> When young people marry, during the marriage ceremony, they ask of God a blessing and help for their mutual future road. With persons who have already completed this road together and many years, they ask of God an affirmation of what they have traversed and a blessing that all may end well in their earthly lives. With Daniel and myself it was more complex. What he was

bestowing upon me as his spouse was his creative work. My obligation was to preserve it and protect it. This was something I had not awaited, to eventually provide it for public distribution. To publish all that Daniel wrote and to read his verses.

We stood before the Lord for our wedding having already lived through all: 10 years of friendship, and the war, and prison, and 10 years of separation, our reunion after the separation, fathoming our cohesion, because I was always alongside him and understood whom I was alongside. This is why our wedding was a genuine vow before God.

The day after the wedding they departed on their honeymoon, taking a river cruise. The route was from Moscow to Ufa, following Moscow River to the Oka, to the Volga, to the Kama to the Belaya River to Ufa, and then the same on the return. They visited Kopanovo, Kasimov, Murom, Gorki (Nizhni-Novgorod), Kazan and of course Ufa. On the return trip they were also able to visit Kostroma, Ulgich and Yaroslavl.

They returned to Moscow on June 23, and immediately departed to visit the Tarasovs in Izmailovo. Daniel and Alla spent a couple of weeks with the Tarasovs and then returned to the Bruzhes' apartment on Podsosenski for 3 days.

About this time Daniel was finishing Book 11 of *Rose of the World, Toward a Meta-History of the Previous Century*, and he dated the end of the book July 5, 1958. Yet, Daniel still planned on one more section.

After their wedding and during their honeymoon, the Andreevs lost the house on Ashcheulov, since they could not afford the rent. From the Bruzhes' apartment on Podsosenski, the couple bounced around staying at various friends for short periods, and at the Bruzhes' summer home. They then traveled to Pereslavl-Zalesski, in Yaroslav province, north of Moscow, arriving July 6. They were mesmerized by the region. As long as the both of them were in Russia, they were never in this area. They only spent 2 days there and then went to the village

Viskovo along the shore of Lake Pleshcheyevo, only a mile or so outside of Pereslavl, and rented a room. As in Kopanovo, they had no electricity and did all their lighting and heating and cooking with kerosene, they remained there for 1-1/2 months. Alla immediately went to work on her sketches of old homes, museums, monasteries and churches. During their stay, Alla completed 4 paintings and a dozen sketches.

During their stay in Viskovo, Daniel worked the entire time on *Rose of the World*, supplementing it with more material and working on Book 12 of the volume, which he titled – *Possibilities*.

Without a nurse or clinic nearly, Alla had to inject medicine into Daniel whenever he had a heart attack. She records the first time she had to do this:

> During one of Daniel's stays in the hospital, a nurse showed me how to inject a needle into Daniel, and she said that if I did not, he would die shortly after. She taught me how to do this in a pillow. So when we were in Viskovo, I had to give Daniel my first injection with a needle.
>
> Daniel said to me, "My little leaf. I feel poor, I need an injection."
>
> I sterilized the needle over a kerosene flame, poured the medicine inside the syringe, as the nurse showed me, wiped my hand with alcohol and jabbed the needle inside a living person, and even then, someone I loved. After I stabbed him I started to cry and pulled it out. It was such a strange experience. But Daniel consoled me, "Why are you scared. Inject me carefully and all will be fine."
>
> So did I sob with my first attempt at an injection. After this, I injected him many times, and even twice a day.

In August, rain started and this had a bad effect on Daniel's health and they took a private automobile back to Moscow. Daniel's heart attacks intensified so they returned to Bruzhes' apartment on Podsosenski, Daniel in almost a flat position.

Back at the Bruzhes' apartment, Daniel began reading a Russian translation of the Hindu *Mahabharata*, just published in Ashhabat by the Soviet scholar Boris Leonidovich Smirnov. He had to read it lying on a sofa. Daniel shared his thoughts of the book in one of his letters:

> So much is found in this book. It contains fathomless philosophic depth, and the colossal concepts of the *Mahabharata,* reflects not only Homer, but everything I decisively know, except for perhaps *The Divine Comedy.*
>
> If this is really the creation of one person, he is a great genius, profound thinker, and so has untilized all the religious and philosophic concepts that have evolved or been developed earlier. This nation that is capable of the creation of such complex philosophic, psychological, religious, ethical and cosmogonic concepts is unexemplified and incomparable. And what an ability to clothe them in a network of majestic and refined verses!
>
> It should not be a surprise that particularly India produced in our age such a gigantic ethicist as Gandhi, the sole person in our recent era with such integrity as a government activist. And yet his intellect was discredited, that as though polity and morality are incompatible.

Their next stop was another vacation in the autumn. They selected Gorachi Kluich, in the mountains in southern Russian, about halfway between Krasnodar and the Black Sea. Alla acquired a couple of discounted tickets from the Union of Artists, and was counting on the warm weather to help Daniel's health.

Not long before their departure to the south of Russia, Daniel had a discussion with Boris Chukov about his fears of the world's future. Chukov later recorded the conversation:

> Meekly, almost deaf, with hoarseness in his throat, he told me how much his thoughts of a threat of a global war, destructive for our civilization, were torturously

painful for his heart. He then had an acute internal pain, rested for a while, and then read to me *Leningradski Apocalypse*.

Daniel gave Chukov a copy of a hand-written collection of poems and prose titled *Predictions*, and asked him to type them out and copy them on a duplicating machine and then pass them out.

Gorachi Kluich is a resort and a very picturesque region in the hills that extend from the Caucasus Mountains. The Psekups River, a tributary of the Kuban River, flows through the city. The city is named on the list of hot springs in the area. However, the Artists Hall, where Alla had her tickets, was unbearable for Daniel and he complained to Rodion Gudzenko:

> It is impossible to live in this place. The radio is always on, and in the evenings it is the accordion playing. In short, the conditions are incompatible with literary work. Eventually we have to move to a mountain that overlooks Gorachi Kluich. Here the atmosphere is cleaner and dryer, and less harmful since we are above the hydrogen sulfide level that seems to pervade the valley.

They moved to a house occupied by the Grechkin family, using one room with a kitchen and a separate entrance. After the primitive life in Viskovo, the conditions here were idyllic. Daniel continues his letter to Gudzenko on his new residence:

> When days are better for me and the weather is good (and both do not occur simultaneously very often), I lie on a couch outside under an apple tree (as I am doing right now), enjoying the distant mountains, the forests slowing turning yellow, and as much as I can, I type letter my letter on my typewriter. Under such circumstances Alla takes advantage of the moment to run and do her sketches. She needs to do a lot of them, so

that at least 2 or 3 will be selected for the Soviet Russia exhibit in Moscow of paintings. Her physical state right now is better, but as far as her psychological attitude is concerned, as you know yourself, is difficult for me. My heart is in tears just to look at her. As far as care for her, there are no nurses here in these parts to be of a benefit.

At nights he would continue reading *Mahabharata*. The October weather did much benefit for Daniel's health and his heart attacks subsided.

Apart from *Rose of the World*, Daniel spent much time on his other collections of verses: *Russian Gods*, *Fugitives of the World*, and *Worlds of Enlightenment*. But the principle effort was still *Rose of the World*, on which he hurried to work, knowing that his health was failing and realizing that his time was running short. He would type with the typewriter on his lap when he was sitting. Daniel rewrote the first book, *Rose of the World and its Place in History*, and completed the final 12th book of the volume. Daniel then supplemented the volume with a short glossary of names, terms and appellations. Daniel recorded his reflections on completing *Rose of the World* in Chapter 1 of the volume.

I finish the manuscript of *Rose of the World* while on vacation, in a gold-colored autumn garden. He, under whose yoke the country weakened, already for a long while is reaping in other worlds the fruits of what was sown in this world. And nonetheless the final pages of the manuscript I hide in the same manner as I hid the first pages, and I am unable to dedicate its contents to even one living soul. And as in the past, and so now, I have no assurance that this book will not be destroyed, or that the religious experience that saturates it will actually be transmitted to at least someone.

I am immensely ill, the years of my life are numbered. If this manuscript will be destroyed or confiscated, I will not have the time to recreate it. But if it will reach at some time even a handful of persons, whose religious thirst will compel them to read it to the end, overcoming all of its difficulties in comprehension – the ideas inherent in it – it cannot but become seeds that will sprout in strange hearts.

In her memoirs Alla recorded the scene of Daniel completing his divine project:

> When I returned with some sketches, I ran into the garden when Daniel was working. Whoever arranged the garden did an excellent job. In front of him was the typewriter and the stack of his hand-written pencil notebooks of *Rose of the World*. A bowl of fruit was also on the table. I walked up to him Daniel sat there with a strange expression on his face. I got real scared and asked, "What? What is the matter?"
> He answered, "I finished *Rose of the World.*"
> And then I felt the same sensation: he completed the work and was now deflated and not happy. I started to comfort him, "Well, I understand. You finished *Rose of the World*, but a lot of work still lies ahead!" But everything still seemed to remain the same: medicine, injections, doctor visits, his illness.
> Daniel's illness just became worse, and I remembered what the doctors told me, I was the one maintaining Daniel's existence in this world. Maybe I was. But not just me, but his guardian Angel maintained him until such time that he would consummate his destined duty.

Alla recorded in her memoirs hiding a copy of *Rose of the World*:

> Daniel made 2 copies of *Rose of the World*, and the 2nd copy I buried at the top of a ridge that partitioned a canyon from west to east. At my back was Gorachi Kluich, in front of me was a river, and beyond the mountains was the sea.[99] I saw a triangular tower and

figured that at least the mound will always survive. I measured 13 steps to a tree split in half, and upon which I etched a cross using a penknife. Under it I buried the copy in a water can, and I thought that no one would ever find it. Since then, the forest overgrew the area.

At the same time, Alla drew a sketch of the area with an indication of the place the can was buried.

About a week after completing *Rose of the World*, on the sleepless night of October 19, Daniel composed the following poem. It was his final composition, a type of prologue and testament and prayer:

> At sometime earlier, in the dawn of strength
> At the age of ten, I asked as a gift,
> To deliver me from inert materials,
> In the name of God, my best endeavor.
> With a malady I existed at the edge,
> And so my petition died:
> Prolong strength for me at least another year
> In the name of selected effort!
> My malady increased,
> I suffocated and withered,
> And started to pray over trivial items:
> To conclude this final chapter,
> Until I be thrown into the jaws of the lions.
> What appeared was the country of shadows,
> For me there remains ten days:
> Although three-fourths of my work is done,
> And peacefully with my head on a desk I will sleep.
> She will preserve it, always, truthfully,
> My girlfriend, my wife.
> But how helpless in such a threatening age
> Is one discarded human!
> You have not observed his request. I do not grumble:

---

[99] This would be the Black Sea.

The hidden one can return the dust
And the rock in his heart. But although then
Direct the protectors to the bitter house:
To the unfinished pages, the destitute books
There the primordial enemy already lairs:
Save them, Lord! Hide them, protect them,
Allow them to see more days.
The second request, at the same incident,
When the light from above predestined me:
Please provide me at least a sign in this darkness
My beloved on the earth.
The third request: so it is destined
For me to again be incarnated,
Allow me to be born in such a country,
At such a time, when the waves
Of divine creativity and veracity of souls prevail
And the Dark one cannot state: Silence!
Give to both of us, wife and myself,
Earth to touch in such a country,
Where temples are built, and the entire nation
Ascends to you generation after generation.

At the end of October, Daniel wrote to Boris Chukov:

Our life here is not deprived of comfort and poeticism. Especially in the evenings, when we ignite the stove, and we read or work or plainly talk. We sit on the terrace outside the kitchen and view the marvelous landscape of the mountains and the valley of Gorachi Kluich. When we arrived the mountains were green, and then they turned a gold-red, and then a bronze-red, and now they seem to be a lilac-blue. Today Alla Aleksandrovna even saw from a distance the snowcapped peaks of the Caucasus.

But the vacation was not so easy for Alla, who was always looking for a doctor, or running to the drugstore, or giving Daniel injections. For his survival he was dependent on daily injections of Euphyllin,[100] and in extreme circumstances he had to receive injections of Pantoseptum[101] with caffeine. Alla's escape was to run into the forest with her easel. The end of October also brought rain and cold and wind, and which aggravated Danicl's health. They celebrated Daniel's 52nd birthday here.

Now Daniel decided to return to the long postponed translation. The interlinear done by Zea Rakhim was unintelligible and many phrases had meaning that were simply incomprehensible. Daniel wrote to Rakhim to provide more clarification on some of the texts, and this resulted in a rupture of their friendship. Apparently the translation proved Rakhim to be less of an orientalist than he portrayed himself. The entire project died at this time.

Meanwhile, Daniel read *The Confessions of Felix Krull* by Thomas Mann.

Daniel and Alla intended to depart from Gorachi Kluich at the beginning of December, but the bad weather did not cease, and already the morning dew had turned into morning frost. Daniel was desperate for strength for the return trip to Moscow and then he would have to go directly to the Vishnevski Institute.

The return trip for Daniel and Alla to Moscow was very difficult, but they did have the money. So they took a private automobile for the trip from Gorachi Kluich to Krasnodar, about 50 miles, and then a train to Moscow. Alla got them tickets in 2nd class, so Daniel would have a soft bed. There were 3 in the compartment, the 3rd worked as a prosecutor for the Soviet government and he was with them all the way to Moscow. Daniel and Alla were free about telling him all about themselves and the difficulties they had with rehabilitation and now with a permanent residence that they could afford with Daniel's pension as a veteran. The prosecutor gave them his name and contact telephone number

---

[100] Also knows as Theophylline.
[101] Also known as Pantopon.

should they need some advice or help should more difficulties arise. The trainmaster, ascertaining Daniel's condition, kept the 4th bunk free in their compartment to make it easier on them.

They arrived at the Moscow train station November 14, and Alla's father waited for them. Daniel was immediately taken to the Vishnevski Institute and he was assigned to Ward 28. Vasili Parin, a cellmate of Daniel at Vladimir Prison, made the arrangements. He was there for almost 3 months.

The daily injections maintained Daniel's life and he even attempted to stand, but the medicine tended to numb and weaken him. The day after his admission Alla was allowed to visit. Visits to the hospital ward were short as it was even difficult for Daniel to breath. A few days into his rehabilitation, Daniel was able to write to Alla:

> My little girl. You left, but my heart ruptures because I was insufficiently nice to you when I bid farewell to you. I allowed you to leave bitter and now you, my poor little one, will wander the streets the entire night, and at the end finally lie in the darkness on our little sofa and in your lonesomeness you will miss me. My little angel, my golden girl, my sunshine! May God preserve you day to day and night to night!

Daniel understood how difficult it was for Alla. The acquisition of a new apartment was not moving forward. In January she had to present her paintings and sketches for presentation at the exhibition, and she was running to stores and drugstores, hurrying to her ill husband, and not seeming to want to admit to herself that his predicament was terminal. They hoped that after a month or so at the institute, he would fully regain his health, and then after his release he would return to the Union of Writers Hall to continue writing.

After a week and-a-half, Daniel regained some of his strength and he would sit in bed and read newspapers, the hot issue being the present discredit of Boris Pasternak. After 2 weeks Daniel was allowed to get out of bed and walk about the corridors for a quarter-hour once a day. Daniel also noticed an exhibit to be held regarding his father's novels and plays, and he made some mental arrangements to attend with Alla and somehow be an active participant. So Daniel wrote a letter from his hospital bed to the organizer, to make sure they would supply tickets to himself and Alla and place him on their agenda. But any short improvements in health were overtaken with subsequent heart attacks, and again, any effort on Daniel's part was painful, and even to speak was difficult. The first complete month of therapy was obviously futile, as Daniels' health only declined and to the point that he was hardly able to just walk to the wash basin in his room.

Daniel explained it in these terms in a letter to Alla:

Dear friend. Know that I am a stubborn and intractable dualist – not in a philosophic sense, but in a religious! And in my eyes, all life, all the universe, is a mystery play of the struggle between providential and demonic powers. Of course, I believe in the inevitable cosmic victory of the Good principle. But in distinct portions and distinct periods of time (and often from the point of view of human dimensions, which are very prolonged) the victories can remain on the side of the dark powers. I do not imagine how to otherwise interpret history. Nonetheless, I do possess this, not as the result of logical deliberations, but conclusions drawn from meta-historical contemplation.

Alla wrote in response:

There is nothing in the world that is so valuable to me, or even half as valuable, as you. There is nothing that I need. I am able to deny it all, as long as you are alive and with me. And my paintings are more precious to me than anything else, because you love my art as I do. And I need life solely for the reason of you not remaining alone, and my desire is to depart following you and as soon as possible.

While Daniel was at Vishnevski Institute, only Alla was allowed to visit him and he was always waiting impatiently for her. As Daniel told her on one of the visits:

I hear them and I can already guess that these are your steps, even far down the corridor. Here my little angel is hurrying.

1959

In January the Vishnevski Institute was quarantined due to a epidemic of grippe and no visitors were permitted. However, Daniel did communicate via letters with Alla and his friends.

Alla went back to her parent's apartment and again applied for their own residence. Her application was denied based on the evidence that her parent's 2-room apartment was enough for 4 people, and he disregarded her argument that most of the room was used for her and her father's work. Alla got hold of the prosecutor with whom she traveled from Krasnodar to Moscow and he intervened.

January 23, Alla received the order for a new residence. She considered this a miracle. The couple was assigned a 9 foot by 15 foot room, one of 2 rooms in a communal apartment on the 2nd floor. The building was at the end of Leninski Prospect, and where the bottom floor was occupied by a store. At the time this was the last building at the end of the street, and the fields were past it. The other room was occupied by a working family of 4: a husband and wife and 2 children, all in one room about the same size. They shared a kitchen. The husband worked every day and the wife would take the children somewhere most of the time. This allowed some quiet for Daniel during the day. They did not have a telephone until several weeks later.

Daniel remained at the clinic until Alla got an apartment because there was no place to take him, and he needed almost 24-hour care for the meanwhile. With some of the royalty money, Alla purchased a few essentials for the room: a desk that doubled as a dining table, chairs, a bookcase with some books, and a bed. She hung some of her paintings on the walls to make the place comfortable for Daniel on his return.

When Daniel arrived from the clinic on February 17, he did not have enough strength to climb the stairs and the elevator was not working, so some of his friends came by and carried him on a chair up the stairs and into their room. The final 40 days of Daniel's life were confined to this room. Prior to his death, Daniel gave Alla a list of persons that he wanted to attend his funeral, and to make sure she would inform them.

Visitors arrived every day and one of those who came each day was Boris Chukov, who was also treated at the Serbski Institute and became friends with Daniel. He could not seem to detach himself from Daniel to his very end, and took several photographs of Daniel and Alla, the last of him before he died.[102] And there were the regulars, such as Irina Yusova and Tatyana Volkova. But with each of them, it was only about a 15-minute visit and by then he was exhausted and had to return to his bed to rest. Daniel impressed them because he never discussed his personal health, but always veered the conversation to their activities, health, children, work and relatives. Not once did he ever complain to anybody, and they all noticed that mentally he was clear and precise with everything he said.

The final 40 days of Daniel's life was a horrible torture for Alla. His heart attacks were more regular and harder on him, and then complications started: his kidneys hurt and his torso started to swell, and Daniel experienced extreme thirst but could not seem to take liquids. Alla continued the regular injections, provided him oxygen, without which he could not hardly breathe.

Alla recollected one of the visits and some of their other conversations the days before his death:

---

[102] One of these is the cover photograph of this volume.

I remember when Sergei Musatov with his recent wife Nina came to visit. She was a student of his at his studio before Sergei was arrested, and she waited for his release the entire term of his sentence. But their marriage did not last long. When time came for them to leave, Sergei and Nina stood, and Nina somewhat bewildered said, "So how should we bid farewell?"

Daniel asked in response, "So do you believe in post-mortem life?"

She replied, "Yes."

Then he stretched his hand out to her and smiled and said, "Until we meet again."

Nina shook his hand. They left and I could hear her sobbing in the corridor just outside our door.

When we alone, Daniel would often ask for me to read his verses to him, and he would listen to them as though detached from them and from a distance. I well remember how he asked me to read *Green Bottomland*. I read as I did naturally, which was from the typewritten copy and not raising my eyes. But when I looked at Daniel, I would notice tears on his eyes.

He said to me, "These are good verses. I listen to them as though they are not mine."

Then he would read *Rose of the World* on his own. Once he asked me to reread the book and make a note of all the places where I disagreed with it somehow, what would cause me to stop and think about it, or any passage where something was not clear. My checkmarks are still penciled into this typewritten manuscript, and at almost every checkmark his correction is made, some kind of comment or something to append to the text.

Once Daniel reread *Rose of the World*, and I was busy with some domestic chores in the communal kitchen, and then I walked back into our room. Daniel closed the portfolio and said, "No. He is not insane."

I asked, "What? What?"

"It was not someone insane who wrote this."

I froze and then said, "What are you talking about?"

And he answers, "You know, I just read this from a different perspective: how should I understand the type of person who wrote this book? Is he insane or not? Well, no, he is not insane."

Doctors came to visit him but nothing could be done any more than the meditation he already had. Some of them even took note of Alla's condition that she was also at the verge of something horrible. But all Alla could do under the circumstances is persevere and stretch Daniel's life a little longer. Fr Nikolai Golubtzov came to their apartment and administered communion and last rites to Daniel and listened to his confession. But since there was nowhere for Alla to go, she stayed in the room and on her knees and prayed. Alla noticed that Daniel repented of other things, but he never repented or regretted composing *Rose of the World* or any of his other writings.

A doctor visited Daniel the morning of his death, and he told Alla to hold him, because only a short while remained and this might comfort him. About 2 hours before Daniel's death, Alla had an inspiration to mention the following to Daniel. She stood on her knees at his bed and said, "I do not know whether you are redeeming yourself with this suffering or acquiring something, but I only feel that this suffering was long destined to occur to both of us." Daniel got enough strength to raise himself and hugged Alla with his weak hands and kissed her on the lips. But he was too weak to talk.

Daniel Leonidovich Andreev died March 30, 1959, at 4 o'clock in the afternoon, and literally in Alla's arms. She leaned over to him and caught his last breath. His death was very painful from another heart attack.

Alla in her later memoirs related the events surrounding Daniel's funeral:

> I decided to wear my white dress, the one I wore when Daniel and I married. I curled my hair and did not wear a scarf over my head. People came to me and asked, "Please. The elderly Orthodox women are asking you to put a scarf on. And why are you wearing this white dress?"
>
> I replied, "Because I decided to attend Daniel's funeral in the dress I wore when we married. And please do not pressure me, but say 'Thank you,' instead, that I am not wearing a veil. This event is tied with our wedding." I was convinced that I was doing the right thing.
>
> The coffin was placed in church in the spot where we married. And Fr Nikolai Golubtzov performed the requiem in the same spot where he stood to marry us.

In his eulogy, Fr Nikolai compared the live flowers on the top of Daniel's casket to Daniel, mentioning that they were not artificial, and so was Daniel, never artificial.

Daniel's funeral was held at the Novo-Devichi Monastery cemetery, where father Leonid purchased graves, and where also Daniel's mother and grandmother and other members of the Dobrov family were buried. About 60 people attended.

For Daniel, the announcer of a future day, the era of ROSE OF THE WORLD arrived and no doubt he ascended to the *sakuala* of the heavenly Russia for all of his merits.

Alla Andreeva summarized Daniel later in her memoirs:

> Daniel was handsome in an original fashion, something different than the typical sense of Moscow beauty. He was talk, agile, thin, and dark complexioned. His face

was narrow and thin, he had a high forehead, thin nose, small lips, and dark eyes. His hair was straight and dark, with a few strands always longer than the rest, and longer than the era, when most men had their hair short. He did not wear a tie, but when he had to, he wore a black bowtie, a small one, almost non-pretentious.

His hands did not match the balance of his stature. Daniel's palms were masculine and large, but his fingers were thick and short. It would seem he was embarrassed of his hands and he would regularly hide them under the table.

Daniel was a genius. As applying to him, there was no pride, no conceit. This was a very difficult burden, a heavy cross, which the Lord only gives to a few. Such people are recognizable, and are distinct due to the awesome qualities and some non-conformity with the balance of men. They seem to know, hear, see what is impossible for another to hear or see. They are like buildings arranged in some locality that are inaccessible to us.

Such special children of God possess a dreadful frailty and infantile vulnerability. I noticed these traits with Daniel, and sometimes attempted to work them out of him, but sometimes I was surprised they were to his benefit, but then finally I just accepted this as his inherent character and no longer tried to change him. At the same time, Daniel was painfully dissatisfied with his external self. He wanted to be a precious and loving figure of a radiant and bright and bold and joyful person. As a result of this attitude toward his external self, he ended up in unexpected situations.

I should also add that Daniel was very attentive to others and very polite with women. He always wanted the best for others, although not every person understood this.

THE LATER YEARS OF ALLA ANDREEVA

Daniel's death was psychologically devastating for Alla. He was her entire life, and what remained of his life was all his compositions, this was all he had to leave and now Alla was rightful heir as well as protector of his legacy. Alla felt herself doomed to death because of her illnesses. She had some surgeries and recovered, probably dealing with her malignant tumor.

Alla then spent her time in typing all of Daniel's pencil-written manuscripts, everything that Daniel forwarded to her from Vladimir prison and what was in the bag when she went there to gather the last of his belongings.

Alla's mother, Yulia Gavrilovna, died in 1962.

In 1963, Alla married again and this time to Evgeni Beloyusov, a friend of Daniel and who likewise was arrested in the alleged conspiracy and was sentenced to 10 years in prison. He was a widow with 2 grown children. Evgeni was not able to get residency in Moscow, but after the couple were formally married, officials granted him a residency permit based on Alla's existing permit. In Moscow, Evgeni worked at the Institute for the Synthesis of Proteins. He retired shortly after and collected pension.

Alla continued to work at various jobs in art and graphics through the Moscow Union of Artists, doing whatever she could just to keep busy. With her marriage, Alla's life definitely became better, now with an income and a husband who wanted to spend his last years in enjoyment and traveling and writing. As with Daniel, Evgeni suffered much during imprisonment, and wanted to make the most of his remaining years, and Alla was as good a person as any with whom to do this.

The following summer, Evgeni and Alla vacationed at the Carpathian Mountains along the Neringa River, at the far western part of Ukraine, near the city of Bukovel and at the Carpathian National Nature Preserve.

In 1971, Alla's father, Aleksandr Petrovich died. She described her father in the following manner:

> It seems to me that in part I have unraveled the secret of such persons as my father: they established themselves on the basis of Christian principles. This was the point of departure for their conduct. Their atheism was purely intellectual.
>
> Other than this, I also possess the following observation: I am convinced that many people do not just live one life, and among them is myself. There are things, often very strange, whose understanding I just cannot fathom based on my present mode of life. And so I think that such persons, as father, have lived not just one life. The Lord, seeing that they have raised themselves to such a high level of integrity, then in some manner deprives them of belief in Himself, they becoming an incarnation of a vacancy, in order for Him to see how they will conduct themselves, now deprived of the fear of God. This is like a final test – and I knew many of such people. And father was so much oriented as a person, that even without God he conducted himself in a manner that believing persons could not.

Later that year and after her father's death, Alla had her first exhibition as a professional artist. It was held at the Artists Hall along Kuznetzski Blvd. Up to that time her paintings were either in the artist's studio, or in her apartment on the floor, or leaning against a chair, or nailed to a wall, and up to this year only 2 or 3 actually made their way to any exhibit. Alla was now 56 years of age and she was finally able to realize herself as an artist. From this time forward, more of Alla's painting were displayed at exhibitions.

Loving leisure in their old age, Evgeni and Alla traveled to the Polar Urals in the summer of 1965, which is the region of the Ural Mountain range north of the Arctic Circle. They traveled by train to Vorkut, on the west side of the Urals, and then again by train across the Urals to Labytnangi, along the Ob River and north of Salehard. The railroad crossed the division between Europe and Asia, but what struck Alla during the trip was seeing remnants of labor camps, so far north and distant from civilization. In July 1968, the couple and 3 other artists made the same trip. With both trips, Alla spent here time with her sketches and paintings of the landscape.

Evgeni Beloyusov died in April 1977, at their apartment in Moscow on Brusov Lane. He had a stroke and then died 2 days later.

On the night of April 29-30, 2005, Alla Aleksandrovna Andreeva died at the age of 90, due to smoke inhalation from a fire that occurred in her apartment in Moscow.

The Formation of
Rose of the World

The manuscript of *Rose of the World* had its own life. In about 1960, Vera Litovskaya in Torzhok retyped the entire manuscript and made 2 carbon copies. Alla sent one copy to Siberia to a friend. However the friend was afraid that if she and her husband should die, then the manuscript would fall into the hands of arbitrary people. The next opportunity this friend had to visit European Russia, she brought the manuscript with her and left it with another friend who lived in Lakhta, near Leningrad. Once reproduced copies of *Rose of the World* started clandestine circulation in Moscow, Leningrad, and other cities in the decade of the 1960s, Alla suspected that this copy was the source of all of them.

Alla gave the other carbon copy to Vadim Andreev during a subsequent visit to Moscow and he took it back with him to New York. Alla of course, kept the original typewritten copy. In 1962, Alla also gave to Vadim a copy of all the compositions, poetry and stories that Daniel composed, all of everything she had a copy, and for him to take on his return and to safe keep there. At the time, not one line of anything that Daniel wrote was published.

Meanwhile in Soviet Russia, copies of *Rose of the World* were distributed, although in distorted and often condensed or redacted versions, or just pages and sections, while others inserted comments into the text. Every person interested seemed to want to supplement it with their personal interpretation. Somehow a few were able to get Alla's telephone number. But because Alla and Evgeni lived in a communal apartment, they all shared one telephone, and whomever would answer the phone would deny any knowledge of the book and tell them they called the wrong number. Alla and the others could not respond otherwise, because they had no idea who was calling and why. Censorship of books was still active in Soviet Russia at the time, and Alla was afraid of them searching her apartment for her one copy, and subjecting her to again arrest and interrogation, as she experienced before. For this reason she kept absolute silence regarding the book.

Daniel's verses were first published in the magazine *Zvezda* (*Star*), in issues of the years of 1966 and 1967. This was done by Nikolai Leopoldovich Braun at the initiative of Vadim Andreev, Daniel's brother. The first issue had 5 poems and the 2nd had 6, but they were only about nature.

Alla's copy of the manuscript of *Rose of the World* continue to lie dormant through most of the decade of the 1970's, as she felt it was still too dangerous a time for a volume of this type to be printed and publicly distributed. But Alla did feel a necessity for some of Daniel's other compositions to be published. But initially there were no takers.

The first actual book consisting of Daniel's poems was published in 1975. This was due to the efforts of Lev Adolfovich Lidin, a writer and editor of poetry books. What he published was an impressive and very satisfactory book as far as Alla was concerned. It was titled *Ranya Sarevo* (*Early Dusk*), but it went unnoticed to the general public for the most part.

In 1978, Alla entered a new stage in her life. Gradually many young people appeared and surrounded her. One day these 2 hippies with long hair and chains of beads hanging from their necks, appeared at her door. There names were Alkhimik and

Valeri. Somehow they acquired fragments of a reproduced copy of *Rose of the World*, and they set out to find Alla and they did. Alla was 70 years of age at the time, and these 2 characters took her by surprise. Alla would not allow them into her apartment, but instead they left the building, and then other hippy-appearing young persons joined them. The group walked about the streets, discussing all the questions that the hippies would propose to her. After she returned home, Alla still did nothing with her complete copy of the manuscript.

It was not until 1986 under Soviet Premier Mikhail Sergeevich Gorbachov and his concept of perestroika that Alla found a good and safe reason to proceed with the publication of *Rose of the World*. Boris Chukov, now the editor of *Novoi Mir* (*New World*) magazine, approached Alla with the intent of publishing excerpts of it. He and a group of young people, all of whom, had read distributed selections from the book and felt the time was opportune for its public dissemination. Alla not only agreed for portions to be published in the popular magazine, but told Boris to proceed with the complete book if at all possible, but as long as there would be no repercussions.

That year, a few of Daniel's verses were published in *Novoi Mir* (*New World*) magazine. It was not until 1987, that Daniel's next volume of verses were published, and this was in the magazine *Sovremmeni* (*Contemporary*). Boris Nikolaievich Romanov,[103] who was a friend of Victor Vasilenko, read the verses in the magazine and which interested him. He then proposed a new and larger volume of a collection of Daniel's poems, and which he published later that year.

Likewise in 1987, Alla traveled to Paris at the invitation of Vadim, and there had a chance to publicly read some of Daniel's poetry to an enthusiastic audience and promote his compositions.

Returning to Russia in 1988, Alla, rather than depending on a clandestine and dubious copy of *Rose of the World* to be used for publication, had her niece Tanya, Yuri's daughter, retype the

---

[103] Boris Romanov also wrote the authoritative biography of Daniel Andreev in Russian, which is the basis of most of this volume in English.

entire manuscript again from Alla's extant but ancient copy. This copy was clandestinely printed in May 1988 using either mimeograph or duplicating machines by friends who contributed to the project, but the number of copies were few and poor quality. Boris Chukov took this final manuscript to *Novoi Mir*. In 1989, the first selections of *Rose of the World* were published and publicly distributed in the magazine *Novoi Mir*.

The complete *Rose of the World* was published in 1991 with 100,000 copies printed, an unheard of quantity for a first printing of something whose success was dubious. Yet, eventually, they sold and the book has been reprinted on a regular basis since.

Enthused over her reception in Paris with reading Daniel's poetry to several interested audiences, Alla decided to do the same in Moscow. Beginning 1988, she invited 20 or so associates to her apartment and read to them. Then she was invited to the home of another, where another group gathered and she read to them, and many of them already by memory. Alla then got the idea of reading in public halls, so she advertised and started to read them at libraries, cultural and literary institutions, museums, theaters, and even churches, and these were not only Russian Orthodox, but also Jehovah's Witnesses, Moonies, and an Adventist Church near Tule. Each reading included an introduction regarding Daniel's life, and this promoted further interest in his writings.

Her most personal achievement was to a packed hall in Smolensk of reformed criminals from various prisons and labor camps. Here she concentrated more on Daniel's and her time in confinement, and many of those who attended were women. With her introductions and biography, most of the audience could identify with Daniel's verses, and of course, promoted perseverance among those listening.

Alla's itinerary led her to speak from London to Vladivostok. She described one event later in her memoirs:

From the first occasion I had to read, the feeling that Daniel was right alongside me, and that he removed from me the sensation of fear of reciting his compositions, or even selections of *Rose of the World,* never left me. These were not easy years, but I presented myself and never let my head down. And there were even strange moments while I was reciting the verses. I would walk in front of the audience, start reading my selections, and then a thought would enter my head. Suddenly something would occur. I would start to read much better, forgetting about my fear of the audience and was totally emerged into the texts. And it seemed that someone was standing right next to me. And it was Daniel next to me. And here it seemed that I could more forcefully project his talents to the audience.

We live in an impersonal, fragmented world. Our lives are often shattered, as well as our understanding of matter. Our physical life is torn from the spiritual, so many religious confessions are broken into pieces. Often what only remains to unite us is the poet and prosaic. So often the poet writes in a lyrical fashion.

But if we were to depart to antiquity, to those who either barefooted or in coarse sandals walked under the blazing sun along dusty or rocking roads in very distant and ancient countries, then without a doubt they would definitely meet some person like this one upon one of these roads, who would seem to be strange, but only to us. But for those with whom he lived, he would be completely understandable. Who is he? The poet and in the ancient significance that we today have long lost.

Individuals of this stature envisioned the world as a whole entity and indivisibly connected with the other world. For them the religious, philosophic, poetic and musical figures of the universe were presented as one whole, not subject to fragmentation, as our present world is fragmented.

Throughout all the ages such individuals surfaced, who possessed a special quality: they heard not the mundane, but the divine. Such were the first Christians, who awaited the imminent arrival of Christ; such were the followers of Avvakum[104] and Savonarola, who feared the end of the world to occur at any time; such were the poets of antiquity, and such was Daniel Andreev in his dream of a global fraternity and the union of all the world's residents in the presence of God. He heard God's truth and God's eras, that it was time to merge the divine into the secular, while he lived himself at this boundary between the divine and the secular.

Circles of readers and adherents to the concepts of *Rose of the World* increased. In 1990, a non-pretentious woman named Tatyana Borisovna Antonyan dedicated herself to the pursuit of creating a library of all of Daniel's compositions, whatever she could find and collect, and create a library of it.

Another woman surfaced from nowhere, Irina Zalesheva, a Russian whose husband was Czech, and she arranged a translation of *Rose of the World* into the Czech language and its publication in Czechoslovakia.. Then in 1990, another woman, Shasha Kazachkov made a translation of a large section of *Rose of the World* into Spanish. A few chapters of *Rose of the World* also appeared in English in 1997, this translation done by Irina Zalesheva. A larger portion of *Rose of the World* was later translated into English by an anonymous scholar from Canada.[105] Yusuiki Sato translated *Rose of the World* into Japanese.

---

[104] Avvakum Petrovich, 17th century, a leader of the Old-Ritualist segment of Russian Orthodoxy.

[105] Presently – 2015 – a new English translation is being prepared by the author.

INTRODUCTION TO *ROSE OF THE WORLD*

Daniel Adreev describes ROSE OF THE WORLD in the following manner:

> ROSE OF THE WORLD can be equated with an inverted flower whose root is in heaven, while the pedal bowl is here, among humanity, on earth. It's stem is the revelation through which the spiritual sap flows, sustaining and strengthening its pedals – the fragrant choral of religion. But other than the pedals, it also has a pith; this is its individual teaching. This teaching is not a mechanical combination of more or less high theses of various theosophies of the past. Other than the new attitude toward religious legacy, ROSE OF THE WORLD materializes the new attitude toward nature, toward history, toward the destinies of humanity's cultures, toward their tasks, toward creativity, toward love, toward the routes of cosmic ascension, toward the subsequent illumination of *Shadanakar*.

Andreev has many meanings assigned to the appellation Rose of the World. As used in this book, in italics, *Rose of the World* is the title of the book composed by In capital type, ROSE OF THE WORLD is Andreev's ideology, his concepts of religion, polity, culture, and history. In Russian *Роза Мира* means A Rose for the World or The World's Rose, although the popular translation prevalent in literature is *Rose of the World*,

It first refers to the future epoch of which Andreev foretold as the golden age of humanity, whose essence will developed fully as history progresses in the close connection between God and people. Second, there is a society of ROSE OF THE WORLD that consists of a world-wide ecclesiastical fraternity. Third, there is a teaching of ROSE OF THE WORLD, an inter-religion or summation of religion. Fourth, ROSE OF THE WORLD is an inter-culture, a meta-culture to encompass all of humanity. Finally, ROSE OF THE WORLD is also a supra-governmental organization or institution, that will possess ethical and moral control over the activities of government.

The teaching of Daniel Andreev has no analogy in global esoteric thought, and it has been subject to tremendous popular interpretation. In his revelations, Daniel envisioned the reign of Rose of the World on earth in the 23rd century, the future epoch being a golden age of humanity, whose essence will developed fully as history progresses into a close connection between God and people.

ROSE OF THE WORLD will install a genuine golden age on our planet. It will abolish the exploitation of one person by another and all violence against the individual. It will motivate the personal strengths of human nature and direct them to the comprehension of nature and continual creativity. With the powers of science it was raise the evolution of animals to possess communication and increase their level of intellect. People will forget words like: tyranny, war, revolution, famine, poverty, and illness, since none of this will ever exist again. Genuinely spirit-filled leaders of all humanity, called pontiffs, will govern the land.

The other facet of ROSE OF THE WORLD is the structure of the universe and the human's part of it.

Daniel records and describes in *Rose of the World,* 248 worlds or strata of the universe, many of them real and many of them allegorical and symbolic.[106] Some are reflective of cultures and civilizations of Earth's history past and present, and some describe those to unveil in the future. Some are descending levels of purgatories and hells and confinements, and some are ascending levels of paradises and heavens and freedoms. An important part of Daniel's ideology is the ascent or development of each individual, and this occurring through successive reincarnations, each one inheriting the karma of the previous to either redeem it in some descending nether regions, or advance due to it in some ascending region of the universal strata. The salvation of souls is possible even from the deepest of abysses. However, there is also a bottom of the galaxy where the infinitely incorrigible are secluded, a place where the annihilation of souls is possible, a second death. At the opposite end is the region of the morally elite at the summit of the galaxy.

Daniel was a dualist, and all of life and existence consists of a struggle between the powers of light and goodness against the powers of darkness and evil, this occurring on an individual basis, to that of the state, and even in the other-worldly spheres of the spirit world.

In Daniel's universe, souls that perish continue to exist, but are not dead. And although he understands the bright hierarchies, but as a messenger, he is enveloped with a struggle with the demonic darkness. He descends into it, as though into the punishment cell, attempting to gaze at all around him and record the powers that reside there. Having experienced the *Duegguer,* Daniel continually seems to be able to almost touch darkness as though it is tangible. Daniel spoke of the *Duegguer* in symbolic language, not finding compatible appellations and

---

[106] Daniel state 242, but further study of his book increases the number to 248.

terms. Then he attempted to devise some, until he started to hear them, some distinctly and some vaguely, in his prison cell at night. The meaning of those voices and images that were earlier nebulous became understandable.

He recorded the activities of powers, he calls one *Aphrodite of All Nations* and the other *Aphrodite of Countries*. He utilizes here a contradistinction of 2 images of the goddess of love: *Urania* symbolizing the heavenly, and *Pandemus* symbolizing the national.

Convinced that the karma of Russian history would predefine the awesome apocalyptic exit, he returned to the visions of almost an inevitable destruction of all that was precious to him, the holy jewels of Moscow. Without a purging fire the liberation of the Russian soul, conditionally called *Navna,* would be difficult to visualize. It seemed to Daniel that *Navna* would exit its captivity upon radioactive ashes. Russian dominion, at the time transformed into a Stalinist demonic citadel, can be liberated only under the ruthless strokes of an external enemy. But Daniel was not the only person within the walls of the Vladimir prison who felt this way. The news of Hiroshima stupefied Daniel when he heard of this while on a vacation, and it remained impressed on him as a premonition of the world's termination.

The demonic principle heavily influences the progress of history, as one *Zhrugr* – the personification of state government – is exchanged for another, such super-terrestrial powers in this unremitting struggle appear in earth's events and national destinies.

THE *ENROF* AND ITS CONSTITUENTS

Andreev calls the physical universe – *Enrof,* and it consists of a layered or stratified structure that includes a large number of parallel worlds, hierarchically organized based on the number of space and time dimensions and, along with this, based on the degree of its perfection or moral development, from the divine to the demonic, and its utilization in the progress of human evolution. Not all the worlds possess dimensions that are relative to the measurements of our universe, but have more than one dimension of time, and more or less than 3 dimensions of space. Some of the strata are concentric circles.

Many heavenly bodies of some universes are connected with the heavenly bodies of others, forming in this manner a complex system of worlds or *bramfaturas*.

The planet Earth, having the name *Shadanakar*, is one of the heavenly bodies of *Enrof* and one of the more than 240 worlds of *bramfatura*. *Shadanakar* is as though located in the sector between 2 poles: the world of the planetary Logos and the world of the planetary Demon, and its name is *Gagtungr*. Meanwhile all the worlds that composes the *Enrof* are defined in a manner that pertains meta-geologically to one another. For example, the greater world of Logos is aligned with the higher levels of the atmosphere.

The common picture that is displayed in *Shadanakar* consists of the creative effort of the bright spirits or monads, and they are incessantly uniting and dividing due to the interference of the dark monads, the demonic, who apostatized from God, and at some time in the past were thrown to *Shadanakar*. The 2 sides co-exist in a continual struggle. The issue is that the demonic monads are nourished by psychic emanations created by suffering. These emanations are called *gavvakhs*. In order to emanate a large quantity of *gavvakhs*, they created worlds of retribution, also known as purgatories and hells. Souls that become burdened due to sins in the earthly life traverse these worlds after death.

Bright spirits enter *Shadanakar* descending from God from the higher worlds of the ascending series, and here they reside. They accomplish the route through *Shadanakar* via the souls they create and direct. (The terms of ascending and descending are defined relative to Earth.) Initially the souls descend to the very lowest and darkest worlds either to work there with the goal of their enlightenment, or else are drawn further down as a result of the their karmic burden. Subsequently, after the defined route of descent, the souls rise to more beautiful and blessed layers, where the possibilities of an even more enlightened and potent existence is opened for them and, once uniting with a monad, they ascend, returning to God.

Rose of the World speaks of a created world populated by a number of entities, the majority of which possess an immortal principle called a monad. These monads are in 2 forms: some are born of the Creator. These are the higher divinely-born monads that reside in heavenly entities. The others are created by the Creator, and these are the human. The incarnation of monads in humanity and participation is its mission.

The possibility of reincarnation is recognized, but Andreev also states:

> Nowhere is it decisively ordained that the route of reincarnation is as though the sole possibility, the only route of progress of an individual soul.

Some souls are incarnated in humanity one time, others – several. This is defined by the specific route of each one independently.

META-CULTURES

Every nation possesses its personal conciliar soul, but the supra-nation as a whole is guided by just one demiurge. It can become close to one of the conciliar souls and, once connected with it, the nation begins to play a leading role in the subject civilization. Subsequently, for one or another reason, this connection can be severed and reattached to another conciliar soul.

Each supra-nation has its heavenly world called a *zatomis*, and its relative demonic antipode called a *shrastra*. The *zatomis*, earthly civilization, and *shrastra* corporately form a meta-culture. The *zatomises*, forming the *sinklit* of the meta-culture, raise the ability of national accomplishment. Here the possibility of a greater creativity and divine inspiration is unveiled to them, and likewise the route that ascends to the higher worlds. The *shrastras* are resident members of a diabolic humanity. They are not former persons, but completely other entities created by the dark powers as a counter balance to humanity.

In addition to the above, there is also another group of entities called *yuitzraors*, and they impose a colossal influence on the life of the Earth's nations, and particularly upon the leadership of government. They inspire the construction of institutions of the empires and concrete governments. Created for the defense of the meta-culture, the *yuitzraors* absorb *eytzekhor*, the demonic element, from the *kaross*, and in the majority of circumstances it will begin to expand dominion, and as a result the governments on Earth evolve into tyrannies. Then the *yuitzraor* enters into a struggle against the demiurge, *sinklit*, and conciliar soul, to retain authority.

THE META-HISTORY OF RUSSIA

As much as a hallmark that *Rose of the World* impresses on the nation of the Russian supra-nation, its meta-history is assigned an immense significance. Five books of the 12 that compose *Rose of the World* are dedicated to Russia. Andreev investigates the events of pivotal moments in the history of the eastern Slavic communities and those nations whose historical destiny is tied with Russia. This includes the evolution of Kievan Rus, the baptism of Rus, the rise of Moscow, the Orthodox schism, the expansion of the country's boundaries, the appearance of the Russian Empire, the revolutions, and the government of Stalin. It should not be unexpected that Andreev would promote his native country as having a role surpassing any other nation in the restoration of true government and true religion in the future, regardless of its failure and tardiness in every area over the entire course of history.

TEACHING OF THE TRIUNE DEITY.

According to Andreev, the entities of Father and Holy Spirit in Christian theology are one and the same in the hypostasis of the Triune Deity. At the same time Andreev states the following in regard to the historical concept of the divine Trinity:

> But I count no one to possess such supreme authorization or empowerment to insist on one sole and absolute validity of this concept, on its dogmatic orthopraxy. The 8th ecumenical council could become the legitimate, generally accepted institution that is empowered to resolve such a question, where representatives of all the other existing Christian denominations, and ROSE OF THE WORLD, would subject this thesis to deliberation. But until this should be accomplished, no one in ROSE OF THE WORLD can affirm the full inerrancy of the old dogma. It seems that a person can only believe as his conscience and his individual spiritual experience dictates, and so work toward a unification of the denominations in order to eventually resolve all dilemmas.

After a few arguments to the benefit of identifying God the Father and God the Holy Spirit, Andreev proposes his personal theological doctrine:

> In this manner, in the teaching of the Trinity and of the Female aspect of Deity what is distinct is not the transfer of something corporeal into the celestial sphere, but on the contrary, the understanding of the objective polarity of our strata – the male and female principles – as the opposite poles in the essence of God that are incomprehensible to us. Apostle John said, "God is love."
> But then the truth that God is love will not lose its veracity. God does not love Himself – such a proposition would be scandalous, but each of the inscrutable facets

that comprise Him and hiding within Him are turned in love toward others, and a 3rd is born out of this love: the basis of the universe. Father – Ever-Virgin Mother – Son.

WOMANHOOD

The Womanhood principle as the identification with the 3rd person of the Triune Deity is then proposed by Andreev:

> It is popularly known that during the duration from the Gnostics to the Christian thinkers of the beginning of the 20th century there lived a vague, although fervent, and persisting sentiment of the Global Womanhood Principle, a sentiment that this principle is not an illusion, not some corporeal category transferred into the cosmic plan, but a higher spiritual reality. The church intended, obviously, to provide an entrance for this sentiment, sanctifying with its authority the cult of the Theotokos in the east and the cult of Madonna in the west. In reality, ahead of the reverential veneration of the Motherhood Principle – a veneration irrationally inherent in the national masses – there appeared a concrete image to which this [principle] endeavored.

The concept of Global Womanhood cannot but grow into the concept of a female aspect of the Deity. *Zventa-Sventana* is the expression of Womanhood in the hypostasis of the Deity. She would then become the spouse of the planetary Logos, Jesus Christ.

It was the despotic and tyrannical consequences of male leaders and male-dominated governments and societies that were at the base of Andreev's necessity of including attributes applying to the motherly and domestic nature of women to his principles and especially elevating it to the rank of deity.

CHRISTOLOGY

As Andreev states, Jesus is the great and supreme divinely-born monad who is the creator and director of our planet. He is not the incarnation in human form of God the Son, not one of the hypostases of the Triune Deity, but the expression of Deity as a divinely-born monad who descended to *Shadanakar* at the very initiation of its existence, in order to become its Logos, the concentration of Providential powers and Divine Spirit in our *bramfatura*. If God the Son is the ecumenical Logos, then the Spirit that was incarnated in Jesus Christ is the planetary Logos. Such a monad does exist in each *bramfatura*.

As far as the incarnation as a human is concerned, Andreev recognizes all the aspects of Jesus' life that are recorded in the Gospels, including his immaculate conception and resurrection, but he does not recognized the veracity of all the details ascribed to the Jesus of the Gospels.

> But Christ was not able to expound his teaching in a book because the teaching was not just his words, but his entire life. His teaching began with his immaculate conception and birth on a quiet Bethlehem night illuminated by the songs of Angels; his conversations with the *Gagtungr* in the desert and his wandering about the roads of Galilee; his poverty and his love, healing of the sick and resurrection of the dead; walking on water and the transformation on mount Tabor; his torture and resurrection. Such a teaching could be expounded, although with some omissions and mistakes, only by living witnesses of this divine path of him.
>
> Each person reading the New Testament tries to remember at least that Christ's teaching is his entire life, and not just his words. The words that are attributed to him are all truth providing they are in accord with the spirit of love.

Interpretation of Original Sin

The sculptor of the chain of posterity in the corporeal worlds, the sovereign of the sexual sphere, is *Leeleet*, one of the 7 supreme *stikialas* of *Shadanakar*. She participates in every act of human sexual intercourse and conception. She possesses the keys of passion of one toward another and represents both genders.

At one time *Leeleet* united with the planetary Logos and provided a beginning to angels.

To understand original sin we need to understand what occurred between *Leeleet* and *Gagtungr*, who was discarded into her world, and the result of this was that her refined composition body was transformed due to the absorption of this demonic element. The *eytzekhor* – which evolved from this union – is the sinful nature of every person. This fall due to her sin – her union with the demonic *Gagtungr* – was a catastrophe. From this time, the *eytzekhor* directed all the further posterity of *Leeleet*. Later she participated in the creation of 3 bright societies: the titans, *daimons* and humans. A mission was assigned to each of them, having a significance for the worlds that they were to inhabit and develop. Nonetheless the titans went astray and traversed a route in the worlds of redemption. The *daimons* were saved due to the incarnation of the planetary Logos – Jesus – among them. Humanity that crucified Jesus goes astray in the same manner as did the titans.

The Incomplete Mission of Jesus Christ

As Andreev interpreted Jesus' mission, there was no need for Him to die, not a violent death or even a natural death. After a long life in *Enrof* and accomplishing all the tasks that He was assigned, a transformation awaited Him, and not death; a transfiguration of His entire substance and His migration to *Olirna*, and in front of all the eyes of the world. Attaining self-perfection, the mission of Jesus would have installed in the course of 2 or 3 centuries an ideal ecclesiastical fraternity in place of the existing governments.

However the *Gagtungr* influenced people to kill Him and which had catastrophic results for all of humanity, and particularly this is the reason for almost all the calamities of global history after Jesus, and toward the end of our world humanity will go astray to such an extent that it will be impossible to continue His mission of redemption. It will only be accomplished by Jesus Himself at his second arrival.

As a result of His murder, humanity had stumbled along a broken, zigzag, unlevel and slanted, fatal route for 20 centuries. It has been equally influenced by both the effort of Providential powers and the ruthless activity of *Gagtungr*. In comparison, the worlds of *daimons*, among whom the mission of the Logos was brought to its victorious goal, entered the route of the followers of enlightenment. At the present, the *daimons* have immeasurably surpassed us in their development.

During the course of the 20th century, an event occurred of such significance that it can only be compared to the incarnation as a human of the planetary logos: a female divinely-born monad having the name of *Zventa-Sventana* descended to *Shadanakar*. As Daniel describes it, while he was writing *Rose of the World*, she resided in the highest strata of *bramfatura*, and later she is to descend into the *zatomis* of one of the meta-cultures. Later Andreev received a revelation that it was the Russian meta-culture. This meta-historical event is reflected in the earthly *Enrof* as the materialization of ROSE OF THE WORLD.

ESCHATOLOGY OF ROSE OF THE WORLD

As mentioned above, Andreev envisioned the reign of ROSE OF THE WORLD on earth in the 23rd century. During the era of Rose of the World, pontiffs will govern the land. They will be selected at Supreme Councils of ROSE OF THE WORLD. With the election of each new pontiff, the capital of the world will be moved to the primary city of that country where the Supreme Preceptor has his origin..

One of the final links in this chain of events will be the reign on Earth of the anti-christ. After his arrival, *Leeleet* will somehow become incarnated or materialize in our world in order to become his spouse. The anti-christ will create a malevolent cult of global sexual perversion surrounding himself and the incarnation of *Leeleet*.

The redemption and salvation of *Leeleet* will arise as one of the tasks of the 2nd Eon, which is the period of history of *bramfatura* after the 2nd arrival of Jesus on Earth. Presently we are living toward the end of the first eon. The fullness of the consummation of ROSE OF THE WORLD will the the era of the 3rd Eon.

Jesus Christ will appear to every person residing on Earth. Diabolic humanity will bodily change and descend into the worlds of retribution for cleansing through the energies of the infra-physical subterranean expanse. The currents of energy of suffering and sexual dissolution from the three-dimensional physical world of the Earth will terminate. Infra-Lemuria and infra-Atlantis will begin to separate into distinct regions.

From this moment, only virtuous people will be born on Earth, since there will no more be any powers from other worlds that would attempt to paralyze humanity and take advantage of the weakness of human nature.

According to Andreev, the hallmarks of ROSE OF THE WORLD are the transformation of government into a religious fraternity and the creation of an intra-culture and inter-religion, enveloping all governments, cultures and religions. This is also the specific purpose for the Russian supra-nation, that is, the union of the nations of Russia, Belarus, Ukraine, Georgia and Armenia. This corporate group was summoned into existence from non-existence to accomplish this mission.

The most important significance of ROSE OF THE WORLD from a meta-historical perspective consists in somehow terminating the quantity of sacrifices of the anti-christ, physical and spiritual, all of whom will now be compelled to traverse after death the worlds of redemption. ROSE OF THE WORLD cannot rectify the results of the unfulfilled mission of Jesus and bring humanity to the accomplishment of His mission.

Even in the most optimistic of scenarios, as Andreev viewed it, the anti-christ will institute a universal tyranny, but after an interval of some time, and as a result of the assigned activity of the planetary Logos, he will be decomposed. After this the world will devolve into a chaos of anarchy and a final global war of all against all. This will be terminated by the second arrival of Jesus Christ. At the time of writing *Rose of the World*, Andreev felt this would occur in about 250 or 300 years.

The posterity of the Brethren of Light will acquire new ethereal bodies and settled all over the world. The new humanity will initiate the transformation and spirit-enlivenment of all that remains from its predecessor on the planet: the crippled nature, cities and civilizations. This period of intelligent life on Earth will recognize only love, creativity and labor for the ascent of those fallen human souls in the worlds of retribution to the bright strata of the planetary cosmos. In the final end, these worlds will be emptied. No emanation of suffering, no emanation of malice, no emanation of lust will any more nourish the lowest levels of the worlds of demonic bases. Such worlds will speedily crumble and as long as it takes for their broken pieces to fall to the bottom of the galaxy.

All the people living in the three-dimensional world will labor for the unification of their souls with the spirit body through the knowledge of the laws of nature, cultural creativity and advancement. Souls enlightened due to their spiritual labors will rise only vertically upward during their post-mortem existence, to the highest worlds of *bramfatura*, our multi-dimensional planetary cosmos. As a result of this progress, the supreme stratum of *bramfatura*, the global *Salvaterra*, will increase the quantity of its space-time dimensions and make it the same as the number of the multi-dimensional Absolute. Then the window into the world of God the Father will open, where the high strata of the planetary cosmos will be transferred by a single space-time dimensional whirlwind. It will attain the quality of the eternal mother of the creations of endless quantities of future worlds. *Rose of the World* states this as follows:

> So, traversing from light to light and from glory to glory,
> All of us populating the world at present,
> And those who lived and those who will appear to life in the future,
> Will arise to the indescribable Sun of the World,
> In order to sooner or later assimilate into Him,
> And to merge into Him,
> To celebrate together, and to create with Him
> More creations of universes and universes.

Interview of Alla Andreeva, Conducted by Olga Skibinskaya and Published in *Rosseiskaya Gazeta*, September 13, 2003, Issue 182 (3296).

Question: So Alla Aleksandrovna, can you tell us in a few words about the gift of Daniel Andreev?

Answer: The uniqueness of Daniel Andreev consists in the amazing visual clarify of his comprehension. He was capable of penetrating through our physical world and into other worlds. His first vision occurred at the age of 15 years. But only in prison, where he was thrown due to betrayals for a supposedly subversive novel, did there occur revelations of spirit audio and spirit vision that awakened a profound memory.

One of Andreev's cellmates was the scholar V.V. Parin, a physiologist of a very material nature, an atheist. He related to me how Daniel worked in prison, "It seem that he was not composing, but recording something that he was hearing from somewhere, as though this was flowing through him, and so he was barely able to write fast enough."

Question: So where did he get the title *Rose of the World* for his book?

Answer: Daniel saw the materialization of a fraternity of all of humanity in a free and voluntary federation of governments uited by an ethical institution – ROSE OF THE WORLD. Particularly one that was ethical. It could not be a political institution or a religion, as far as Daniel conceived it, that could unite all of humanity.

In his book, Daniel Andreev relates how the universe is multi-stratified. Our Earth is the most reliable stratum since we reside here, and it is the crossroad where the system of worlds of other dimensions meet. I say this conditionally, since Worlds of Enlightenment rise above us and eventually enter into the residence of Christ. Beneath us, as Andreev describes, descend Worlds of Retribution, and which center is the residence of the Devil. All living existence and the meta-history of the human race proceeds from these structures of the universe. Its reflection in our daily cognizance materializes what we call history.

From this point of view, Daniel Andreev in *Rose of the World* reviews the history of Russia. Every nation possesses a bright conciliar guide – their Demiurge, that leads them to the Light. Every nation possesses a holy conciliar soul, its female counterpart, the inspiration and preserver of the bright creative principle. All the demiurges are brethren, and all the conciliar souls are sisters.

The book contains chapters that are dedicated to the most recent history of Russia, among them are chapters regarding Stalin, as the most potent concentrated personification of evil. A significant portion of *Rose of the World* is dedicated to nature, its hidden activating strengths. These are the stikials or spirits, or the elements of nature.

Question: The notorious statutue 58 was codified in this manner: Anti-Soviet agitation, terror, preparation for attempts against Stalin. But in reality, was the reason for the arrest of Daniel Leonidovich and youself, and your close associates, the manuscript of his novel *Night Wanderers*?

Answer: Daniel started writing this novel in 1937. He wrote at nights and without any hope of it ever being published. His work was not finished until after the war, in the spring of 1947. A circle of friends and relaives read or listened to Daniel reading it, and this is where people surfaced and the matter started. The manuscript of the novel was destroyed by the agencies after Daniel was sentenced. The prison hand-writen manuscripts of Daniel Andreev are located in the Russian archives of the university at Leeds in Great Britain. I was successful enough to have them transferred there, not having any hope that they would even be published in the author's homeland. In volume 3 of the *Collected Works of Daniel Andreev*, which was published in the 1990s, what fragments remained of the novel are published.

The activity of *Night Wanderers* occurs in Moscow at the end of the 1930s. The title of the novel means the following: We, the Russian people, wander through the night that encompasses all of Russia. One of these episodes is where the arrested guide of an underground group, the ideologue Glinski, is secluded in a cell at Lubyanka, which is crowded with other inmates. There is an Orthodox priest and Islamic mullah also sitting in the cell. Not speaking one word to one another, they pray in order for all the rest. Silently. When the person who is praying is summoned for interrogation, with a facial gesture he transfers his prayer duty to the next person remaining.

Canonically this of course is impermissible. But I do not think that some clergyman would condemn such people. A general objection to non-spirituality was conceived on its own in the labor camps and prisons of this godless era.

As far as the accusations that were created are concerned, there was never any conspiracy. The proceedings even proved this, and they continued for 19 months. This however did not interfere with the sentences they seved: 25 years prison for Daniel and 25 years labor camp for myself.

Question: On your own you resisted the entire system, such a person so morally strong. No doubt you felt you were doomed to perish. Fifty years have now passed since you were sentenced. How were the prison years and labor camps' years a struggle for you?

Answer: Of course, we did support. And not only faith, but people were also a support for us, those who were alongside us. I already mentioned the scholar Parin. The hand-written manuscripts of *Rose of the World*, the poetry of Daniel, twice perished due to searches in prisons. But some were saved from the sentries and hidden, and these were not only Russians, but Germans and Japanese. We are grateful for the help they provided Daniel Leonidovich, and who was able to finish his primary project after he was released.

Something else was very difficult. After the sentence was served, during the years 1948 to 1950, Daniel and I had no news at all about the other. We did not even know if the other was alive. And only when correspondence was permitted, I found out from my mother that Daniel was alive. And it was only beginning in 1954 that we were able to correspond with one another. One letter a month was all that an inmate was allowed, but this was still a luxury. And we persevered.

I stare at the Andreev family photographs.[107] His wife is alongside him, happy, a warm glow seems to emmanate from her and her expression is so much like Daniel Leonidovich. His father appears concentrating, withdrawn or elsewhere, as though alone.

Statement by the questioner:

Alla Aleksandrovna was born in 1915. Of course, her health over the course of time has decreased, she has undergone several medical surgeries and is gradually losing her vision. In unfamiliar places she cannot find her way without help from someone. But this woman has always struck me as possessing indestructable optimism, regardless of her difficult fate. A passionate glowing fire resides in her.

---

[107] Referring to Leonid and Aleksandra Andreev, Daniel's parents.

In 1998, Alla Andreeva published her memoirs, having the title, *Sailing to the Heavenly Kremlin*.

Question: Daniel Leonidovich was a deeply religious person. However after the public distribution of *Rose of the World*, a conflict with Orthodox Church seems to have surfaced. One priest in a radio program mentioned that the author of *Rose of the World*, when on his death bed, rejected his book, asked for it to be destroyed, and said that any effort to publish it would be against his will.

Answer: This is false. Daniel Andreev never rejected any of his compositions and he did not object to any of his conviction. Not in prison, not when free. I was inseparably next to him all the final months of his life. And Daniel shared with me all of his thoughts and ideas, and I think that Daniel would not have hid from me anything so important as this. We had no secrets between us.

Question: Let me return to this disagreement with the [Orthodox] Church.

Answer: I think that it is possible, and I also notice this myself, to find in this composition concepts that do not agree with Orthodox dogmas. Know that Daniel Andreev is a poet, and not a philosopher and in no way is he a theologian. This allows him the right for special poetic visualizations of the world, although this does not stop him from making such mistakes that we would consider our personal interpretation. However, I do not know of one person that *Rose of the World* caused to leave the Church. But I do know of many that it has brought to the Church.

Several years ago I received a letter from one bishop, who wrote, "Reading *Rose of the World* attached a vivid religious comprehension to my previous concepts of belief." So this negative attitude of the [Orthodox] Church toward Andreev cannot in any manner be considered unanimous.

Russian Bibliography

Андреев, Даниил Леонидович, *Роза Мира*

Андреев, Даниил Леонидович, *Стихотворения и Поэмы*

Андреева, Алла Александровна, *Плаванье к Небесной России*

Бежин, Лионид, *Даниил Андреев, Рыцарь Розы*

Романов, Борис Николаевич, *Даниил Андреев*

Романов, Борис Николаевич, *Путешествие с Даниилом Андреевым*

Штеренберг, М. И., *Роза Мира, Д. Андреева и современность*

www.ingramcontent.com/pod-product-compliance
Lightning Source LLC
Chambersburg PA
CBHW020728160426
43192CB00006B/157